Protecting
the
Consumer
Interest

Private Initiative and
Public Response

edited by
Robert N. Katz

Ballinger Publishing Company • Cambridge, Massachusetts
A Subsidiary of J. B. Lippincott Company

Protecting
the
Consumer
Interest

This book is printed on recycled paper.

International Standard Book Number: 0–88410–282–3

Library of Congress Catalog Card Number: 76–7502

Printed in the United States of America

Library of Congress Cataloging in Publication Data
Main entry under title:

Protecting the consumer interest.

"The edited version of selected papers from sessions on consumerism presented at the National Affiliation of Concerned Business Students' (NACBS) three-day Second National Symposium conducted in October 1974."
    Includes bibliographical references.
    1. Consumer protection—United States—Congresses.
I. Katz, Robert N.   II. National Affiliation of Concerned
Business Students.
HC110.C63P77   381'.3   76–7502
ISBN 0–88410–282–3

Contents

List of Figures and Tables

Preface

Protecting the Consumer Interest: Private Initiative and Public Response is the edited version of selected papers from sessions on consumerism presented by the National Affiliation of Concerned Business Students (NACBS) at a three-day Second National Symposium conducted in October 1974.

Originally a student organization, the NACBS today is a cooperative effort among business executives, business school faculty, and graduate business students. Since being incorporated as a nonprofit educational foundation in 1971, the organization's main objectives have been to promote research on the role of the corporation society and to contribute to development of business school curriculum relating to the business and society interface.

A companion volume, *New Perspectives in Environmental Management*, edited by George Rohrlich, is based on papers given on this subject in concurrent sessions at the symposium and focuses on the most cogent aspects and emerging issues in environmental management.

Joining *The Unstable Ground: Corporate Social Policy in a Dynamic Society* (S.P. Sethi, editor), a book published last year based on the NACBS First National Symposium, these volumes represent thoughtful and constructive viewpoints of university scholars, business executives, labor leaders, public interest advocates, and students concerned about the role of business in dealing with contemporary social problems. Donald MacNaughton, Chairman of the Prudential Life Insurance Company has said, "Abundant evidence exists and keeps growing that the interface between government and business is the critical linkpin that will determine our nation's socioeconomic future."

Since we have a representative form of government, reflecting the aspirations of a broad and diverse society, the NACBS believes that a logical extrapolation of MacNaughton's observation is the conclusion that the business and society linkage is the most critical determinant force shaping our nation's socioeconomic future. The pivotal importance of the field has attracted dedicated young professionals interested in the survival of a private sector and the health of society—in America and globally. Guided through its formative period by Kirk Hanson, who served as co-chairman for the Second National Symposium, NACBS activities and programs have become widely recognized under Douglas J. Westervelt, the organization's current president and executive director.

Recognizing the critical need to prepare today's MBA student to cope with the rapidly broadening social dimensions of management, thirty-eight corporations currently sponsor the NACBS and make its independent activities possible. They are:

American Can Company	Hoffman-LaRoche, Inc.
American Telephone & Telegraph	Honeywell, Inc.
Arthur Andersen & Company	McDonald's Corporation
Atlantic Richfield Company	McGraw-Hill, Inc.
Bank of America	3M Company
Bethlehem Steel Corporation	Montgomery Ward Company
Borg Warner Corporation	Newsweek, Inc.
Chase Manhatten Bank	Olin Corporation
Chrysler Corporation	J.C. Penney Company, Inc.
CPC International, Inc.	PepsiCo, Inc.
Cummins Engine Company, Inc.	Prudential Insurance Company
Dow Chemical Company	Quaker Oats Company
Equitable Life Assurance Society	Scott Paper Company
Exxon Corporation	Shell Oil Company
Ford Motor Company	Standard Oil Company of California
General Electric Company	Standard Oil Company (Indiana)
General Mills, Inc.	Syntex, Inc.
John Hancock Mutual Life Insurance	United California Bank
H.J. Heinz Company	Universal Oil Products

Special acknowledgment is due S. Prakash Sethi and Hazel Henderson, who served as co-chairpersons for the second national symposium and who were responsible for arranging the consumerism and environmental tracts of the program, respectively.

McDonald's Corporation provided funds to cover a portion of the cost of the symposium and a grant from the General Electric Foundation made possible the attendance of forty students representing twenty-seven leading graduate business schools. Their contributions are greatly appreciated.

Introduction

Robert N. Katz

Harry Truman is reputed to have said that "the only person in Washington who speaks for the individual is Harry Truman." Whether or not he was correct, his statement suggests that a spokesman for the individual cr consumer is indeed hard to find in the nation's capital. Many have claimed the mantle but no one has clearly worn it. As a result, clear and unequivocal representation of the individual consumer has been less than consistent at best. Thus, we must ask not only who speaks for the consumer, but also when they will be heard and in what forum.

Even today, spokesmen for consumers do not agree on issues, tactics, or constituencies. For instance, the *Los Angeles Times* for June 1, 1975 contained three articles dealing with consumerism, each from a completely different perspective. One discussed the consumer's lack of clout and inadequate handling of consumer problems in the regulatory agencies. Another article described municipally funded legal groups enforcing consumers' rights, and the third described a consumer group opposed to Naderesque and regulatory activities that result in increased government spending.

Unlike the lowly consumer, special interest groups with clear focus and power are easily identified and have no difficulty making themselves heard when public policy is being formulated. Congressional committee staffs, for example, can readily call upon industry leaders or spokesmen to set forth their position in public hearings on a given piece of legislation. The nonindustry interested parties are so fragmented, however, that it is not easy to determine who should be asked to testify. When congressional hearings were conducted on such issues as products labeling, food additives, or sugar import quotas—all of which affect the consumer—no unified consumer groups testified. But a variety of industries were represented at each of these hearings.

Efforts to organize consumers have produced a mushrooming of "consumer interest groups" as well as formation of what may be termed "counter groups." The first section of readings in this volume addresses this issue. Lee Preston notes, "It is not yet clear, however, who does speak for the consumer, and no one seriously claims that the Independent Regulatory Commission (IRC) could do so effectively." Vogel and Nadel cite case situations to illustrate the lack of unanimity among consumer groups. And Sturdivant discusses a special group, which he argues has been without voice and without champion.

Whenever a "movement" is identified, there are attempts to pinpoint its genesis; the difficulty of doing so is illustrated in *Consumerism* by Aaker and Day [1]. The authors state that consumerism as movement had a resurgence with the appointment of Esther Peterson as Presidential Advisor for Consumer Affairs and that the movement began with the appearance of *Silent Spring* and *Unsafe At Any Speed* [2]. Those works did indeed bring emphasis to consumerism. But concern for the consumer has been present throughout recorded history in varying degrees. As defined by Aaker and Day, consumerism is the response of people and organizations to consumer problems and dissatisfactions. Certainly "response" can be found throughout history: controls were found in Europe in the twelfth century, and standards for product integrity and penalties for misrepresentation were present in the thirteenth and fourteenth centuries [3].

I would submit that consumerism has been an aspect of broader societal concerns since the early sixties, and is rather a recognition that at various times and in various areas there is an imbalance of power between components of our society. The sixties marked a decline in public trust in all large entities, and marketeers were among those whose power was resented. Not only was business criticized, but the church, the university, and government also were subjected to the combination of increased scrutiny and decline of esteem. It is against this background of increased public response and awareness that consumer protection must be examined.

This, of course, raises the broader issue of the legitimacy of the economic enterprise. Thus, an increased imbalance between consumer and producer has led to increased interest in and intensity of the consumer movement. Consumer needs (as opposed to "rights") can be summed up in one word—protection. An analysis of how best that protection has been and can be provided, and by whom, would be appropriate and perhaps fruitful.

It is easy to point out that the consumer does not have all the protection to which he is entitled, nor all the rights he is due. It is more difficult to offer solutions. Clearly we wouldn't have books like these or seminars dealing with consumerism if all those who are charged with responding to consumer problems and dissatisfactions were responding fully, effectively, and consistently. Nor will consumers ever be fully satisfied, if for no other reason than the continuing changes in our needs, our technology, our expectations, and our aspirations. Consequently, the consumer will always need protection. The search is thus for this protection.

The ultimate source of protection for the consumer—perhaps his last resort—is the courts. It could be argued that the courts indeed have been the only source of meaningful consumer protection. The development of strict liability in tort for defective products has caused manufacturers to increase their concern for product integrity to avoid injury to users. This has been a tremendous boon to consumers, and it came about only through court action and judicial decision, not through public outcry or group pressure.

Proponents of consumer rights have decried the concept of caveat emptor and feel that there should be greater emphasis on and attention to caveat venditor. Today this may well be true. It is noteworthy that at one time—namely when the guilds were weak and craftsmen unorganized—the buyer had as much or more power, as much or more knowledge, and as much (or, most likely, more) wealth than the seller. In a buyer's market there may be more justification for caveat emptor. But even so, the defrauded, the deceived, the gullible and easily misled have not been totally without recourse, for the courts have long granted relief for victims of fraudulent misrepresentation and have long recognized the existence of implied warranties.

But consumerism implies more. It implies alternative choices, informed buyers, and prevention of injury before the point of purchase rather than relief after the fact. Mayer and Nicosia address the issue of the informed customer in Part 1. Yet the question of how much the consumer listens remains unanswered. At least the consumer could make an informed decision if information about products were readily available in understandable form.

Sethi also has a proposal for assuring availability of countervailing data for the consumer, in his article beginning Part 2. Can the press inform? Will it? Pollock and Kandel address this issue. In a free society, a free and independent press is essential. This was clearly illustrated quite recently with the role of the *Washington Post* in uncovering the Watergate scandal. There is some concern, however, about how effective the media is in protecting the consumer. The threat of media exposure of fraud and other wrongdoings can serve as a deterrent and thus provide some consumer protection. Unfortunately, though, at the point of exposure the injury has already occurred.

What about the role of government? The consensus today appears to be that the government, or at least the IRC, is ineffective in protecting the consumer and in fact increases the cost to the consumer without offsetting benefit. The regulatory commissions are casting about for justification of their roles. In Part 3, Krattenmaker discusses the efficacy of the Federal Trade Commission and sets forth proposals for making it more effective. The FTC has been long maligned and much criticized. To say that it has been a failure would be unfair, for we don't know what would have befallen the consumer in the absence of the FTC. But to say that it has been less than fully successful would be generous. It is startling that the FTC has had any success when one compares the size of its budget to that of other agencies. Certainly the work of Ralph Nader has focused attention on the shortcomings of this agency. That report, followed by the report of the American Bar Association committee [4], led to a revitilization of the commission. This did not, however, lead to the FTC's filling a role that many would have desired.

To accomplish protection of the consumer's safety, Congress created a new agency, the Consumer Product Safety Commission, rather than expanding the function or responsibility of the FTC. The functions and activities of that relatively new IRC are discussed by Pittle. The proposed federal consumer protection agency will, if created, have as one of its goals that other agencies consider and protect the consumer's interest.

The consumer, individually, cannot rely on self-help, for obvious reasons. What self-help can be employed? Only to exercise the choice of not purchasing, and as many people say, if there is no alternative purchase available the choice of declining a specific item or brand is not a viable option for the consumer. Can—or will—industry itself protect the consumer? There are a number of problems in relying on this. First, there is the problem of competitive viability when one's competitor is not exercising the same degree of concern [5]. The possibility of industry self-regulation is argued by Katz as an alternative to government regulation.

Regardless of whether industry or government regulates, formulation of standards for products or services is critical. It is here that the voice of the consumer is essential. Rosenberg discusses ways in which meaningful representation of consumer interests can be effected in standards programs [6]. It might be appropriate here to point out that in many ways we have a dual standard. The consumer is rightfully upset if a product does not last or if he overpays. The same individual, however, may be one who seeks to get "special" prices for services or transportation in violation of appropriate tariffs. This writer thus feels that "corporate social responsibility" is a worthy goal that is currently fashionable, but product quality and prices are not the only areas in which increased responsibility may be needed. By no means do all businesses exploit the consumer, nor does business have a monopoly on lack of ethics. It is essential, though, that in areas that do not really concern "ethical" decisions, but rather standards, there be a forum for the consumer to help establish the standards.

As mentioned previously, the courts play a vital role in our system for orderly resolution of conflict. In Part 4 of this volume, Kass discusses quasi-judicial actions on which activists and consumers may rely. Other aspects of activity in the courts are discussed by Barton and Phillips. Some special situations in the insurance and pharmaceutical industries are discussed by Orren and Cady. This broad overview, with suggestions, proposals, and alternatives, would perhaps lead one to conclude that while some progress has been made in protecting the consumer interest, much remains to be done. It is worthwhile to evaluate how effective some activities have been, and where prospects for success in consumer protection are greatest.

Today the courts recognize that the greatest incentive for the seller to provide "prepurchase protection" is for the courts to invoke sizable "postpurchase sanctions." This has been done substantially and significantly in one area without imposition of any "fault" or moral stigma. We here speak of strict liability in tort for products. This concept, which might be extended to other areas of the consumer field, provides great hope for the consumer. Justice Roger Traynor probably did more for direct benefit to the consumer than did Ralph Nader:

> ... it should now be recognized that a manufacturer incurs an absolute liability when an article that he has placed on the market, knowing that it is to be used without inspection, proves to have a defect that causes injury to human beings. *McPherson v. Buick Motor Co.*, 217 N.Y. 382 [111 N.E. 1050, Ann. Cas. 1916C 440, L. R. A. 1916F 696], established the principle, recognized by this court, that irrespective of privity of contract, the manufacturer is responsible for an injury caused by such an article to any

person who comes in lawful contact with it. (*Sheward v. Virtue*, 20 Cal. 2d 410 [126 P. 2d 345]; *Kalash v. Los Angeles Ladder Co.*, 1 Cal, 2d 229 [34 P. 2d 481].) In these cases the source of the manufacturer's liability was his negligence in the manufacturing process or in the inspection of component parts supplied by others. Even if there is no negligence, however, public policy demands that responsibility be fixed wherever it will most effectively reduce the hazards to life and health inherent in defective products that reach the market. It is evident that the manufacturer can anticipate some hazards and guard against the recurrence of others, as the public cannot. Those who suffer injury from defective products are unprepared to meet its consequences. The cost of an injury and the loss of time or health may be an overwhelming misfortune to the person injured, and a needless one, for the risk of injury can be insured by the manufacturer and distributed among the public as a cost of doing business. It is to the public interest to discourage the marketing of products having defects that are a menace to the public. If such products nevertheless find their way into the market, it is to the public interest to place the responsibility for whatever injury they may cause upon the manufacturer, who, even if he is not negligent in the manufacture of the product, is responsible for its reaching the market. However, intermittently such injuries may occur and however haphazardly they may strike, the risk of their occurrence is a constant risk and a general one. Against such a risk there should be a general and constant protection and the manufacturer is best situated to afford such protection [7].

There was a time when a manufacturer would avoid liability for a defective product if he had exercised the degree of care in production that any other reasonably careful manufacturer would have employed. The strict liability concept in effect makes the manufacturer an insurer of the integrity of his product. What greater incentive can there be than imposing severe economic sanctions for sale and distribution of a defective product as an inducement to the greatest degree of care in manufacturing? Thirty-eight states have, by statute or case decision, adopted the strict liability concept. The Federal Restatement of Torts (2nd) Section 402A also adopts this concept. The number of product liability claims has risen from approximately 35,000 in 1960 to some 600,000 in 1974, according to insurance industry estimates. While this growth may reflect an increased consumer awareness, it directly reflects the courts' trend of giving a different priority to economic consideration.

In the past, the courts excused absence of safety devices at railroad crossings on the theory that requiring such devices would impose an unreasonable economic burden upon the industry. Today the predominant position of the courts is that since the industry is better able to bear the loss as a cost of doing business, industry should sustain the loss. That constitutes a 180-degree shift and can afford great protection to the customer when personal injury or death is involved.

According to consumer advocates, much remains to be done for the consumer with respect to protection from defective or misrepresented products that cause economic loss, annoyance, and inconvenience. Perhaps the recently passed Warranty Act [8] will provide partial solution, as might the creation of a federal consumer protection agency. But, in conclusion, it might be argued that the major hope for increased protection for the consumer lies in the consumer's asserting rights that have already been judicially established, tested, and found to exist. For that hope to be fully realized the consumer must be educated, informed, and have ready access to the courts.

NOTES TO INTRODUCTION

1. David A. Aaker and George S. Day, *Consumerism: Search for the Consumer Interest*, New York: The Free Press, 1971.

2. *Ibid.*, pp. 1–5.

3. F.S.F. Lerner, "Quality Control in Pre-Industrial Times," *Quality Progress* (June 1970).

4. Miles W. Kirkpatrick, "Report of the ABA Commission to Study the Federal Trade Commission," (pamphlet; September 1969).

5. Phillip I. Blumberg, Eli Goldston, and George D. Gibson, "Corporate Social Responsibility Panel: The Constituencies of the Corporation of the Institutional Investor," *The Business Lawyer* (March 1973): 177–213.

6. Richard E. Caves and Marc J. Roberts, *Regulating the Product: Quality and Variety*, Cambridge, Mass.: Ballinger, 1975; and David Hemenway, *Industrywide Voluntary Standards*, Cambridge, Mass.: Ballinger, 1975.

7. Justice Roger Traynor, California Supreme Court, *Escola v. Coca-Cola Bottling Co.*, 24 Cal. 2d 453 (1944).

8. Public Law 93–637, 15 US C 2301, et. seq.

Part 1

Who Speaks for the Consumer?

Commentary

VOGEL AND NADEL

The consumer movement is not the united front that might be sup-
posed, nor is business always unanimously against consumer groups
on all issues. Rather, four case studies show that consumer and busi-
ness interests were united respectively for and against only one pro-
posal—creation of a federal consumer protection agency with broad
powers. More common in recent times has been the tendency for
traditional consumer coalitions to divide over specific issues. For
example, both consumer groups and business interests have been split
on the question of no-fault auto insurance. The position of many
insurance companies has moved toward no-fault, but some consumer
advocates, notably Ralph Nader, have declared that no-fault is not
reform enough—the entire insurance industry must be overhauled. ·

STURDIVANT

Despite the growing consumer movement, three groups of consumers
remain relatively unprotected—the poor, the aged, and the very
young. The lack of comprehensive protection for these groups, who
often are the most exploited as consumers, at least partially results
from prevailing cultural and economic patterns in American society.
One way that this imbalance in consumer protection and social atti-
tudes might be alleviated is through creation of a consumers' special

prosecutor, who would see that federal agencies actually perform their regulatory and consumer advocacy functions.

MAYER AND NICOSIA

Consumers are bombarded with advertisers' claims, salesmen's pitches, consumer groups' warnings—a veritable information explosion. Yet consumers have not been sufficiently educated in how to obtain appropriate information and how to use it. This situation could be improved if business and government were to reduce the financial, time, and psychological costs of getting information, and if the data available were consistently useful and beneficial to consumers in evaluating products and services.

BRADLEY

The consumer affairs professional within industry can do much to represent consumers both individually and collectively. This person serves as a bridge between top management of an industry and its consumers, whose concerns, problems, and needs might not otherwise be represented or even heard. Likewise, the consumer affairs professional can convey valuable information about the industry to consumers, perhaps forestalling or eliminating some of their concerns, and certainly keeping open the lines of communication. Such consumer representation within the business community will help promote and augment cooperation between these two important segments of society.

Chapter 1

Who Speaks for the Consumer?

Lee E. Preston

The question, Who speaks for the consumer?, can be answered in many different ways, and out of the articles the following spectrum of answers has emerged.

The consumer speaks for himself. That is, by his purchase behavior in the market, the consumer indicates his own tastes and wishes, and producers and sellers must respond accordingly. This is, of course, the traditional theory of the market mechanism, and a theory that can scarcely be challenged when the consumer has adequate purchasing power, adequate knowledge, and a suitable range of choices from which to make his selection.

Market research speaks for the consumer. The main purpose of market research is to discover in advance the potential consumer responses to alternatives not at the moment present in the marketplace. Since it is in the interest of buyers and sellers to discover which among the unlimited number of potential products and services consumers would be most interested in obtaining, and the conditions under which purchases might be made, we would expect the market economy to generate specialized organizations and individuals to perform this function. Commercial market researchers and the research staffs of supplier organizations thus attempt to speak for the consumer, or, in a slight variant, to make the consumer speak for himself about alternatives not in fact available in the market place.

The political and legal systems must speak for the consumers, by providing them with a forum in which to generate nonmarket pressures and a means of redress in the event of market disappointments. What is involved here is not simply the enforcement of traditional

3

contract and liability laws through the courts, but a broader access to the entire political power apparatus—including the possibility of coalitions with other groups in order to bring about political results. According to the four case studies presented by Nadel and Vogel, a united consumer movement can have considerable political power, particularly if other power blocs (for example, a "business" bloc) are divided or uninvolved. More important, the consumer movement can form coalitions with other groups or political segments to bring about results in its own best interest.

Prominent activist leaders have spoken vigorously for the consumer at many times in the past, and increasingly throughout the last decade. Some of this leadership activity has led to the formation of political power blocs. A larger effort has been made to push individual cases and issues through the existing legal system in response to specific problems that have arisen. This is essentially an after-the-fact approach; it reflects negative or undesirable appraisals of past experiences in the marketplace. According to Kass, the individual activist approach is now on the decline, partly because serious activists and concerned groups can see that the ex post resolution of problems tends oftens to be "too little and too late." He predicts a shift of activism toward the development of group services (such as group legal services, product testing, consumer advice, and so forth) and voluntary business-consumer interactions that will shift into an anticipatory rather than a reactive mode.

The new breed of corporate consumer affairs officers and other types of "scanners" and ombudsmen are attempting to survey consumer interests from a broad perspective and bring the results of that analysis into the internal management of the corporation. Their orientation is not simply conventional market research, but broader analysis of consumer needs and overall life styles, environmental and social efforts of business activity, and so on. Bradley speaks openly and very frankly about the problems and potentials of such a role—which he himself occupies—and stresses the importance of an active posture for individuals in that role vis-à-vis both the external environment and the internal strategic decision systems of the organization. The dilemmas faced by a serious consumer affairs officer when confronted by questionable products and unethical advertising are frankly acknowledged in his article (5).

What is the appropriate paradigm for the consumer-producer relationship? Is it one of conflict and exploitation, or one of cooperation and symbiosis? Certainly the latter possibility is more desirable, but it may not be realistic. Moreover, even in an open and interactive relationship, producers and sellers face genuine problems about whom to listen to and how to balance the views and interests of various consumer, and potential consumer groups. The appropriate aggressiveness of the consumer affairs officer with respect to his management colleagues also has been questioned. Clearly, if he fails to ennunciate consumer concerns, then he is worthless; on the other hand, if he makes every consumer question or criticism a crucial issue, his ability to bring about internal change may be undermined.

On the consumer side, the costs, problems, and delays involved in individual consumer complaints and their resolution have been strongly stressed. These factors seriously limit the effectiveness of formal legal avenues of consumer redress. Furthermore, individual consumers can gain little benefit from generating bad publicity for individual firms and products. In short, all the available modes of consumer expression have been and will continue to be of importance.

Chapter 2

The Consumer Coalition: Dimensions of Political Conflict

David Vogel
Mark Nadel

CRACKS IN THE COALITION

When consumerism emerged as a political issue in the 1960s, consumer activists were fighting for fairly clearly defined goals and there was little dissension in their ranks. As the organizations and issues got older, however, some cracks in the coalition began to appear. There have first of all been angry spats within the big consumer organizations. Unhappiness with the style of leadership and positions on some issues led to an unsuccessful attempt by some Consumer Federation of America (CFA) leaders to oust executive director Erma Angevine. In addition, labor unions are a major source of support for the Consumer Federation. When issues involving tariffs have surfaced, the CFA has been notably reticent about pursuing the consumer interest in free trade—which often conflicts with the position of organized labor. This backing away has led to considerable strain within the organization.

Even in that traditional bastion of consumerism, Consumers Union, there has been considerable divisiveness and bickering over a variety of organizational and policy questions [1]. Indeed, we could view Consumers Union as something of a surrogate for the consumer movement and the problems it faces. First, there is the problem of monopoly and economic concentration. In order to make its ratings useful to a national audience, *Consumer Reports* necessarily rates nationally distributed products made by the major industrial corporations. This tends to increase the already sizable advantage of the national brands. Furthermore, a negative rating can be disastrous for a small company, while it simply rolls off the back of an industrial giant like General Motors. This problem parallels the general strategic dilemma of consumerists over whether to target in on smaller local firms or large centers of economic power.

In addition, there has been considerable disagreement within Consumers Union over which kinds of products to rate. It has been charged that rating items such as outboard motors and full-sized sedans makes the magazine appropriate only for upper middle class audiences and deprives lower income consumers of a rating service that they need more than upper income consumers. Furthermore, some of the products rated, such as small boat depth sounders, are trivial or of very limited utility. Again, this parallels the priority problem of consumer activists.

Finally, there has been controversy over the degree of activism to be pursued by Consumers Union. In 1969 Consumers Union opened a Washington office; since that time the organization has become more actively involved in following and promoting legislation and administrative actions of interest to consumers. But this activism has not been without opposition, for some subscribers, members of the board of directors, and the staff object to CUs doing anything other than rating products. As consumerism has become a more important and visible political issue, the complexities and controversies surrounding that issue thus have been inevitably reflected in Consumers Union.

There have also been splits between former allies. For example, in early 1973 two aides of Senator Abraham Ribicoff prepared a report in response to charges that General Motors has misled Ribicoff's subcommittee in regard to alleged defects in the Chevrolet Corvair. The Ribicoff report concluded that GM had not misled the subcommittee. Two weeks later, members of Ralph Nader's staff blasted the Ribicoff report as a "whitewash" and issued a 120-page report of their own [2]. Ribicoff and Nader, it should be noted, had previously joined forces on a number of important consumer issues. In general, while Nader's power remains substantial, his popularity in Congress substantially diminished in 1972, largely as a result of widespread unhappiness with his Congress Project.

Furthermore, there is evidence that consumers themselves are balking at measures on the farther edge of consumer protection and that consumer dissatisfaction is being eagerly reflected in Congress. Thus, as part of an automobile safety bill in 1974, Congress enacted the first reversal of auto safety regulations: the Department of Transportation was prohibited from requiring the controversial seatbelt-ignition interlock system or even the continuous warning buzzer. The amendment passed by lopsided margins in both houses of Congress— margins that included previous supporters of auto safety.

These observations are not meant to suggest that the consumer groups or the consumer movement is falling apart. Rather, after the heady early days of fighting just to get a foot in the door, organizations have gotten older and different perspectives have increasingly emerged. The same phenomenon has afflicted crusades such as the civil rights movement and the environmental movement. The politics of consumerism can no longer be seen as a struggle between the children of light and the children of darkness. As the issues have become more complex, it has become progressively more difficult to assert unambiguously the nature of the "consumer interest." The purpose of this article is to suggest some emerging characteristics of the politics of consumer protection as the movement goes into its second decade.

THE CONSUMER PROTECTION AGENCY: AN UNRESOLVED CONFLICT

For nearly five years a key political issue of contention between the business community and the consumer movement has centered on the establishment of an independent consumer protection agency. Consumer organizations have pressured Congress to create a governmental body with broad powers to advocate the consumer interest before government regulatory agencies and in the courts. The business community has argued that a consumer protection agency would only increase the harassment of businessmen by the government and disrupt the work of other agencies. These spokesmen contend that if performance of existing agencies is inadequate they should either be improved or abolished, not surplanted by yet another government bureaucracy. Business opposition has been intensive and, to date, effective.

Enactment of legislation authorizing the CPA has been a major priority of the consumer movement for over three years. In 1971 Ralph Nader stated, in an interview published in *Fortune*, that he would readily trade in all pending consumer protection legislation for a consumer protection agency [3]. In 1974 he made the establishment of a CPA his New Year's resolution. Nader's growing interest in a government agency whose exclusive function would be to represent consumer interests reflects his concern with institutionalizing the ad hoc pressures that have made the consumer movement one of the most powerful and consistently effective challenges to business power during the last decade.

Nader's political strategy and outlook have undergone a subtle yet important shift since he emerged into public prominence eight years ago. In the beginning he sought primarily legislative solutions to corporate abuses: nearly a dozen pieces of legislation, ranging from automobile safety to nonflammable pajamas, bear the imprint of his lobbying and journalistic efforts. Unlike previous generations of reformers, however, he quickly saw the limitations of the legislative process: laws, however impressive sounding, do not enforce themselves. Rather, they require the continuous dedication and political energies of government administrators. Hence the two-foot-wide shelf of exposés of the bureaucratic process that Nader and his associates have produced since 1971.

At first glance, to demand creation of yet another governmental body to protect the public welfare seems almost a parody of the findings of Nader's own study groups. The subversion of regulatory agencies by the interests they are entrusted with regulating is the closest thing political scientists have formulated to a scientific law; the corruption of the regulatory process has become by now a commonplace observation of commentators across the political spectrum. Why should the experience of this agency be any different? The *Wall Street Journal* confidently predicted in this vein that "Mr. Nader's New Year's resolution in, say, 1977, will be to win repeal of the Consumer Protection Agency" [4].

Yet in another sense there is a curious logic behind the position of the consumer movement. Much of the policy making process of the federal government is remarkably decentralized. In a process that Lowi has described as "interest-group liberalism," the various policy making powers of the federal administration are parcelled out among the constituencies most affected by their decisions [5]. The survival of each agency or bureau rests upon its ability to form a partnership with the particular interest group with whom it interacts most continuously. Consequently, the dominant pattern of conflict in Washington is not between private groups and the government, but rather between coalitions of various government agencies and their respective interest group constituencies.

The airline industry has a government body that protects its interests, as do defense contractors, veterans organizations, and wheat farmers. Why, then, should not the consumer movement have a "captured" agency to look out for its interests in the administrative anarchy of the bureaucracy? Critics of CPA have contended that the consumer interest is too diffuse to be represented by a single governmental institution. This contention is logically flawless but politically naive. While it does seem somewhat paradoxical for the consumer interest, which is an exceedingly general one, to be represented by a particular group of administrators, it is a paradox that is built into the nature of a liberal society. Is a consumer protection agency really any more strange a notion than a "public interest lawyer" or a lobby that calls itself "Common Cause"? In each case, in a society divided into private interests, the "public interest" can only be represented by a particular interest [6].

Since 1973 the debate in Congress has focused on the power of CPA to represent the consumer interest before other government bodies. Fully appreciating the "subversion" of the regulatory process, pro-consumer forces have been attempting to give the new agency as wide as possible latitude in advocating the consumer point of view throughout the government bureaucracy. Unlike other regulatory bodies, the CPA is not to regulate business directly; it is to serve as a sort of watchdog over the behavior of the existing regulatory agencies. Its purpose is to drive a wedge between these agencies and their constituencies. To the charge that the CPA would create legal and administrative chaos (the *Wall Street Journal* predicted a plethora of cases titled *United States of America vs. United States of America* [7]) and vastly complicate and delay both governmental and corporate decision making, the bill's proponents might well plead guilty; that is, in fact, the real purpose of the new agency.

Accordingly, the agency's critics have attempted to restrict its power as much as possible. While the consumer lobby wants the CPA to be able to intervene in the proceedings of other agencies as a formal party, Congressmen hostile to the bill have sought to restrict its role to *amicus curiae* status. A similar debate centers on whether the CPA should be allowed to participate in the informal deliberations of other agencies. In addition, critics of the bill have sought to restrict the agency's ability to gain access to trade secrets and other confidential business material. Antonin Scale, chairman of the Administrative Conference of the United States, told the Senate Governmental Operations subcommittee on Reorganization:

> The inquisitorial powers . . . not only give the CPA a substantial weapon unavailable to private parties appearing in the same proceeding, but in some cases . . . give it access to information that the staff of the regulatory host agency itself cannot obtain [8].

More important, consumer and business lobbyists differ on whether the consumer agency should be allowed to appeal the decisions of other government agencies even if it had not participated in the original agency proceeding.

In a critique of the American policy process similar to that of Lowi, McConnell argues that public policy tends to systematically favor private, organized interests because of the restricted scope of decision making. The constituencies of administrative agencies tend to be relatively small, thus encouraging in each bureau and agency of the government a somewhat narrow and restricted view of the public interest [9]. The CPA is clearly an attempt to arrest this pattern: its constituency is universal. Yet it is precisely the agency's wide scope that defines its potential strength as well as its weakness. The mandate of the bill favored by the consumer lobby gives the agency's directors considerable discretion in defining the consumer interest and determining the optimal strategy for achieving it. By in effect abdicating consumer policy to a branch of the executive, the bill's congressional sponsors are forcing the CPA to rely upon its own political resources to survive; its statutory authority is so broad as to be without any legal impact.[a] In the best tradition of interest group liberalism, the CPA will be forced to depend for support on the organized consumer movement. If the consumer interest remains a relatively popular one, the new agency will in all likelihood be relatively successful.

By establishing an agency two steps removed from private pressures, the consumer movement is attempting to delay and perhaps even prevent its eventual corruption by business. Consumer advocates seem to have virtually abandoned the possibility that a government agency with supervisory and administrative responsibilities can ever be relied upon to protect the consumer interest. Instead, they have chosen to place their faith in the political effectiveness of the legal process. CPA is based on a judicial rather than administrative model: it substitutes the legal clash of adversary interests for the decrees of administrative regulation [10]. This strategy is a novel one, but its success will be marginal. As soon as public interest in consumerism wanes—as it has twice before in the century—CPA will be added to the list of governmental bodies muckraked by the next generation of reformers. To appoint a guard for the guardians, even if it is a legal one, only delays the question, "Who will guard the guardians?"

The struggle over the establishment of the CPA has become an increasingly bitter one. Senator Ribicoff, one of CPA's strongest supporters, told a press conference on July 31, 1974:

A tightly organized group of trade associations representatives, through confusing and misleading alarms circulated throughout the country have

[a]This argument is the substance of Lowi's attack on the pattern of public policy making by liberals.

launched a tremendous lobbying campaign to kill the bill. . . . They [business] don't want their power in Washington challenged, counterveiled or appealed; they don't want to share the soapbox with the consumer in an effort to sway federal action [11].

The *Wall Street Journal* in turn editorialized:

What is emerging . . . is an agency empowered to force its subjective view of the consumer interest into almost every administrative procedure. . . . There are too many classes of consumers, both those consuming today and those who will be consuming in the future. . . . What can only happen with a CPA, which presumes it can somehow represent all these views and strike a balance, is an inexorable erosion of Washington's concern for the consumer movement . . . the CPA will be ground to bits by Capital politics [12].

In addition to Ralph Nader and his associates, the consumer coalition consists of the Consumer Federation of America (an alliance of 185 local consumer organizations), Consumers Union, the AFL–CIO, the UAW, Friends of the Earth, and Sierra Club. The participation of organized labor in the pro–CPA lobby was presumably purchased by a provision specifically exempting labor negotiations from the agency's scrutiny. Business opposition has also surfaced along a broad front. Only one firm, a subsidiary of Montgomery Ward, has publicly endorsed the need for a consumer agency. Opposed to the establishment of any consumer protection agency, but particularly one with wide legal authority, are the Chamber of Commerce of the United States, the National Association of Manufacturers, National Association of Food Chains, Business Roundtable, and an ad hoc group of 300 firms and trade associations called the Consumer Issues Working Group.

The Senate passed a CPA bill in 1970 by a vote of 74 to 4. It subsequently died in the House Rules Committee. In 1972 the Senate bill was filibustered to death. The consumer forces were unable to muster sufficient strength to force cloture. Two years later this pattern was repeated. A bill authorizing a CPA was approved by the House on April 3, 1974 by a vote of 293 to 94, yet was again defeated by a Senate filibuster. Supporters of the bill in the Senate attempted unsuccessfully to cut off debate four times—and thus the agency will in all likelihood remain stillborn for another two years.

TARIFFS: LABOR DESERTS THE COALITION

In his study of the Progressive Era, *The Age of Reform*, historian Richard Hofstadter writes that consumer issues represented "the lowest common political denominator among classes of people who had little else to unite them on concrete issues" [13]. If the debate over establishment of an effective consumer protection agency illustrates the consumer coalition at its broadest, the controversy over tariff reform demonstrates the fragility of "the common political denominator" that purportedly unites the consumer forces in Washington.

From its origin at the beginning of this century, the consumer movement has consisted of two segments. During the Progressive Era these factions consisted of upper middle class professionals and the blue collar working class. The former were largely white, Protestant, native born; the latter disproportionately immigrant or black. Popular reaction to Upton Sinclair's *The Jungle* furnishes a graphic illustration of the different priorities of the two groups. Written to awaken the sympathy of the public to the brutal oppression of stockyard workers, the book instead upset a middle class audience concerned about the quality of the meat on its dinner tables. Sinclair later wrote, "I aimed for the public's heart and I hit its stomach instead" [14]. While working conditions improved, they did so only as a by-product of consumer pressure.

A similar uneasy alliance exists today. On one hand, the relative affluence of the organized working class has led it to take consumer interests more seriously. The AFL–CIO has lobbied extensively for much consumer legislation. Yet the consumer movement still conceals an important political tension. The organized consumer movement consists of public interest lawyers and the membership of such organizations as Consumers Union. In terms of education and income they are well above the national average: the subscribers responding to CU's most recent questionnaire had a median income of $14,000 and 58 percent were college graduates [15]. A survey in the *California Management Review* reports, "as income increases the tendency to support consumer protection by the government increases" [16]. Surveying the active membership variety of public interest groups which have emerged to do battle with business over the last decade, Simon Lazarus, a former assistant to Bess Meyerson, wrote:

> [Its] leaders are drawn from those professional and educational backgrounds that take political ideals seriously. In practice, this means that many of them come from the same relatively elite social or educational backgrounds that provide an active constituency for financial and organizational support [17].

By contrast, organized labor is apt to take the financial stake in consumerism more seriously. There is a direct conflict between the financial objectives of their membership and those of management. The fight for consumer protection is an important part of their struggle for a higher standard of living. Consumerism can be understood as the collective bargaining process carried out by other means.

This contrast in motivation reflects a more fundamental tension. Both factions relate to the corporation in their roles as consumers; this is the basis of their alliance. But organized labor, unlike middle class professionals, also interacts with the corporation in its worker role. Workers thus have a dual loyalty—on one hand, they are interested in improving their bargaining position in the marketplace, yet on the other hand they also have an important stake in the continued growth and expansion of the industries in which they are employed. When these interests conflict, it is the latter that logically receives priority. Maintaining employment is clearly more in the worker's self-interest than marginally reducing the cost of goods and services he consumes [18].

The current political controversy over government tariff policy vividly illustrates this conflict. Few government policies have a more direct impact on the costs and variety of goods and services available to the American public than tariff restrictions. According to Ralph Nader's Study Group Report on Regulation and Competition, the total cost to the American consumer of government restrictions on free trade is almost $20 billion a year. In his article "The $20 Billion Import Protection Racket," Howard Knee, a lawyer working for Nader's Corporate Accountability Research Group, contends that free trade increases competition and hence reduces domestic inflationary pressures. He concludes his blanket indictment of tariffs and quotas by arguing:

> The consumer is entitled to government policies that save him money, bring him the largest selection of products, satisfy his need for goods not produced in the United States, and which maintain a competitive impact on domestic prices, product efficiency, and innovation. These are the policies of free trade [19].

Accordingly, consumer organizations are firmly committed to the principle of free trade.

Historically, unions have been strong supporters of more liberal trade policies. Their political backing was critical to the passage of every major liberal trade initiative since the 1930s. Since 1970, however, unions have become increasingly concerned about the loss of jobs stemming from growing foreign market penetration of American markets. This has been particularly the case for industries such as steel, consumer electronics, autos, apparel, textiles, and shoes. The AFL–CIO estimates that imports claimed 900,000 jobs between 1966 and 1971 [20].

While individual unions have usually been divided on the merits of foreign trade (some, like textiles, shoes, and ceramics, have leaned toward protection, while others, like the auto workers, have been strong supporters of free trade) the balance of opinion within the national union leadership has shifted decisively over the last four years. The AFL–CIO strongly opposed the Trade Expansion Acts of 1970 and 1973, which would give the President broad power to negotiate trade agreements and instead has lent its support to the Burke-Hartke bill, which is designed to limit American investment abroad. Even the UAW, traditionally the strongest advocate of free trade, has moved toward a more protectionist position.

Unions have not confined their activities to lobbying; they have also sought to encourage consumer boycotts of foreign goods. The latter strategy is particularly revealing. Unions are asking their membership, as well as the public at large, to place their interests as workers above their interests as consumers. The plight of a former shoe worker who lost his job because of imports dramatically conveys the union's dilemma. He confessed to a reporter for *Fortune*: "I have seven kids and I'd buy imported shoes to save money" [21]. Middle class consumer organizations and organized labor have thus taken diametrically opposite positions. The consumer movement continues to identify the public interest with the lowest possible prices on goods and services. Organized labor, on the other hand, has given this interest a lower priority. They have deserted the coalition to protect their interests as workers.

THE DEFEAT OF THE SUGAR ACT: THE CONSUMER INTEREST TRIUMPHANT

On June 1, 1974, *Congressional Quarterly* reported that opponents of the Sugar Act had little hope of defeating it. Yet on June 4 the House killed a renewal of the 1937 Act by a 209 to 175 vote. This surprising upset and the background to it offer a revealing illustration of the fate of the consumer interest in tariff policy.

The government sugar program in its present form began with the Sugar Act of 1937 and has been repeatedly and routinely renewed through the years. The act established quotas on domestic production and assigned specific quotas on foreign imports on a country-by-country basis. It also provided a program of subsidies to domestic producers financed by an excise tax paid by manufacturers on the processing of sugar. The result was invariably a domestic price for sugar that was higher than the world price. Thus, a stable and guaranteed market system was indirectly subsidized by U.S. consumers.

This arrangement, which started in response to harsh economic problems for domestic producers, came to assume a political life of its own. The political forces behind the continuation of the program became among the most powerful in Washington—so much so that Douglass Cater pointed them out as a classic example of a "subgovernment" that succeeded in making self-serving public policy in a relatively closed policy system [22]. The sugar subgovernment has consisted of the producer's lobby, the agriculture committees in Congress, and the Department of Agriculture. Foreign producers were also a part of the subgovernment through their lobbyists, who earned thousands of dollars for their efforts to increase the quotas for their particular client countries. Thus, there were a substantial number of interests who benefited from the system at the expense of domestic producers. For over 35 years the sugar subgovernment has faced no effective opposition, and certainly no countervailing political weight by consumers.

A major factor behind the upset was the change in world economic conditions. Like most quota systems, the sugar program was based on a world surplus. But, as with most other commodities, that surplus has become a deficit. The Agriculture Department forecasts relative scarcity for at least the rest of the decade. As a result, sugar prices tripled in 1974. The rise in prices was only the precipitating factor behind the upset. Although the House Agriculture Committee partially took new conditions into account by reducing subsidies and eliminating the excise tax, they were unwilling to come to grips with the full import of the drastic change in the agricultural situation. As consumer and congressional critics pointed out, there is simply no longer any rationale for a quota system in a time of worldwide scarcity. Nonetheless, the sugar subgovernment attempted to respond in terms of its perceived political power rather than in the context of new economic realities.

The self-serving utilization of political "clout" and the ignoring of new economic realities can be seen in the position of the domestic industry and the statements of House Agriculture Committee Chairman W. R. Poage. Thus, a representative of the domestic producers proposed as a response to "a period of unusually tight world supplies" that the Puerto Rican quota be cut and domestic quotas be increased [23]. Poage simply ignored the market of the last two years and stated in the House debate: "Were we to let the price of sugar drop to the levels of the world market as it has existed for many years, there simply could be no sugar produced in the United States" [24].

Thus the defeat of the Sugar Act came not as an automatic response to new economic realities, but as a result of a political process stemming from those new economic realities. A variety of consumer groups opposed the extension of the Sugar Act, as they had all along. But, ultimately, it was pressure not from retail consumers but from industrial consumers that changed the political balance of forces. Grocery manufacturers account for about 75 percent of the domestic consumption of sugar. Shortly before the vote in the House, the Industrial Users Group representing those manufacturers actively began lobbying against the bill.

Additionally, sugar refiners and export-import firms opposed the bill in the fear that higher prices would lead to increased use of sugar substitutes. Thus, in the case of sugar quotas, it was not simply a case of consumer pressure for lower prices prevailing—at least not directly. Rather, the consumer interest in lower prices prevailed when it coincided with extremely important industrial interests. Here we have a case of John Kenneth Galbraith's theory of countervailing power, in which broadly based public interests are advanced by more powerful organized economic entities that have coinciding interests [25].

Of course, the interests of industrial consumers are affected by any tariff issue, and it is unlikely that it was only the greater political power of the retail food industry that made all the difference. Another important factor was evidently the role, or more precisely, the passivity, of organized labor. The farm workers, unlike workers in other protected industries, simply were not reaping great benefit from the legislation. Although the present Sugar Act requires that producers pay a minimum wage set by the Secretary of Agriculture, representatives of the farm workers and labor leaders claimed that the Act was not in fact benefiting the wages or working conditions of laborers.

Consequently, prior to ultimate defeat of the entire bill, several amendments to protect farm workers were inserted into the bill as reported by the committee. Nonetheless, although labor leaders pressed for these amendments, they did not press for final passage of the legislation, nor is there any indication that the farm workers themselves expressed much interest in ultimate passage. In any case, farm workers are certainly among the most politically powerless segments of the economy.

As it turned out, the political forces favoring the sugar quota system consisted only of the sugar producers themselves allied with the major farm organizations. Unlike the case of other tariff legislation, organized labor did not join forces with the business interests who favored protection. In one sense, the main outlines of the conflict simply boil down to a conflict between economically competing commercial interests, which provided a spillover victory for consumer interests. In another sense, however, the Industrial Users Group acted as an exceptionally powerful consumer group itself. The conflict of business interests did not simply provide spillover benefits to consumers. Rather, different kinds of consumer interests were pitted against the sugar subgovernment. The major grocery manufacturing corporations, acting in their role as consumers, provided most of the political muscle for an ad hoc coalition of consumer interests that overcame previously entrenched political power.

NO-FAULT: PROFESSIONALS AS WORKERS

The present system of automobile insurance is an outgrowth of the law of torts and depends on a finding of fault. Unfortunately, the finding of fault in an automobile accident is often not a simple matter and frequently involves protracted litigation—litigation that denies accident victims prompt compensation. There has long been dissatisfaction with the auto insurance system, and criticism of the system intensified during the period of increased consumer awareness in the late 1960s. By that time, a number of legal scholars began pressing for the adoption of a so-called no-fault system, in which all accident victims would be compensated by their own insurance companies without a finding of fault in an accident situation. A major thrust in this direction was the publication in 1967 of *After Cars Crash: The Need for Legal and Insurance Reform* by Robert Keeton and Jeffrey O'Connell—a book that helped to provide the legal and intellectual rationale for no-fault reform [26].

Although there have been important developments toward reform in most states, and at least seventeen states now have some form of no-fault law, our analysis will focus on the play of political forces at the federal level. The first major federal action was a congressional resolution in 1968 directing the Department of Transportation to undertake a study of the automobile insurance system. In 1969 the Senate Judiciary Committee's Subcommittee on Antitrust and Monopoly, under the chairmanship of Senator Philip Hart of Michigan, concluded extensive hearings on a variety of automobile policy problems. Hart introduced a no-fault bill along with several other pieces of auto-connected legislation late in 1970, but no action was taken on them. The present form of federal action and no-fault actually began in 1971, after Hart again introduced legislation.

In the meantime, the Department of Transportation study was released in March 1971. It showed that consumers had good reason to be dissatisfied with the present system. The report harshly criticized current practices as being inadequate for society in general and accident victims in particular. It charged that the present system allocates benefits poorly, discourages rehabilitation, burdens the legal system, and does little to minimize crash losses. A supplemental study by the Senate Antitrust and Monopoly Subcommittee found that only 42 percent of total premium payments were returned to accident victims and that those returns were poorly allocated. Victims who suffered losses of more than $25,000 received, on the average, compensation covering only 30 percent of their losses, while victims with losses of $500 or less received an average compensation of twice the amount of their actual loss.

In 1972, after extensive hearings by the Senate Commerce Committee, a no-fault bill was reported out under the sponsorship of Hart and Senator Warren Magnuson of Washington. The Hart-Magnuson bill required the states to enact legislation meeting minimum federal standards or they would come under more stringent federal standards. Tort liability was eliminated except for very limited circumstances. The bill was effectively killed on August 8, 1972, when the Senate voted 49 to 46 to refer the bill to the Judiciary Committee— where it was bottled up until the end of the 92nd Congress.

In 1973 the Senate Commerce Committee held further hearings on no-fault and this time the legislation, S 354, survived the legislative process in the Senate and was passed on May 1, 1974. The bill required each state to enact a no-fault law meeting federal standards or it would come under more stringent federal requirements. The bill required motorists to purchase insurance that guarantees payment of minimum benefits for bodily injury without regard to fault. States were given the option of including property damage under the existing tort liability system. As the bill went through the Senate legislative process, several amendments and compromises somewhat broadened the circumstances in which a lawsuit could be brought, but still the no-fault principle survived without serious incursion. Hearings were held in the House Commerce Committee, but further action was not taken because the Committee and the House in general had a backlog of other legislation that had been assigned higher priority as Congress rushed to adjourn prior to the 1974 elections.

The major parties at interest have been the insurance industry, lawyers, and consumer groups. It is hardly surprising that consumer groups favor no-fault because it promises faster victim compensation and lower insurance premiums as a result of a sharp decrease in tort litigation and the attendant cost of such litigation. Also not surprising is the opposition of trial lawyers, represented by the American Trial Lawyers Association (ATLA), out of whose pockets would come the savings in legal costs.

The position of the insurance companies is somewhat more complex. When the no-fault concept was first seriously considered at the federal level, the insurance industry was solidly against it—in large part because the industry has traditionally fared much better in state legislatures. By the time the Hart-Magnuson bill came up in 1972, most insurance companies still opposed no-fault but the opposition was no longer uniform. Instead, the companies, represented by the three major insurance trade associations, took positions completely coincidental with their economic interests—but always justified in terms of the consumer interest. Two associations, the National Association of Independent Insurers (NAIA) and the American Mutual Insurance Alliance (AMIA), represent the bulk of insurance companies. Both associations represent companies that generally sell through salaried rather than commissioned agents and both sell to predominantly good risks: thus their premiums have been relatively low. Additionally, the AMIA companies are mutual associations owned by policyholders whose dividends are converted into lower premiums.

Because these companies would have had to take all insurance applicants under the Hart-Magnuson bill, they would tend to lose their competitive advantage of lower premiums. The American Insurance Association (AIA) represents 119 large publicly held companies selling through independent agents on commission. They also have a greater number of low income, high risk clients than the other companies. Under no-fault there would be a comparative advantage to insuring such low income customers since their personal economic losses from accidents tend to be lower—and it is only their own losses that would have to be reimbursed. Thus no-fault would reduce the competitive advantage of NAIA and AMIA companies over AIA companies. Although many AIA companies endorsed the Senate bill, AIA itself did not take a formal position in 1972 because some of its members favored a state-by-state approach. The other two associations came down hard against federal no-fault [27].

The position of the insurance industry continued to change in the 1973—74 period. In December 1972 the representatives of the industry met at a conference at the Camelback Inn in Arizona and approved a compromise proposal for a very limited no-fault plan to be enacted by the states rather than the federal government. But the industry's united position did not last long. The American Insurance Association endorsed the Senate no-fault bill in 1973, and some of the giant companies such as State Farm also shifted in favor of Senate bill S 354. In general, the thrust of the insurance industry position shifted toward approval of the no-fault concept with differences in approach pertaining primarily to jurisdiction (state versus federal) and to limitations on liability. In addition to the American Insurance Association, S 354 has been supported by consumer groups, led by the Consumer Federation of America and bolstered by the Teamsters, United Steelworkers, and United Auto Workers; in short, the classic consumer group–labor union alliance.

As the issue developed in the 93rd Congress, the main anticonsumer business group was the American Trial Lawyers Association. Additionally, the American Bar Association opposed the bill and the Nixon Administration professed to favor a state-by-state approach. In fact, as the insurance industry shifted position, the legislative battle began to take the shape of a rather bitter fight between two powerful industries—insurance and law. Thus, former ATLA president J. D. Lee testified at the Senate Commerce Committee hearings, "It must be true that lawyers generally do represent their clients effectively or else the insurance industry would not be so anxious to abolish the role of the personal lawyer for private claims." As Lee's statement indicates, the trial lawyers claim to be representing the true consumer interest—although that interest, as defined by most of the consumer groups, was being represented by the insurance industry.

In fact, the case of no-fault insurance is an area where there has been ambiguity and conflict over what was in the consumer interest and who most appropriately represented it. This can be illustrated by the position of Ralph Nader and the controversy that swirled about Nader over this issue. An article in *The New Republic* [28] reported that Nader was not lobbying at all for the 1972 Hart-Magnuson bill, and in fact was somewhat opposed to the bill. The article also noted that other consumer advocates considered no-fault to be major priority consumer legislation. It went on to charge that Nader's position was influenced by an offer by the American Trial Lawyers Association to donate $20,000 to the Center for Auto Safety—one of the Nader spin-off organizations.

There was, in fact, a contribution made to the Center for Auto Safety but it was quickly rejected and returned—Nader hotly denied that the link between the ATLA offer and his own position on no-fault. More important, in terms of the ambiguity of the consumer interest, he stated his own position, which attacked the pending legislation as a mere palliative. Nader asserted: "With such widespread revulsion [against the present insurance system] at a rising peak, the opportunity for reform should be broader and deeper than the Hart no-fault bill. . . . My judgment is that Congress has one chance in this decade to make a clean new policy revolution" [29]. He argued for a major overhaul of insurance practices that would tie accident insurance into a system of preventing accidents in the first place. If Nader is correct, we can speculate that the insurance companies were wise enough to realize that no-fault is a cheap price (or no price) to pay for preventing the kinds of reforms and tough regulation that Nader has in mind.

The position of the trial lawyers is also more complicated than it first appears. Trial lawyers have previously been active in behalf of consumer interests generally and have represented consumers in injury cases against manufacturers. Even as no-fault is being fought, the ATLA is underwriting a program to compile data on injuries stemming from hazardous consumer products and refer that data to appropriate federal agencies. While the $100,000 program will no doubt benefit consumers, it should be noted that it also can aid lawyers by providing better evidence for lawsuits against manufacturers.

In the case of no-fault, however, the interest of lawyers as workers is squarely opposed to the broader consumer interest (at least as defined by most consumer activists). Thus their primary economic interest has led this segment of the professional middle class to desert the consumer coalition on this issue. No-fault insurance, then, is being fought out in the context of a battle between primary business interests, with consumer interests generally identified with one of the contending producer interests.

CONCLUSION

These four examples by no means exhaust recent political developments in consumer protection. Nonetheless, they do suggest some important generalizations about the nature and impact of the consumer coalition in Washington. In *Labor in American Politics*, J. David Greenstone argues that the conflict between consumers and producers has emerged as the central political cleavage in advanced industrial societies. He writes:

> [T]he instrumental character of economic rationalization (i.e., a concern for improving productive methods for their own sake) means that the

activities of the economic authorities continuously disturb the physical, social and economic environment . . . those who hold economic authority positions have an interest in advancing the instrumental rationalization of production . . . in order to successfully perform their entrepreneurial and managerial roles. Conversely, those who do not occupy authority roles have an interest in curbing such instrumental rationalization. . . . Contemporary class conflict is a cleavage between economic authorities in their role as producers and economic non-authorities in their role as consumers [30].

Greenstone's formulation has the virtue of dividing the society into two distinct sets of interests with respect to consumer issues. He suggests that the conflict between those who wield economic authority and those who are subjected to it has replaced the struggle between the bourgeoisie and the proletariat that defined the politics of nineteenth century industrial society. Increasingly, Greenstone contends, the focus of conflict between business and its critics has moved from the sphere of production to the sphere of consumption. To advance the protect the interests of their members, labor unions are forced to devote a larger share of their political resources to battling business on consumer protection issues.

The dispute over the establishment of a consumer protection agency clearly validates Greenstone's analysis. On one side were arrayed the wielders of economic authority, namely the business community; on the other side, groups represented social interests who wield no authority over the production process, namely labor organizations, the consumer movement, and environmentalists. From this perspective, the CPA case study can be seen as representing a "classic" alignment of social and political forces with respect to consumer issues.

The other three case studies, however, suggest the need for a somewhat different analysis. In the examples of tariff reform and no-fault insurance, various economic nonauthorities deserted the consumer coalition to support policies that were opposed to their interests as consumers. Why should this be so? By including the immediate families of economic authorities in the category of producer interests, Greenstone recognizes that, at least in the case of the bourgeoisie, the consumer interest is not always paramount. Businessmen and their families allow their roles as producers to take priority over their interests as consumers. Why then should not similar behavior be expected from other groups in the society when their producer (or worker) interests are threatened?

Seen in this light, these examples are not exceptions to a broader rule. Rather, in the case of each proposal to advance the interests of citizens in their role as consumers, a critical factor that determines the eventual policy outcome is the impact of the proposed change on citizens in their roles as workers. The broader that impact, the more likely that various economic nonauthorities will join segments of the business community to effectively oppose consumer legislation. If, as in the case of the sugar quota, worker interests are not affected, the outcome will be determined by the relative strength of competing corporate interests.

In fact, we would suggest that the CPA is actually the unusual case. Most consumer issues involve what Lowi would classify as falling under the rubric of "regulatory policies." They affect the welfare of specific and relatively narrow economic interests but have no impact on their distribution of power and privilege in the policy as a whole [31]. With respect to such issues, coalitions are fluid, and the victory of any particular set of interests is problematic. To analyze the structure of corporate power in America will tell one relatively little about whether auto safety, no-fault, or truth in lending will or will not be enacted by Congress. Each issue attracts a particular constellation of political interests.

By contrast, the stakes in the struggle over the enactment of CPA are of a different order. CPA affects the interest not just of a specific firm or industry but of American business as a whole. The agency would have the authority to interfere with the decisions of virtually every commercial enterprise. The more extensive the scope of jurisdiction of a government agency, presumably the more difficult for business to anticipate—and eventually neutralize—its deliberations. CPA threatens to upset the accommodations most industries have painstakingly worked out with the government agencies responsible for supervising their conduct.

Accordingly, CPA can be understood as a "redistributive" or "class" issue, even though it remains within the pattern of "interest-group liberalism." Lowi reserves this classification for legislation that threatens to change the balance of power within the corporate system. Other examples would include tax policy and the right of labor to bargain collectively. In terms of the scope and intensity of business opposition (no other consumer protection measure has ever before been filibustered), the struggle over CPA most closely resembles the controversy over the Wagner Act in the thirties. In each instance the business community perceived a fundamental threat to the autonomy of management and has reacted accordingly—although in the case of CPA this "class threat" appeared under the guise of a proposal to create another government agency. On CPA, in sharp contrast to the other three issues, the business community was not divided among itself. It presented an unusually broad front and waged a vigorous struggle.

Our analysis of the dual role of both workers and producers thus suggests that political conflict over consumer protection legislation can be understood in terms of four categories. This typology can be illustrated graphically in the following way.

Business

		united	divided
	united	CPA	Sugar
Consumer	divided	Tariff	No-fault

As the economic implications of consumer protection become more important, particularly during the current period of inflation and rising unemployment, relatively few issues will fall neatly into the CPA category—the "classic" model of consumer-business conflict. Forms of class conflict will, of course, increase under such circumstances, but they are more likely to center on work-place issues, such as wages and productivity, than on marketplace ones. (The no-fault category is, in a sense, a residual category; it reflects not so much the complexity of consumer conflict as its occasional ambiguity.)

The most interesting—and potentially important—categories are the sugar and tariff ones: in the former, producers acquire a consumer consciousness, while in the latter consumers become aware of their interests as workers. The pattern of conflict over tariff reform and the sugar quota is prototypical of situations that are likely to develop on a growing number of issues. Much of the impetus for deregulation of various sectors of the economy is likely to come from corporations that, in their role as consumers, would benefit from more competitive markets in such areas as transportation and agricultural production. On the other hand, unions are likely to appraise more critically their automatic support for stricter consumer product safety standards, particularly for commodities for which the costs of federal safety requirements are seen as directly contributing to increased costs and hence higher prices and fewer sales.[b]

---

[b]Nonmanual lawnmowers and bicycles are obvious examples. The attitude of organized labor toward the recent vigilance of the Consumer Product Safety Commission bears watching.

In sum, the politics of the consumer coalition are a function of the nature of consumer policies. These policies are not static, and they are becoming more complex.

NOTES TO CHAPTER 2

1. See Morton Mintz, "Consumers Union: Institution in Trouble," *Washington Post*, 22 April 1973, p. 1. The present analysis draws from Mintz's report.

2. Morton Mintz, *Washington Post*, 28 May 1973, p. 3.

3. Richard Armstrong, "The Passion that Rules Ralph Nader," *Fortune* (May 1971): 144–147.

4. "Mr. Nader's New Year's Wish," *Wall Street Journal* 10 April 1974, p. 14.

5. Theodore J. Lowi, *The End of Liberalism: Ideology, Policy, and the Crisis of Public Authority*, New York: W.W. Norton, 1969 (especially pp. 55–93).

6. A classic statement of this position may be found in Karl Marx, "On the Jewish Question," in T.B. Bottomore (ed.), *Early Writings*, New York: McGraw-Hill, 1964, pp. 1–40.

7. "Mr. Nader's New Year's Wish," *op. cit.*

8. "Consumer Protection Agency," *Congressional Weekly*, 14 April 1973, p. 867.

9. Grant McConnell, *Private Power and American Democracy*, New York: Alfred A. Knopf, 1966 (especially pp. 91–156). Along with Lowi, McConnell's boon represents one of the most important contemporary critiques of pluralism by a political scientist.

10. American reformers have historically been fascinated by law and the legal process. A disproportionate number of contemporary anticorporate activists are lawyers. For an intriguing critique of the contemporary reform movement that draws heavily upon this legalistic tradition, see Simon Lazarus, *The Genteel Populists*, New York: Holt, Rinehart Winston, 1974.

11. "Senate Fails to End Filibuster on Consumer Bill," *Congressional Weekly* 3 August 1974, p. 2064. For a typical editorial supporting Ribicoff's position see "Consumer Interests," *New York Times*, 19 August 1974, p. 24. The *Times* wrote: "The ferocity of minority opposition to a relatively modest and limited proposal is something to behold." A somewhat more neutral source, *Congressional Quarterly*, titled its article on the political struggle over CPA "Consumer Protection: Mismatch of Lobbyists," *Congressional Quarterly*, 20 July 1974, p. 1873.

12. *Wall Street Journal, op. cit.*

13. Richard Hofstadter, *The Age of Reform*, New York: Vintage Books, 1955, p. 172.

14. Upton Sinclair, *The Jungle*, New York: New American Library, 1960, p. 349.

15. Robert Herrmann, "Consumerism: Its Goals, Organizations and Future," *Journal of Marketing* (October 1970): 59.

16. William Wilson, "Consumer Reality and Corporate Image," *California Management Review* (Winter 1973): 89.

17. Simon Lazarus, *op. cit.*, p. 144.

18. Anthony Downs makes a similar point. See Mark Nadel, *The Politics of Consumer Protection*, Indianapolis: Bobbs-Merrill, 1971, p. 240.

19. Howard Knee, "The $20 Billion Import Protection Racket," in Mark Green (ed.), *The Monopoly Makers*, New York: Grossman, 1973, p. 345.

20. Irwin Ross, "Labor's Big Push for Protectionism," *Fortune*, March 1963, p. 94.

21. *Ibid.*, p. 92.

22. Douglass Cater, *Power in Washington*, New York: Vintage Books, 1964, pp. 199–205.

23. Congressional Quarterly, *Weekly Report*, 9 March 1974, p. 629.

24. Congressional Quarterly, *Weekly Report*, 8 June 1974, p. 1529.

25. J.K. Galbraith, *American Capitalism: The Concept of Countervailing Power*, Boston: Houghton Mifflin, 1956, pp. 108–134 passim.

26. Robert Keeton and Jeffrey O'Connell, *After Cars Crash: The Need for Legal and Insurance Reform*, Homewood, Ill.: Dow-Jones, 1967.

27. Karen Lewis, "No-Fault Insurance Bill Moves Toward Senate Floor," *National Journal* 8 July 1972, pp. 1117–1125.

28. Leah Young, "A Chink in Nader's Armor?" *The New Republic*, 2 September 1972, p. 11.

29. *The New Republic*, 9 September 1972, pp. 13–14.

30. J. David Greenstone, *Labor in American Politics*, New York: Knopf, 1969, pp. 374, 388.

31. In a seminal analysis of the politics of public policy, Lowi distinguishes among distributive issues, regulatory issues and class or redistributive issues. It is the latter two that are relevant to our purposes. Theodore J. Lowi, "American Business, Public Policy, Case Studies and Political Theory," *World Politics* (July 1964), pp. 677–715.

 *Chapter 3*

The "Unprotected" Consumers: The Young, the Old, the Poor

Frederick D. Sturdivant

According to John D. Rockefeller III, the revolution known as consumerism "is directed at entrenched economic power, [and is] spurred by those who want to have influence over the economic decisions that affect their lives" [1]. While Rockefeller's description of the objectives and motivations of consumerism is very much on the mark, it should be clear that progress in the struggle for consumer welfare has been uneven. The purpose of this article is to focus on the peculiar problem of three relatively "unprotected" consumer groups—young children, the poor, and the aged—and to develop a broad analytical framework to serve as the basis for understanding and corrective action.

THE "UNPROTECTED" CONSUMERS

Given the proliferation of consumer legislation at the state and federal levels, the existence of numerous regulatory agencies and the sharp rise in ombudsmen and consumer-action groups, it is clear that no large body of American consumers is unprotected. Hence, the term "unprotected" is used here in a relative sense. One dominant characteristic of this society is that economic and political power beget "protection" and advantage. Thus in both respects the poor, the elderly, and young children are disadvantaged.

Among the three groups, the most numerous are the poor. The most current federal data indicate that approximately 23 million—or about one out of every nine—Americans are below the poverty level. A poverty definition based on the relationship of income to family size, sex of the head of household, and so forth, reveals that the incidence of poverty is greatest "among the aged, black people, those with relatively modest schooling, and households headed by women" [2]. The second largest group is the 21 million-plus Americans aged 65 and over [3]. The age 65 deliniation for defining older Americans is compatible with the Older Americans Act of 1965 and the Older Americans Comprehensive Services Amendment of 1973, which outline federal policy concerning the elderly [4]. With the exception of the nutrition program (qualify at age 60) and the part-time work program (qualify at age 55), federal policy and programs are clearly oriented to the 65-and-over population. The four-year-and-under classification for children is also based on federal government practice rather than any specific physiological or psychological grounds. In 1973 there were about seventeen million children under five years of age in the U.S., down from a high of over twenty million in 1960 [5].

In short, while there is a problem of double counting between the groups, nonetheless this category of relatively unprotected consumers represents a very large segment of American society. It is likely that the poor have received the greatest attention in their role as consumers. Since the publication in 1963 of David Caplovitz's *The Poor Pay More* there has been a growing recognition of the serious plight of the poor in the marketplace. The list of problems is all too familiar: the pervasiveness of illegal and unethical practices in the ghetto marketplace (bait and switch, used goods for new, excessive interest charges, high pressure selling techniques, and a variety of deceptive practices); relative immobility; poor nutrition; dependence on credit; prevalence of small, inefficient merchants; and so forth [6]. The 1971 White House Conference on Aging listed income maintenance, health, transportation, shelter, and food as major endemic problems for most older Americans [7]. The list of consumer concerns for young children has been less thoroughly researched and studied, but certainly it includes the influence of television commercials, nutrition, flammable fabrics, and dangerous toys [8].

Although certain consumer problems are shared by the three groups, there is no doubt that the problems are polycentric in nature. Therefore, it is not the objective of this article to develop a full list of issues and trace their origins, analyze their complexities, evaluate extant legislation, or propose specific corrective actions. Instead, a single matrix or framework is presented as a means of organizing one's thinking about the issues and the ways in which the problems are being impacted by various institutions and agencies (see Table 3−1). Illustrations of action or inaction for a selected problem faced by each group are presented to suggest how areas requiring attention may be identified.

CONSUMERISM AND CULTURE

With the definition and size estimates of the three "unprotected" consumer groups established, and at least a general list of problem areas noted, it is important to move to a broader frame of reference for viewing a recommended course of action to upgrade the welfare of these groups. That broader frame is culture and its relationship to these groups and to effective action on their behalf.

Thomas Petit has argued persuasively that "Society always controls the economy through the cultural norms that govern economic activity" [9]. In this sense it is important to view the consumerism movement as part of this profound and relatively slow-moving cultural process. While there is no question that the marketing system has significantly influenced the values of this society (for example, attitudes toward credit use), we tend to be much less aware of the influence of culture on marketing practices. Indeed, as W.T. Tucker has noted,

> Most of us are naive about culture. Even the adult who knows perfectly well that his eating habits are dominated by cultural patterns he has internalized does not say to himself, "I am hungry. Because I live on the North American Continent, I have learned to assuage that hunger with roast beef. If I were a native of India, the notion of eating roast beef would appall me" [10].

The relationship between culture, the market system, and consumer behavior is fundamental to an understanding of unprotected consumers and the consumer movement in general. For example, the relatively unprotected state of poor consumers is directly traceable to the negative way this segment is viewed by the dominant elements of the culture. As Charles Valentine has so effectively argued, there is a deeply rooted pejorative tradition, even within the social sciences, about the poor [11]. The Calvinistic roots of our culture create an atmosphere conducive to a callous attitude toward the poor, who are often described by adjectives such as apathetic, ignorant, lazy, alienated, and inferior. These negative attitudes are further reinforced by the large numbers of poor who are also minority group members [12].

Table 3–1. Consumer Problems of Special Consumer Groups

Consumer Problems/ Group	Action/Response Sources			
	Major Corporations	Federal Government	State and Local Government	Private Consumer Groups
Children *1. Influence of TV commercials 2. Flammable fabrics 3. Dangerous toys 4. Nutrition	Television Code Review Board limits on frequency; use of hosts and cartoon characters in commercials; sponsorship of high quality shows; pretest of commercials with mothers	FTC hearings; FCC regulations on programming	(N.A.)	Attempts to ban TV advertising for children; distribution of a "TV Survival Kit"
Poor 1. Atomistic ghetto market structure *2. Illegal and unethical sales practices 3. Nutrition 4. Dependence on credit 5. Transportation	Better Business Bureaus	FTC; FDA; Commerce Department; Consumer Product Safety Commission regulations; FTC authority for corrective ads, counter ads, and ad substantiation; consumer rebates	Ombudsmen; state laws on deceptive sales practices; small claims courts; offices of consumer protection	Boycotts; pickets; class action suits; filing of complaints with appropriate regulatory bodies

Older Americans

1. Income maintenance *2. Health maintenance 3. Transportation 4. Shelter 5. Nutrition	Senior citizen discounts on drugs; marketing of low salt, low cholestral, and iron supplement products; innovations in detecting, monitoring, and treating chronic diseases of the elderly	Medicare; Medicaid; support of research through Administration on Aging	Community Health Clinics; Mobile Health Care facilities; innovations in delivery of health-care services	Expansion of non-profit prepaid health plans; volunteer services

*Selected for illustration.

The treatment of older Americans seems also to have a cultural explanation as simply stated as "our culture places a high value on youth" [13]. Unlike some cultures, we do not treat older members of the community with great respect and deference. The decline of the extended family too often has brought loneliness, isolation, and indifference for the elderly. As a people we seem to shun the elderly as unpleasant reminders that the youthfulness that is so treasured in this society is but a temporary state. If the belated and grudging acceptance of the concept of Social Security by this society is not sufficient evidence (even then one wonders if such a law might ever have been passed had it not been for the economic and political turmoil of the Great Depression), one can cite the case of medical care for older Americans. In spite of vigorous efforts during the Roosevelt-Truman New Deal–Fair Deal era to correct the often scandalous condition of health care in this country, Medicare did not become law until July 1, 1966 [14]. Less than full attention to the consumer problems of older Americans, therefore, is quite compatible with historical attitudes.

Much more puzzling has been society's apparent lack of concern for consumer protection aimed at young children. The reluctance to take corrective steps to protect children from inherently dangerous products such as lead-based paint, poisons, medicines, insecticides, and the like are as baffling as the needlessly hazardous toys that remain on the market. The attitude may well be rooted in the assumption that the parents, not the children, are actually the buyers—if not the users—of such products and that the traditions of parental supervision and caveat emptor prevail.

This tentative and doubtless partial explanation of the enigma of relative unconcern for consumer protection for children is also relevant to a broader discussion of consumerism. Just as consumers are generally naive about culture and its relationship to the market system, so have been many of the leading consumer advocates. Much of the criticism of business practices fails to recognize that the system is delivering what the customer wants. Even the most casual observer of American culture recognizes that one of the dominant social values is materialism. Indeed, it appears at the top of Rescher's "register of American values" [15]. Too often consumerists have failed to recognize the dominance of materialism and have ignored Petit's argument that "Chief among the determinants of the particular shape which an economic system takes are the dominant social values of the society of which the economy is a part" [16].

In short, realistic action programs will reflect an awareness of dominant social values (which is not to say that values cannot be altered, but it is clearly a gradual process, even in a dynamic society). Thus Max Lerner has suggested that in order to understand "the truth about American 'materialism' " one must identify "the dominant gods in the heaven of the American . . . consumer" [17]. Lerner's gods are comfort, cleanliness, and novelty. The American obsession with novelty represents a good example of quixotic confrontations by consumerists. Many fads, gadgets, and "new and improved products" may well be trivial or wasteful. But the utilitarian view of the marketplace too often ignores the noneconomic dimensions of that arena. Certainly it should not be necessary in the mid 1970s to restate the demise of the myth of the economic man. Consumerists forget that excitement, fun, and dreams are often more significant in the minds of consumers than concerns about deception, unsafe products, or full disclosure of product information.

This position is not offered as an apologia for the system or as a defense of marketing practices that violate consumer rights. But rather than trying to protect every consumer from personal foibles and weaknesses for superlatives and sizzle, the effort would be better spent on larger issues. The balance of this article, therefore, proposes a new venture on behalf of consumerism which, it is felt, meets these criteria. It deals with very major issues. It is in conformance with dominant values. And finally, the timing is right to get widespread support for the effort.

THE CONSUMERS' SPECIAL PROSECUTOR

While there is always a danger of assigning too much long term importance to current events, they can provide a measure of the public's mood. If any clear lesson has emerged from Watergate it is that people in powerful positions of public trust are not above violating that trust. Hence there is a need for periodic, objective scrutiny of their conduct and performance. The remarkable popularity of the Office of the Special Prosecutor is an important indicator of the attractiveness of the concept. Indeed, the firing of Archibald Cox and its aftermath (the "Saturday Night Massacre") are cited by some as the beginning of the end of the Nixon administration. Even those staunch Nixon supporters who argued that the President and his associates "didn't do anything that others hadn't done before" are providing at least implicit support for the *necessity* of the prosecutor's role.

In recent months this nation has witnessed the resignation of a President under a cloud of criminal conspiracy, the "no contest" plea of a vice president to a felony charge and his resignation from office, the indictment of several former cabinet level officials, and the sentencing of a federal judge and former state governor to prison for accepting bribes. The current public enthusiasm for careful scrutiny of public officials, coupled with the widespread and intense concern about inflation, sets the stage for the appointment of the Consumers' Special Prosecutor. The characteristics of this office would be as follows.

1. Unlike most proposals calling for action by government, this one will not lead to the creation of a permanent bureaucratic agency. In fact, the office should be limited to a life of not more than five years, to avoid encrustation with vested interests and cooptation. Government agencies have an uncanny ability to perpetuate themselves long after their usefulness has expired, but such would not be the case with the Consumers' Special Prosecutor (CSP). If the need arises again in the future, as it surely will, a new temporary CSP can be appointed.

2. The mission of the CSP would be to investigate those federal agencies directly charged with protecting the welfare of consumers. Unlike the presidential commissions that appear from time to time, the CSP would *prosecute* any agency officials or commissioners found in violation of the law. Instead of passive resignation to ineffective or even corrupt regulators, these agencies would now be held to the letter of the law. The CSP might find it fruitful to follow up on the kind of situation described in a recent article in the *Wall Street Journal*, which was captioned "CAB Is An Enthusiastic Backer of Moves to Trim Airline Service, Increase Fares" [18]. The article referred to the Civil Aeronautics Board as a "friendly watchdog." A thorough analysis of the CAB coupled with full disclosure of findings might be quite enlightening to the public and the Congress.

It could be argued, of course, that Ralph Nader and his associates have been fulfilling this role. They have documented the failings of the U.S. Department of Agriculture in protecting consumers from unsafe food [19], how the "Food and Drug Administration has shirked its duties" [20], and the ineptitude and corruption of the Interstate Commerce Commission [21]. However, in spite of their generally thoughtful and sound work, the impact on board or commission appointments and policies has been limited. Public awareness of their reports is very restricted, and of course they have had neither the force of law nor the credibility and visibility of a CSP. Since the problems are widespread, there is no reason to believe that the CSP would put Nader or Common Cause or Robert Choate or Herbert Denenberg out of business.

3. One aspect of the CSP's mission that would deserve top priority would be to assign particular urgency to investigating those governmental bodies having the greatest potential impact on the poor, the elderly, and young children. While the potential savings to consumers in general could be staggering, it would make sense to focus initially on those groups which have received the least attention in the past.

CONCLUSIONS

In essence, this paper has outlined the plight of relatively unprotected consumer groups, noted the importance of consumer action programs that are responsive to the dominant values of society, and suggested an approach for effective action. The recent reaffirmation of the worth of the legal process, coupled with rising concerns about consumer injustice (especially in the face of spiraling inflation), suggests that the time is ripe to deal with some deeply rooted causes of consumer problems. The notion of the Consumers' Special Prosecutor recognizes that all too often those charged with the public trust of representing the best interests of consumers have violated that trust. As Andrew Jackson warned in his first inaugural address in 1828:

> There are perhaps few men who can for any great length of time enjoy office and power without being more or less under the influence of feelings unfavorable to the faithful discharge of their public duties. Their integrity may be proof against improper considerations immediately addressed to themselves, but they are apt to acquire a habit of looking with indifference upon the public interest and of tolerating conduct from which an unpracticed man would revolt.

It is time to take dramatic and vigorous action on behalf of consumers. The concept of a Consumers' Special Prosecutor offers one means of pursuing this goal.

NOTES TO CHAPTER 3

1. John D. Rockefeller III, *The Second American Revolution: Some Personal Observations*, New York: Harper and Row, 1963, p. 54.
2. Fabian Linden, "The New Profile of Poverty," *The Conference Board Record* XI (8) (August 1974): 62. "The poor" as a category clearly overlaps

with the other two groupings—i.e., young children and the aged may also be poor.

3. "It's Older Americans, Not Senior Citizens, Month Now," *Aging* (May 1974): 6.

4. "Congress Passes Compromise Older Americans Act Amendments," *Aging* (May 1973): 5.

5. U.S. Department of Commerce, *Statistical Abstract of the United States, 1973*, (Washington, D.C.: U.S. Government Printing Office, 1973, 6–7.

6. David Caplovitz, *The Poor Pay More*, New York: The Free Press, 1963; Frederick D. Sturdivant (ed.), *The Ghetto Marketplace*, New York: The Free Press, 1969.

7. White House Conference on Aging, *Toward a National Policy on Aging*, Washington, D.C.: U.S. Government Printing Office, 1971.

8. No single source is available that covers the full range of consumer issues relative to young children. The following are representative of the available literature: Jean Carper and Warren G. Magnuson, *The Dark Side of the Marketplace*, Englewood Cliffs, N.J.: Prentice-Hall, pp. 123–127, 141–151; Jean Mayer, *Human Nutrition: Its Physiological, Medical, and Social Aspects*, Springfield, Ill.: Charles C. Thomas, 1972; Edward M. Swartz, *Toys That Don't Care*, Boston: Gambit, 1971; Scott Ward, "Kids' TV-Marketers on Hot Seat," *Harvard Business Review* L (4) (July/August 1974): 16–28, 146, 150–151.

9. Thomas Petit, *Freedom in the American Economy*, Homewood, Ill.: Richard D. Irwin, 1964, p. 277.

10. W.T. Tucker, *The Social Context of Economic Behavior*, New York: Holt, Rinehart & Winston, 1964, p. 22.

11. Charles A. Valentine, *Culture and Poverty*, Chicago: University of Chicago Press, 1968, pp. 18–47.

12. Frederick D. Sturdivant, "Subculture Theory: Poverty, Minorities, and Marketing," in Scott Ward and Thomas Robertson (eds.), *Consumer Behavior: Theoretical Sources*, Englewood Cliffs, N.J.: Prentice-Hall, 1973, pp. 469–520.

13. Tucker *op. cit.*, p. 24.

14. For an excellent review of the early struggle see Roy Lubove, "The New Deal and National Health," *Current History* XXXXV (264) (August 1963): 77–86.

15. Kent Baier and Nicolas Rescher (eds.), *Values and the Future*, New York: The Free Press, 1969, pp. 92–95.

16. Petit, *op. cit.*, p. 1.

17. Max Lerner, *America as a Civilization*, Vol. *I*, New York: Simon and Schuster, 1957, p. 250. Other discussions of materialism may be found in Harry K. Girvetz (ed.), *Contemporary Moral Issues*, Belmont, Cal.: Wadsworth, 1968, pp. 153–176; and Frederick D. Sturdivant, "Values and Marketing: Some Thoughts on Consensus and Materialism," in Fred C. Allvine (ed.), *Public Policy and Marketing Practice*, Chicago: American Marketing Association, 1973, pp. 19–31.

18. *Wall Street Journal*, 13 August 1974, p. 32.

19. Harrison Wellford, *Sowing the Wind*, New York: Grossman, 1972.

20. James S. Turner, *The Chemical Feast*, New York: Grossman, 1970, p. vi.

21. Robert C. Fellmeth, *The Interstate Commerce Omission*, New York: Grossman, 1970. For an overview of several regulatory bodies, see Mark J. Green (ed.), *The Monopoly Makers*, New York: Grossman, 1973. For an especially interesting account of the impact of a regulatory agency on the life of an individual, see D.H.V. Erickson, *Armstrong's Fight for FM Broadcasting: One Man vs. Big Business and Bureaucracy*, University, Ala.: The University of Alabama Press, 1973.

Chapter 4

Consumer Information: Sources, Audiences, and Social Effects

Robert N. Mayer
Francesco M. Nicosia

INTRODUCTION

The purpose of this article is to report some of the descriptive findings that were produced as part of a study of the interface between technology and consumers [1], and to draw out their implications for consumer protection and other issues of public policy. Our empirical focus is the flow of information *to and from consumers*, with special attention to the roles of federal agencies and private consumer organizations. This approach differs from most earlier attempts to study consumer information.

Ten years ago, a discussion of consumer information would have meant addressing, first, the degree of information contained in advertising and other communications from business to consumers, and second, the propriety of government regulation of these business initiated communications [2]. In other words, little attention would be paid to the flow of information from consumers (complaints, for example) and to sources of information other than business and informal personal contacts [3]. The corresponding view of people was that they were passive, powerless, and easy prey for the manipulative mass media [4].

The relevant research literature reveals two perspectives. One is an adaptation of the classic communications framework to information disseminated by firms and the business sector in general—that is, asking who says what, by which channel, to whom, and with what effect? To make this research more useful to managerial decision making, a sixth question was usually added: What are the costs and expected benefits to the firm of transmitting certain information? Hence, this "communication" approach takes the perspective of the information sender or source, and is concerned with message exposure, perception, credibility, informativeness, and influence.

The second perspective, in contrast, takes the viewpoint of the consumer and stresses the importance of consumer search for information. The "consumer search" approach seeks to identify the social and psychological characteristics of consumers, as well as the circumstances surrounding particular purchases, which are associated with varying degrees of search for information. It also attempts to determine the conditions under which one *type* of information source rather than another (usually businesses versus friends and relatives) will be sought or, as illustrated by the recent work of Jacoby, and associates, to measure the amount of information necessary for optimal decisions. [5].

The difference between these two perspectives is exemplified in their treatment of the cost of information. From the consumer search perspective, information cost refers to the consumer's expense (time, money, psychic energy) in obtaining the information, and it is the perception of this cost that is balanced against the perceived need for it and its anticipated value. From the communication perspective, cost is defined by the expense of producing and transmitting information. Its cost to consumers is relevant only inasmuch as it affects the message's accessibility and therefore its impact.

Our strategy in this article is first to discuss the roles of the federal government and private consumer associations in the flow of information to and from consumers, relying primarily on the communication perspective. Then, in order to draw the implications for consumer protection and public policy, we add the insights of the consumer search perspective and develop a third perspective, a societal perspective, which allows for analysis of the role of consumer information in the economy and society.

AN OVERVIEW OF INFORMATION FLOWS

In focusing only on consumer organization and federal agencies, we do not mean to imply that these are the only or the most important institutions involved in the flow of information to and from consumers. Certainly communications from the business sector, as well as personal and informal sources of information, play a tremendous role [6]. Our choice of concentration was dictated in part by a glaring gap in the literature and, more important, by our desire to make policy relevant recommendations concerning the technology–consumer interface. Figure 4–1 represents the range of institutions

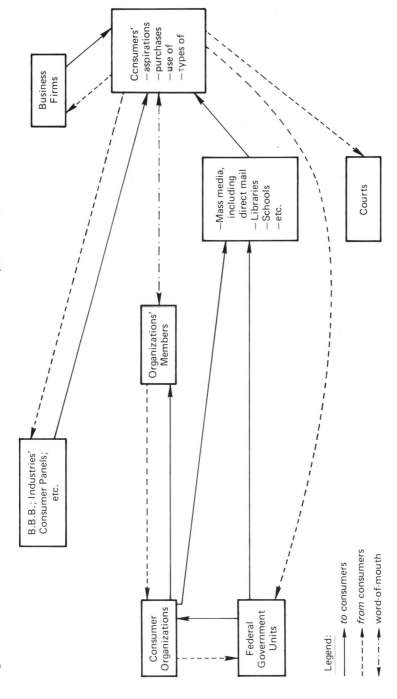

Figure 4–1. Information Flows *To* and *From* Consumers: A Blueprint Derived from Observed Activities

which *we* found in our research to be implicated in the flow of information to and from consumers.

The Roles of Private Consumer Organizations in Information Flows

Before presenting our findings, we must emphasize that our survey of private consumer organizations was not based on a systematically drawn random sample. Besides being biased toward consumer groups in California, New York, and Washington, D.C., our sample was drawn judgmentally in an attempt to represent all the major types of consumer organizations (consumer cooperatives, public interest law firms, and business sponsored consumer oriented organizations were excluded). We have a high degree of confidence that we succeeded in this attempt. Nevertheless, it must be remembered that our findings are extremely qualitative, and, when quantitative, of questionable generalizability.

Information Related Activities in the Context of Overall Activities. We factored the activities of the private consumer organizations studied into twenty-eight categories. Of these, fourteen could be said to involve the *dissemination of information to consumers*, and three related to *receiving information from consumers.* The most common type of activity was the publication of a newsletter; thirteen of the twenty-four organizations analyzed had one. In addition, two of the remaining eleven organizations published a commercial periodical. Hence, the majority of the organizations studied were involved in the *regular* dissemination of consumer information.

In addition, eleven of the organizations released special reports, although not on a regular basis. Typical topics include:

Chemical additives in food and
  alcoholic beverages
Asbestos in the air
Toxic substances in gasoline
Health hazards of asbestos
Concentration in the food industry
Pesticides
Cosmetics
Dangerous toys
Household cleaning products
Air and water pollution

Consumer education legislation
Voting records of members of Congress
Medicines and drugs
Life insurance
Family planning
Consumer credit
Buying clubs
Banking services
Public records relevant to consumer
  redress of grievances

Other activities that involved disseminating information to consumers included the production of special materials such as informative posters and calendars; issuing media releases, writing regular newspaper columns, making public appearances, holding public meetings and conferences, serving as a clearinghouse for consumer complaints (referrals), aiding and advising in grievance resolution, making available firm evaluations based on complaints received, and engaging in community activism such as informational picketing.

In terms of information from consumers, the organizations' most important functions are receiving and compiling consumer complaints. In fact, receiving these complaints and helping individual consumers solve their problems was the *raison d'être* of two of the organizations studied. An additional activity of relevance to the flow of information from consumers was the stimulation and encouragement of communication between individual consumers and their legislators.

It can be concluded that the exchange of information with consumers is the lifeblood of many private consumer groups. Further, several of their activities involve the dissemination of information to groups other than consumers, lobbying, testifying before legislative committees, commenting on legislation, representing consumers before various public agencies; and imparting skills such as training public servants in consumer affairs and training citizen lobbyists. It would not be too much to say that the exchange of consumer information is the most important function of private consumer organizations.

Major Type of Information Exchanged. The content of the information disseminated by consumer organizations shows a great variety both among these organization and within them. Some organizations specialize in reporting the results of comparative product testing or in reporting several different types of information. The following classification of types of information (by content) was derived from our analysis of the documentation we compiled.

1. The specific product (or service) attributes of a brand or the practices of an individual firm—e.g., results of comparative testing.

2. An entire product class or industrywide practices—e.g., drug pricing; guidelines for buying safe toys.

3. Particular substances that may be used in the manufacture or production of one or several goods—e.g., chemical additives in foods; asbestos; fluorides.

4. Federal consumer action, either legislative, regulatory executive, or judicial—e.g., Nader Report on the FTC; proposed laws.

5. Consumer action of state and local governments.

6. Activities of the particular consumer organization—e.g., petitioning of regulatory agencies.

7. Activities of other nongovernmental, consumer oriented organizations, especially private consumer groups—e.g., Consumer Federation of America reporting on activities of member organizations.

8. The services, resources, and information available from various organizations—e.g., grievance handling; publications.

9. Consumer attitudes and practices on an aggregate level and problems related to these patterns—e.g., price surveys; depletion of resources.

10. Negative (and positive) experiences of an individual consumer—e.g., misrepresentation; failure to honor warranty; particularly satisfactory repair job.

It is difficult to speak of the content of a given communication without also addressing its intended effects. It is clear from this list of types of information that the purpose of these communications is to alter knowledge, awareness, attitudes, or behavior. More specifically, some of this information takes the consumer's values as given and attempts to help him maximize them. Other types try to change or add to the criteria that are taken into account in a purchasing decision, while still others suggest changes in behavior with respect to buying, using, maintaining, and disposing of goods. Other goals of communication include preventing consumer disappointment and problems, increasing propensity to use information, and in the case of information from consumers, being responsive.

The Audience for Consumer Information. The size of the audience reached by a given communication depends on (1) the channel through which the message is sent; (2) the resources that can be committed to disseminating the information; (3) the cost to the consumer of obtaining the information, including the promotion given to the information; and (4) the characteristics of information receivers, especially their level of interest and education.

Consumer organizations typically rely on the print and broadcast media as well as on personal interaction as the principal channels for their information; they do not have access to point-of-purchase media such as labels or displays. While personal interaction may make for effective communication, it is not conducive to reaching a wide audience. The print and broadcast media are capable of exposing many people to a given message, but consumer organizations, because of their limited resources, often must depend on the good will of the media. If consumer issues are not considered newsworthy, they may receive little coverage.

Few private consumer organizations have the resources to distribute information free of charge on a large scale or to invest in promoting the sale of information. Because most consumer group publications offer little, if any, short term savings to the consumer, their cost must be kept low. Further reduction in their cost would probably not attract enough new readers to offset the loss in revenue; in other words, the price elasticity of consumer information is low. Consequently, the price of most consumer publications is either nominal or not calculable (as when one buys a membership in the organization and receives its newsletter). Only the comparative testing magazines can compete in price with other magazines.

Finally, it appears that purchasing consumer information publications depends more on an interest in consumer affairs and the desire to be a well informed consumer than on the hope of saving money. Several studies have shown that consumer publications attract a certain type of reader—high in education, middle-high in income and occupational status, and low in age [7].

It can be concluded that the actual audience of consumer publications will remain limited unless (1) the resources of consumer groups can be substantially increased (which would probably require increased revenue from publications—a Catch 22); (2) consumer information becomes more oriented to saving the consumer money on an immediate, purchase-to-purchase basis; (3) the publications become more entertaining or sensational; or (4) there is a significant increase in interest in consumer affairs among the general public. Until one or more of these conditions is met, information from most private consumer associations will continue to be exchanged with their members, those who use their services, those particularly concerned with developments affecting consumers, and the various levels of government.

The Roles of the Federal Government in Information Flows

While we were only able to study twenty-four private consumer organizations of the seventy-eight we were able to identify in the United States, we were able to collect at least some documentation on all of the federal agencies involved in consumer related areas. Of the sixty-nine federal offices listed in the Office of Consumer Affairs publication, *Guide to Federal Consumer Services* (1971), we selected for further study the twenty agencies most significantly involved in consumer affairs. We sent them questionnaires that probed their information related activities and asked for documentation that reflected these activities. Only one agency did not respond to our requests; consequently there is no problem of generalizability of our findings. Because of the broad range of activities engaged in by federal agencies, the vast amount of literature that they produce, and the proliferation of consumer oriented committees, panels, and offices within the agencies we studied, however, our findings may be less accurate and complete than they were in the case of the private consumer groups.

Federal Activities Influencing the Flow of Information to Consumers

We factored the activities of the forty-five federal agencies most significantly involved in consumer related activities into twenty-five categories (we eliminated twenty-four offices from the OCA list because we felt that they did not deal with citizens *as consumers*). Activities that affected the flow of information to and from consumers constituted a much smaller proportion of the activities of these government agencies than they had of the private consumer organizations. Only five of the twenty-five activities clearly involved the flow of information to consumers; (1) requiring or strongly suggesting the provision or public availability of certain types of information; (2) ensuring that all information provided to consumers, whether offered voluntarily or not, is accurate and not misleading; (3) producing and disseminating information to consumers on its own; (4) providing counseling services for special consumer groups such as the aged or non-English-speaking; and (5) being involved in consumer education, a crucial aspect of which is the provision of information.

Encouraging and Requiring Business to Provide Information to Consumers. When the federal government requires or encourages the provision of certain facts to the consuming public, it is difficult to say whether this information has really been provided by the government or by the firm involved. Nevertheless, this type of information to consumers, whether required by law or merely encouraged, differs from direct provision by government in two important respects. First, the costs of providing this information are primarily spread among the consumers of the given product rather than among the taxpayers as a whole. Similarly, it is less expensive for a firm to disseminate information that it has at its disposal than for the government to collect this information on its own. Second, this practice tends to encourage business to present facts that are relevant to consumer purchasing decisions before they are required or even encouraged by government.

Guaranteeing Information Accuracy. Federal action aimed at preventing and prosecuting fraud to ensure the accuracy of information reaching consumers usually involves the regulation of advertising, labeling, or packaging. In some cases the information intended for consumers must be approved in advance. For instance, the Agricultural Marketing Service of the Department of Agriculture approves all labels for meat, poultry, and their products prior to use in the marketplace. In other cases practices are merely monitored. The Department of the Treasury, through its Bureau of Alcohol, Tobacco, and Firearms constantly reviews the advertising for these products but does not require advance approval.

These regulatory activities tend to be organized on the basis of types of products rather than on the basis of the means by which this information is communicated to consumers. Only the Federal Trade Commission has the responsibility to prevent and prosecute consumer deception in general. Usually a particular agency watches over the advertising, labeling, and packaging of a group of products. The Food and Drug Administration looks after foods, drugs, devices, and cosmetics, while the Securities and Exchange Commission regulates securities. Whereas this type of system allows for the development of expertise in guaranteeing accurate consumer information for specific types of products, it puts a huge responsibility on the organization charged with the residual categories, namely, the Federal Trade Commission. Table 4–1 lists the federal agencies involved in this type of activity and their duties.

Federal Dissemination of Consumer Information. Regardless of the debates over the propriety of federal dissemination of consumer information, the government does supply a great deal of valuable information. This is not confined to information regarding the activities of agencies involved in consumer related areas, explanation of new laws, listings of publications available from agencies, and explanations of how to use government produced information such as grades and standards. Such information would not upset those who feel that it is inappropriate, or even dangerous, for the government to provide consumers with information. But the government also disseminates bibliographies of consumer resources, guides on how to buy and use particular types of products, ways to save money or make consumption more efficient, and even comparisons of specific brands (e.g., EPA's gas mileage ratings).

In fact, all ten types of information that are characteristic of the communication between consumer groups and consumers can be found in the exchange of information between federal agencies and

Table 4—1. Ensuring the Accuracy of Consumer Information

Agency	Activity
USDA-Agricultural Marketing Service	Approves all labels for meat, poultry, and related products in advance of their use
Federal Trade Commission	Prevents deceptive packaging and advertising; monitors TV, radio, and printed advertising for possible deception and fraud Assures truthful labels on wool, fur, and textile products
HEW-Food and Drug Administration	Assures that foods, drugs, devices, and cosmetics are honestly and informatively labeled and packaged
Department of Justice	Enforces federal laws pertaining to consumer fraud through cases referred to it by other government agencies
U.S. Postal Service	Polices mail for possible fraudulent schemes
Securities and Exchange Commission	Sets up regulations to prevent fraud in the securities markets
Department of the Treasury	Prevents consumer deception in the labeling and advertising of alcoholic beverages, tobacco products, and firearms (the FDA and FTC also have authority in this field but refer cases here)

consumers. There are differences of emphasis, to be sure. Relative to consumer organizations, the government provides less information that is brand specific and less information concerning substances used in the production or found in one or more products, but more information regarding available services and more information describing consumer attitudes and practices on an aggregate level. From the point of view of *content*, though, the federal government and private consumer associations provide the same *types* of information.

In terms of the intended effects of this information, the government's goals appear to be more limited than those of the consumer groups. That is, most of the government's information takes the consumer's values as given and tries to increase the efficiency of his choices (for example, the Department of Agriculture's "how to buy" series). One exception is in the area of consumer rights. There appears to be a substantial effort to explain the meaning and impact of new laws, such as the Federal Reserve System pamphlet, "What Truth in Lending Means to You", and to clarify consumer rights in situations in which they are often abused (e.g., the Interstate Commerce Commission's "Public Advisory No. 2: Arranging Transportation for Small Shipments—Shipper Rights, Remedies, and Alternatives"). In general, however, government provided information does not address consumer choices among brands or consumer decisions on whether to buy from within a product class. It does try to prevent consumer disappointments and problems.

In reporting their own activities, the agencies are extremely diligent in providing information. But this information provides no explicit criteria with which the consumer can form an opinion of the kind of job a given agency is doing. Finally, there is a great deal of literature whose apparent purpose is to make government produced information more accessible to the consumer. Besides the publications lists of various agencies, among the most important of these is the Consumer Product Information Center's "Consumer Information Index" and the Office of Education's "Consumer Education Bibliography."

Counseling Services and Consumer Education. Having just mentioned the provision of information about information, we have but to add the second key function of consumer education—increasing the propensity to use information. The federal government's involvement in consumer education tends to be rather limited. Only the Federal Trade Commission, Office of Consumer Affairs, Office of Education, and the Agriculture Department's Extension Service are significantly involved in consumer education. Further, the federal government prefers advising and supporting consumer education programs to running them. For instance, the Office of Consumer Affairs does not conduct consumer education programs but prepares guidelines to assist educators in formulating and implementing their individual courses.

Similarly, the FTC is more involved in providing consumer education materials and training consumer educators than it is in actually running such programs. The Extension Service's programs focus on family problems, using a home economics perspective, and cover topics such as nutrition, housing, clothing, health, and decision making regarding financial management of the home, in addition to more community oriented issues. The Office of Education supports local projects designed to prepare youth and adults for the dual roles of homemaker and wage earner. Therefore, taken as a whole, federal involvement in consumer education has been largely indirect and partial.

The Flow of Information from Individual
Consumers to the Government

Of the twenty-five categories into which we placed the activities of the federal agencies studied, only two involved communications from consumers—receiving consumer complaints, and investigating and acting upon them. Of these, only the reception of consumer grievances is a direct part of the communication between consumers and the federal government.

Although agencies such as the Office of Consumer Affairs and the Food and Drug Administration have as part of their mandates the conducting of investigations, conferences, and surveys concerning the needs, interests, and problems of consumers, our investigation of these agencies' activities showed that these methods of securing consumer input were relatively untapped. Hence, we concluded that the primary means by which these and other agencies receive information from individual consumers is through the handling of complaints and problems. Table 4—2 shows the federal agencies that receive consumer complaints and the specific offices to which complaints should be directed.

It can be seen from Table 4—2 that the federal system of receiving complaints is highly specialized and fragmented. Each agency is responsible for a particular type of complaint. In some instances these areas of responsibility are relatively narrow (the Civil Aeronautics Board only entertains complaints pertaining to air service), while in others the area of jurisdiction is quite broad (the Consumer Product Safety Commission will entertain most complaints involving issues of safety). Although in some cases these agencies will aid the consumer in achieving redress of his individual problem, the agencies tend to be more interested in using these reported problems as the first step in preventing other consumers from being similarly victimized. The FTC for example, will accept a wide variety of complaints, but until very recently never sought restitution for the individual complainant.

The Office of Consumer Affairs is the only federal agency charged with handling consumer complaints per se. But it is only empowered to serve a clearinghouse function—to promptly transmit the complaint to the appropriate agency. When a complaint does not fall within the clear jurisdiction of any particular agency, the office is supposed to transmit the complaint to the "Federal, State, or local agency whose regulatory or other authority provides the most effective means to act upon" the grievance (Executive Order 11583).

Table 4-2. Receiving Consumer Complaints

Civil Aeronautics Board	Complaints, either formal or informal, may be filed with the CAB by contacting its Office of Consumer Affairs in Washington, D.C.
Department of Commerce National Bureau of Standards	Any group of consumers (or manufacturers, distributors, etc.) may request the Department of Commerce to set in motion its standard-making procedure upon making the proper application to Washington, D.C.
Consumer Product Safety Commission	Telephone hotline, toll-free
Environmental Protection Agency	Inquiries should be sent to Director of Public Affairs in Washington, D.C.
Federal Communications Commission	Complaints should be sent to the Secretary of the FCC in Washington, D.C., but there are also Commission Field Engineering Bureaus in thirty-one major cities
Federal Power Commission	Consumers may make complaints directly to the FPC, but complaints relating to retail rates and service are beyond the jurisdiction of the FPC and should be taken up with local or state regulatory agencies. Interested individuals or consumer groups may intervene in FPC proceedings, including those involving licensing of hydroelectric power dams, electric and gas rate cases, and construction of natural gas pipeline facilities, on either economic, environmental, or service grounds
Federal Trade Commission	Complaints may be directed to the FTC office in Washington, D.C. or to any of the eleven field offices; however, the FTC does not seek refunds or adjustments in individual matters and it does not disclose the identity of the complainant
Department of Health, Education and Welfare—Office of Consumer Affairs	Complaints may be handled if one writes to Washington, D.C. office
Food and Drug Administration	Alleged violation should be reported to the nearest FDA district office; the consumer will be provided with a complaint form which he must file

Table 4—2. continued

Interstate Commerce Commission	Special consumer affairs office to handle household goods carrier complaints, including a telephone hotline. Other complaints and alleged violations should be reported to any regional office or to the Commission in Washington, D.C.
Department of Justice	Alleged violation of the antitrust law should be written to the Antitrust Division of the Department of Justice in Washington, D.C. or reported to one of its regional offices or to the local FBI office
Securities and Exchange Commission	Complaints may be directed to any of the Commission's regional offices or to the SEC in Washington, D.C.

Similarly, although the Office of Consumer Affairs is supposed to conduct investigations and surveys concerning problems, it does not have the power to collect data pertaining to consumer complaints from all the federal agencies. Thus there is no overall monitoring of consumer complaints, and this inhibits the development of an overall perspective on consumer experience and problems.

The Audience for Information from the Federal Government

In terms of the exposure of its communications, the federal government has several distinct advantages over private consumer organizations, but these are counterbalanced by one major disadvantage. One major advantage is that the federal government can use point-of-purchase media in addition to the broadcast and print media. This usage can take two forms. First, it can be direct intervention, as would be the case if unit pricing were made manatory. Second, and more commonly, the government's usage of point-of-purchase media is indirect, as when it makes mandatory the provision of certain information by businesses. These requirements can be quite specific, including the wording, size, and placement of the information, such as the health warning on cigarettes.

Not only do federal agencies have access to this additional means of reaching consumers, they also have more resources to commit to the dissemination of consumer information, including communications that promote their information. In addition, information from the government is more likely to be given free air time as a public service. A third advantage, which also has its roots in the greater resources of the federal government, is the ability to make consumer information publications available at little or no cost to consumers. The vast majority of federal publications of interest to consumers are individual booklets or pamphlets that either cost less than a dollar or are free of charge. Annual subscriptions for the consumer related newsletters and magazines are more expensive, but they are still quite inexpensive per issue. *Consumer News*, a bimonthly newsletter published by the Office of Consumer Affairs, was until recently available for only $2.00 a year, approximately ten cents an issue. One of the most expensive federal publications is the *FDA Consumer*, which informs consumers of recent developments in the regulation of foods, drugs, and cosmetics. Ten issues per year cost $6.50.

Despite these several factors favoring the exposure of federal communications relative to those of consumer groups, differences in the characteristics of the audiences to which these organizations address their communications make it an open question as to which information source achieves greater *exposure and impact*. We have already seen that the publications of private consumer organizations appeal to an audience that is high in education, medium-high in income and occupational status, and low in age. Members of this group are certainly interested in saving money and maximizing quality in their purchases, but they are also interested in long term cultivation of their purchasing efficiency and in being well informed about more general developments in consumer affairs.

The federal government, in contrast, is less likely to produce information that attempts to aid consumers in saving money or maximizing value when deciding among specific brands. Further, it is committed to disseminating information to those consumers who buy least efficiently and experience the greatest number of problems in the marketplace—the aged, the poor, the non-English-speaking— but these groups are least likely to have the propensity or competence to use consumer information. Thus, the government finds itself with powerful means and ample resources with which to reach consumers, but those who need this information the most are also least likely to be sensitive to these communications. It is left little choice but to hope that by continuing to direct information to and gearing information for the groups that need it most, interest in and receptiveness to it will be created. In the meantime, the government must continue to produce and require production of information that, while of potential interest and value to all consumers, is only used by a minority of them.

INTERNATIONAL COMPARISONS

When looking at the experiences of other nations, the most striking observation that many of the consumer organizations in other countries are sponsored by consumers *and* government simultaneously [8]. This is not just the case in the Scandinavian countries with their socialist governments; in fact, Scandinavian consumer information organizations are just as likely to be supported entirely by the government as they are to be sponsored jointly by consumers and government. But we also find joint sponsorship in such countries as Austria, Belgium, France, Germany, and Great Britain.

Several of these jointly sponsored organizations attempt to represent consumers as well as to inform them about a broad range of issues (Arbeitsgemeinschaft der Verbraucher in Germany; the National Union of Consumers in Italy). Most of them, however, focus more narrowly on purchase relevant information concerning specific brands through the use of comparative testing, informative labeling, and quality certification. While it is true that consumer organizations with primarily political and legislative goals are less likely to receive financial support from the governments of other countries and must relay more heavily on the contributions of women's organizations, cooperatives, trade unions, and consumers in general, the fact remains that in the United States, private consumer organizations bear a major portion of the cost of supplying consumers with information, a cost that in most other countries would be borne largely or entirely by the government.

In some respects this has not adversely affected American consumers. For instance, although dozens of other countries have comparative testing organizations, no such organization, regardless of how it is funded, can compare with Consumers Union in terms of total subscribers and the size of its budget. On the other hand, there are some indications that the *proportion* of a country's total population that subscribes is related to the extent of government support in this area. In Norway, for example, 14 percent of all households subscribe to the comparative testing magazine of the Norwegian Consumer Council (Forbrukerradet) [9].

Similarly, a lack of government funding may help to explain the relative lack of informative labeling organizations in the United States and may result in a greater reliance on mandatory rather than voluntary labeling requirements. The most successful informative labeling organization is the Swedish Institute for Informative Labeling (VDN). Manufacturers apply to use their label and are licensed by the VDN Institute and charged an annual fee for the privilege. The manufacturer decides what to put on the label; the Institute only controls the style of layout and the typography on the label. Information put on the labels, however, must be capable of precise measurement—that is, subject to standard tests—and it must be clear and unambiguous. Thus, a VDN label on an armchair might give the chair's precise dimensions, the materials from which it was constructed, and its strength as measured by standard tests. What is noteworthy about the Swedish experience with informative labeling is its popularity with manufacturers [10]. In 1969, for example, 868 licenses were in force [11].

Not all informative labeling programs have been able to enlist the support of manufacturers and consumers—as in the case of the British "Teltags" for example—but two points remain relevant for American consumer policy. First, while a successful informative labeling program can *eventually* generate a substantial proportion of its own budget, adequate funding from goverment, business, or consumer sources is necessary to get the program off the ground. Consumers must be taught to look for the labels and to use them, not as certificates of minimum quality, but as tools for selecting products that best meet their individual preferences and requirements. Second, when labeling information is provided only when made mandatory by government (which is largely the case in the United States), information tends to be made public only when it can be justified in terms of honesty, safety, or danger to health (i.e., "motherhood" issues).

Consequently, we have or will have truth-in-lending laws, cosmetic safety labeling, drug effectiveness duration labeling, and perhaps we will even have energy efficiency labeling. However, if consumers of a floor rug differentially value fastness to light, color fastness, and strength, they are unlikely to find standardized measures of these qualities on rug labels. (They might find such information in a Sears Roebuck or Montgomery Ward catalogue, but the ratings in each will not be based on the same standardized tests.) Thus, the selling point of informative labeling that should be emphasized is that it "counteracts the trend under mass production towards standardized goods which meet average needs, by separating out the distinctive characteristics of a product in order that they be set against individual needs" [12].

BROADER VISTAS

Kinds of Information and Public Policy

In the previous section we explicitly distinguished types of consumer information according to their content and the purposes of their sender. Furthermore, we implicitly discussed information according to its source, that is, either government or consumer groups. In order to discuss the public policy issues related to consumer information, however, a classification based on the needs of consumers, both as individuals and as members of a society, would seem more useful.

1. Information relevant to purchasing decisions. This is perhaps the most familiar type of consumer information. It may refer to the attributes of a particular brand, to the activities of a specific firm, or to certain product ingredients and components. In addition, information relevant to consumer buying decisions can also refer to the characteristics of a given product class, industry, or commonly used substance. Hence, the quality of consumer choice and consumer demand (its well informedness) and their effect on market performance and structure are the central issues for public policy.

2. Postpurchase activities—use, maintenance, repair, and disposal. This would include, for example, instructions on how to care for a garment or on how to make minor repairs on a car. The central concerns here are (a) the extent to which interaction with a good or service involves acquisition of knowledge and skills, and (b) consumer satisfaction with his experience with a good.

3. Information relevant to one's "social" position as a consumer. This would include information about the activities of various public and private organizations that affect the "political" position of consumers, consumer buying patterns, buying power, and attitudes, and the aggregate effects of national or community consumption activity. Hence, the key issues here are the degree to which consumers are aware, interested, and ethically engaged (the same qualities that are said to be necessary for the optimal functioning of our political system).

We could use the same tripartitie division of prepurchase, postpurchase, and social or nonpurchase information to classify information flowing *from* consumers. We prefer, however, to distinguish simply between information that is essentially expressive (suggestions, responses to surveys, letters of commendation) and that which is goal oriented and clearly requires a response (complaints, problems). Thus, the main issues are the quality of monitoring activity and the degree of responsiveness to purposive communications.

The "Adequacy" of the Current Supply of Consumer Information

Let us start with the issue of whether or not consumers currently have adequate information available to them. When this question is posed, it is generally assumed that the purpose of the information is to aid the consumer in making purchasing decisions that are "rational" given the consumer's preferences. It is further assumed that we are talking about information *to* consumers. Using our classification of kinds of information, however, we not only see that the sufficiency or adequacy of consumer information can be assessed from the point of view of postpurchase activity or nonpurchase considerations, but we also see that the flow of information *from* consumers can be inadequate, whether from the perspective of an individual consumer, a business manager, or a government official.

The major problem in determining the adequacy of the supply of any kind of consumer information is finding a criterion for judgment. The safest criterion is that of consumer preferences—that is, how much information consumers say they want, or how important they consider the provision of specific bits of information.

There are two drawbacks to this criterion, however. First, more consumers will express a desire for information than will actually use it. For example, Lorna Opatow found in a survey of consumers that 61 percent of the respondents had heard of open dating. When a description of open dating was given to all respondents, regardless of whether or not they had heard of it, 85 percent said that open dating was either important or extremely important to them *personally* [13]. Add to this the well known finding in advertising research that much information is actually used for no other purpose than to reinforce a previously made consumer decision. Consequently, an expressed desire for information on the part of consumers does not necessarily indicate that the information will be used or even how it will be used.

Second, expressed consumer preferences for information will tend to be limited by the supply of information currently available, so the desire for more information, especially for new types of information, may exist but not find expression. Further, since consumer desire for information depends in part on the perceived value of information (which varies among different types of products) relative to the perceived cost of obtaining it, if information is made more useful, more convenient, or less costly (that is, more efficient), then the consumer will want more information. For example, a label telling consumers what a tea kettle is made of is valuable if this information can be related to the product's durability and the speed with which it boils various quantities of water, and even more valuable if these attributes can be compared to other kettles made of the same or different materials.

Thus, any determination of the adequacy of consumer information based on the expressed desires of consumers is likely to overstate the extent to which consumers actually use the information available to them, but it might underestimate the extent to which consumers might use new types of information that are perceived as more valuable or less costly, or both.

Social and Economic Effects of Consumer Information

Since scientists are not likely to discover a basic human need for consumer information against which to measure the adequacy of the current supply, social criteria must be used. This is essentially what is meant by those who assert the consumer's "right to know." Although it has been argued that the right to information is basic and therefore justifies itself, consumer information as a right (and the substantial expense it requires) is more often justified in terms of its effects on the market and society. Much the same argument can be made in the case of the consumer's "right to be heard."

The individual's rights to express his opinions and have his grievances fairly addressed are certainly important in themselves, but their greater justification lies in their ability to keep business and government attuned to the feelings of consumers and to aid these institutions in preventing problems for large numbers of consumers. Let us look, then, at some of the socioeconomic effects of consumer information.

First, it is commonly asserted (with more logical than empirical proof) that well informed, rational consumers are essential to the efficient operation of a competitively organized market economy. Even if rationality in purchasing can only be defined in terms of maximizing one's own values, firms that offer the greatest amounts of these values should be rewarded with "intelligent dollar votes" when consumers choose carefully and deliberately, not when they reach their decisions in a state of wonder and perplexity [14].

Richard Holton, former chairman of the Consumer Advisory Council and Assistant Secretary of Commerce, summarizes these arguments in his notion of the "quality" of consumer demand [15]. By this Holton means the nature (information from previous product usage in contrast to information resulting from external search, for example) and the extent of the information that the consumer brings to bear on a given purchasing decision. He contends that by considering the quality of consumer demand across markets, one can understand why certain markets are likely to yield results approximating the competitive model more closely in some cases than in others.

Holton is quick to note that under some circumstances, the quality of consumer demand may be quite complete even if the state of information is limited to what is in the mind of the consumer when the purchase is first contemplated—that is, prior to any external search. When these conditions do not apply (for example, when the item is bought infrequently and the rate of technological change in the product is rapid relative to the frequency of purchase), however, the requirements of the competitive ideal will not be fulfilled on the demand side. For instance, when relevant information is absent or when consumers do not use the information, consumers will tend to rely on national, well advertised brands, thereby excluding the small competitor who may be offering superior value. Thus, imperfections in the quality of demand become translated into imperfections on the supply side.

While this first example of the socioeconomic effects of consumer information refers primarily to the impact of prepurchase information and only secondarily to information pertaining to postpurchase activities, the reverse is true of our second example—the impact on consumer satisfaction. While satisfaction with a product is related to the quality of the process by which it was chosen, consumer satisfaction is more intimately connected with experience in using the item, which in turn becomes a key element in prepurchase information for the next purchase. Therefore, the extent to which information covering use, maintenance, and repair is provided or available to consumers can affect the quality of the consumer's experience with a product.

In the case of an automobile, if the owner is informed about ways of driving that will minimize wear on the car, ways of maintaining it that will reduce the need for major repairs, and ways of performing minor repairs that will save him money, consumer's satisfaction with the car is likely to be higher than without this information. This might be true even if he doesn't use the information!

Thus, information designed to increase consumer satisfaction quickly takes on broader social dimensions. If added information can teach consumers to use products more efficiently and to maintain them so they will last longer, natural resources will be conserved. In addition, if information can add to the consumer's satisfaction with the goods he has acquired, not only will trust and respect for the firms directly involved tend to increase, but a more positive attitude toward the entire business community might result. Once entrusted with this confidence and respect, the process can become self-reinforcing. The implications of such a development are enormous [16].

As a third example, let us point out how the provision of information that is not particularly relevant to specific purchases can also have far-reaching effects. If government agencies are going to accept the role of safeguarding the consumer, isn't it important that consumers be aware of how their interests are being formulated, so that, if necessary, they can redirect consumer policy through their power as voters? On the other hand, if consumers are only one of several groups whose interests the government seeks to advance, the reasons for consumer awareness and involvement in these activities hold all the more strongly.

Information regarding the aggregate effects of a society's consumption activity is a final example of the potential effects of information that has little relevance to a specific purchase. For example, statistics on the amount of aluminum used annually by Americans in comparison to the consumers of other countries, or facts on the amount of water pollution, air pollution, and solid waste generated in one's community may raise consumer awareness at least to the point that the ethical choices involved in consumption and the possibility of social responsibility on the part of consumers become issues in consumer activity and decisions.

Consumer behavior does not occur in isolation. It affects one's fellows and generations to come. When consumer information can increase a person's efficiency in buying and using (for instance, save him money), the calculus of expected gain and perceived cost determines information search. The gains from obtaining and processing this information are either imperceptible or of a social or moral, rather than financial, nature. Hence, in several problem areas in which a well informed and involved consumer population could do the most good, the incentives for consumers to acquire information and increase their awareness are the weakest.

Finally, information *from* consumers also has its social and economic consequences. From the point of view of individual firms, communications from consumers provide an alternative to and a richer measure of consumer satisfaction and reaction than sales figures. Yet we have also seen that information from consumers provides private consumer organizations and public agencies with indicators of consumer problems and thereby serves as a catalyst for action that will prevent further harm to consumers.

Although we have already noted that the federal system of receiving complaints is highly specialized and fragmented and that there is little overall monitoring of consumer complaints and problems, there appears to be a growing awareness of the importance of communications from consumers as a source of information to social managers. The Consumer Product Safety Commission, for example, is currently considering a new set of rules that would force all companies (other than retailers) to keep records of all customer safety complaints for five years, even if the firm thinks the complaint isn't valid. These records would then provide a source of information for the Commission to draw from in discovering whether products with safety defects are being turned out.

Some private consumer groups have already realized the usefulness of consumer communications with regard to their experience with products and firms, and they provide this information to other consumers as a form of prepurchase information. Thus, information from consumers can have positive socioeconomic effects both through its ability to alert business managers and public officials to consumer problems and through its ability to direct consumers away from firms that are not responsive to consumers (and, of course, toward firms that are responsive).

Should Consumer Information Be Subject to Cost-Benefit Analysis?

The foregoing examples of the *possible* social and economic effects of increased consumer use of information should not be taken as a call to provide consumers with more and more information from any and all sources, for if marketing and communications research have taught us anything, it is the following:

1. The existence of an informative communication does not imply that it will be received or perceived. Consumer perception is very selective.

2. Information is not objective. The meaning consumers attach to a given bit of information may bear little resemblance to what the communicator intended to impart.

3. Even if a message is perceived and internalized, it may not be used by the consumer. The information may have no behavioral consequences.

Therefore, we have not asserted the desirability of any and all information on the grounds of a basic consumer right but have, rather, tried to indicate some of the potential economic and social benefits of government and business (and hence, ultimately, consumer) expenditures on consumer information, and thereby justify its costs. Different parties can expect different benefits from providing consumer information. Similarly, different types of information have different costs and different means of distributing these costs. For example, if a private firm adds an informative label to its product, it hopes to increase its sales and the cost of this information is borne primarily by the firm and its customers.

If, on the other hand, the government requires the firms of an industry to include a label on product care, the expected beneficiary is the entire consuming public, and the costs are absorbed by all consumers in their roles as taxpayers. Further, if a private consumer group publishes a report on the health dangers of certain food additives or on air pollution caused by asbestos, it attempts to increase the awareness of its readers and to raise the level of public debate on these issues, while it hopes that enough sales are generated to allow for its continued organizational existence.

Hence, consumer information is subject to a kind of cost-benefit analysis. For government, the benefits must remain loosely defined and temporally inexact, for the expected gains are largely qualitative and societywide in scope. For business firms and private consumer groups, though, it is a rather strict relationship. When not subject to government regulation, private firms will spend on consumer information to the extent that it can be justified in short term revenues or good will (long term revenues and stability). The private consumer group essentially lives to exchange information with consumers, for as long as consumers will pay for this information.

Since much of the information provided by the private consumer organizations does not lead to direct financial gains for consumers, the existence of many of them is precarious. Therefore, the government can only allow them to go under if it is willing to provide the same information itself or deems the information of minimal social importance. Otherwise, it should be ready to assist these groups financially under certain conditions. There is certainly ample international precedent.

It should be emphasized that just because calculation of benefits from government expenditures on consumer information is inexact and difficult, this by no means implies that efficiency in expenditures should not or cannot be sought. For example, it might be decided that to encourage consumers to look for safety features when they buy their cars would be in the national interest. Whether to achieve this goal by spending on television spots showing devastating accidents or by rating cars according to their crashworthiness and then requiring manufacturers to put these ratings on a label (or present the results on TV spots) then becomes the crucial question. An adequate answer would require drawing on the knowledge of advertisers, marketers, and survey researchers to estimate and compare the costs and effects of alternative methods. We should not necessarily believe those who claim that advertising can convince consumers of anything, whether they be the critics of advertising or its proponents.

Consumer Protection Through Information?

Providing consumer information is clearly not the only means of attempting to advance consumer interests. Different methods may be more or less appropriate to the solution of certain types of problems. For example, consumers can be protected from monopoly prices by the encouragement of more vigorous competition. Consumers can be protected from dangerous products through safety standards—that is, regulation of the behavior of producers. During the recent energy crisis, it appeared that even the behavior of consumers would have to be regulated, in the form of rationing, in order to protect them from gasoline shortages. In these cases, increased provision of information to consumers would represent either a less efficient or totally inefficient means of protecting consumers.

The distinctions among different means of advancing consumer welfare are not always sharp. For instance, should labeling requirements be considered an example of increased provision of information or regulation of the behavior of producers? There is a basic distinction, however, between information provision and all other means of consumer protection. Regulation of products and producers involves a change in the *quality* or nature of the alternatives open to the consumer (he cannot choose a new car without an anti-smog device or seat belts). Promotion of competition tends to *increase the number* of alternatives available. Regulation of consumer behavior *decreases the options* open to the consumer. Providing consumers with more information, though, leaves both the number of choices and the quality of the alternatives unchanged. It is therefore the means most compatible with freedom of choice, which includes the freedom to choose in a self-destructive manner.

Consumer education has not been given a chance to live up to its potential in increasing the consumer's propensity to use information. Further, as cultural norms continue to favor the well informed consumer, people and especially children may begin to internalize the value of consumer search for information for its own sake. For the time being, however, consumer use of information will be largely determined by its expected return relative to its perceived costs. Thus, business and government can increase the consumer's propensity to use information by decreasing the financial, time, and psychological costs of obtaining information and by increasing the usefulness of information.

One way of increasing the value of consumer information is to make it more comparable across brands. Another is to provide information along those dimensions that are salient to different types of consumers and that allow for a better matching of distinctive product characteristics and individual needs. Reduction of the perceived costs of consumer information might involve placing more information at the point of purchase or in the media consumers routinely use. Finally, consumer information can be made more entertaining, thereby reducing the psychic costs of processing information. Thus, both the argument that consumers should be given more information and the argument that consumers don't use the information they already have may miss the mark: it all depends on the form in which the information is presented and the expected benefits relative to the perceived costs of using it.

Let us conclude by raising one final issue. Even if all consumers had plenty of information at their disposal—*and used it*—this would not necessarily predict the nature of their choices. People have accepted their right to consume, but not the ethical responsibility in choosing what they consume. Yet it is precisely a consciousness of the moral and social dimensions of consumption, and action following from this awareness, that is essential if the programs of both government and business concerning recycling, energy conservation, nutrition, and pollution control are to be effective.

Hence, to what extent do we wish to influence, and by what right do we try to change, the values consumers use in making their decisions? Are the sanctity of the environment, the welfare of our fellow citizens, and the rights of future generations more important values than our comfort and convenience and the maximization of individual, short term self-interest? It is not the American tradition to legislate morality, but perhaps we can try to make consumers—not just businessmen—more aware of the ethical and social dimensions of consumption activity by providing information, from all sources, that promotes self-consciousness and awareness of the values we bring to bear when we buy, use, and dispose of consumer goods.

NOTES TO CHAPTER 4

1. Robert N. Mayer and Francesco M. Nicosia, *Technology, the Consumer, and Information Flows*, a report prepared for the National Science Foundation's Office of National Research and Development Assessment, 1974.

2. Louis P. Bucklin, "The Informative Role of Advertising," *Journal of Advertising Research* (September 1965). *Freedom of Information in the Market Place*, Freedom of Information Center, 1967.

3. Exceptions are, for example: Ralph M. Gaedeke, "Filing and Disposition

of Consumer Complaints: Some Empirical Evidence," *Journal of Consumer Affairs* (Summer 1972); and Hugh M. Sargent, *Consumer Product Rating Publications and Buying Behavior*, Urbana, Ill.: Bureau of Business and Economic Research, University of Illinois, 1959.

4. Herbert Marcuse, *One-Dimensional Man*, Boston: Beacon Press, 1964; C. Wright Mills, *The Power Elite*, New York: Oxford University Press, 1956; Vance Packard, *The Hidden Persuaders*, New York: David McKay, 1957.

5. Examples of this perspective include: George Katona and Eva Mueller, "A Study of Purchasing Decisions," in Lincoln H. Clark (ed.), *Consumer Behavior: The Dynamics of Consumer Reaction*, New York: New York University Press, 1955, pp. 30–87; Louis P. Bucklin, "Testing Propensities to Shop," *Journal of Marketing* (January 1966), pp. 22–27; Louis P. Bucklin, "Consumer Search, Role Enactment, and Market Efficiency," *Journal of Business* (October 1969), pp. 416–438; Donald F. Cox, "The Audience as Communicators," in Donald F. Cox (ed.), *Risk Taking and Information Handling in Consumer Behavior*, Boston: Division of Research, Graduate School of Business Administration, Harvard University, 1967, pp. 172–187; Donald J. Hempel, "Search Behavior and Information Utilization in the Home Buying Process," in Philip R. McDonald (ed.), *Marketing Involvement in Society and the Economy*, Chicago: American Marketing Association, 1969, pp. 241–249; and James F. Engel, David T. Kollat, and Roger D. Blackwell, *Consumer Behavior* (2d ed.) New York: Holt, Rinehart and Winston, 1973, pp. 349–435; Francesco M. Nicosia, *Advertising, Management and Society*, New York: McGraw-Hill, 1974, Chapters 12 and 13.

6. For a comprehensive examination of the private sector or sender of information to consumers via mass media, including unpublished data and new elaborations of federal statistics, see Nicosia, *op. cit.*, Chapter 11 through 14.

7. See, for instance, Hugh W. Sargent, *Consumer Product Rating Publications and Buying Behavior*, Urbana, Ill.: Bureau of Business and Economic Research, University of Illinois, 1959, pp. 37–51.

8. There are also a few instances of consumer information organizations that are funded jointly by consumers and business organizations, in Finland, France, and Switzerland.

9. Hans B. Thorelli, "Consumer Information Programmes," *International Consumer*, Proceedings of the 7th I.O.C.U. Congress (Autumn 1972), p. 16.

10. John Martin and George W. Smith, *The Consumer Interest*, London: Pall Mall Press, 1968, pp. 204–205.

11. Thorelli, *op. cit.*, p. 17.

12. Martin and Smith, *op. cit.*, p. 216.

13. Lorna Opatow, "Consumer Opinions of Open-Dating, Nutritional Labeling, Packaging and Pollution," *Proceedings of the American Marketing Association*, 1972, pp. 236–240.

14. Examples of this assertion can be found in Louis P. Bucklin, "Consumer Search, Role Enactment, and Market Efficiency," *Journal of Business* (October 1969), p. 416; Arch W. Troelstrup, "The Consumer Interest and Our Competitive System," in *Freedom of Information in the Market Place*, Freedom of Information Center, 1967, p. 77.

15. Richard Holton, "Consumer Behavior, Market Imperfections, and Public Policy," in J.W. Markham and G.F. Papanek (eds.), *Industrial Organization and Economic Development*, Boston: Houghton Mifflin, 1970.

16. In a thoughtful assessment of information disclosure practices, George S. Day concludes that although "the available evidence strongly suggests that past disclosure efforts have had little effect on consumer behavior . . . the important conclusion is . . . that more information enhances confidence" in the decision process, the product, and the seller ("Information Disclosure as a Consumer Protection Strategy," 1974 Albert Wesley Frey lecture, University of Pittsburgh Graduate School of Business, May 7, Pittsburgh, Pa.).

Chapter 5

Does Industry Listen?

William W. Bradley

This article concerns the consumer-affairs professional in business and what he is trying to bring to the business-consumer relationship. First of all, we need to recognize two things: (1) business and consumers need each other, and these mutual needs can best be met within an open, honest relationship; and (2) there have been problems in business-consumer relationships, some of which are not yet solved. A basic purpose, then, of the consumer affairs professional is to help solve the problems existing in the business-consumer relationship so that both business and consumers can be of mutual help.

Successful businesses grow; and when they grow, they become more complex. This isn't necessarily bad, but it does usually create some problems in the business-consumer relationship. Department managers often are specialists who are not necessarily conversant with overall corporate goals. When one has the stated responsibility for the growth and health of his own "tree," it is easy to overlook the "forest" of factors that contribute to its well-being. Thus, the business forest and the necessity of good consumer relationships may be missed by those responsible for tending the departmental trees.

The insulation of top business management from consumers often effectively prevents the transmittal of information either from or to the consumer. If the business has a consumer affairs professional, the consumer can write or speak directly to him, for he has the knowledge to answer most consumer questions. If he doesn't know the answer, he has contacts within the company to obtain it quickly.

Although many people in a business have "more important" things to do than to listen to consumers, the consumer affairs professional does not. His primary responsibility is to listen to consumers. If they have a complaint, he has the authority to resolve the complaint without getting entangled in red tape. Although a specific complaint is usually handled very quickly, elimination of the cause of the complaint often is not so simple. By analyzing and communicating complaints, the consumer affairs professional can get action started where it can do the most good. This might be in virtually any area of the company.

If a product is involved in a complaint, the problem may be with the design of the product, the materials from which it is made, the manufacturing process itself, inadequacies in the quality control system, or even faulty distribution practices. Regular communication of consumer complaints and inquiries to all of these areas of a company offers two distinct advantages.

1. The department manager can see where his departmental activities interact with the consumer. He may see where certain cost-cutting measures, for example, have created a problem with consumers that was not evident in the department.

2. The departmental managers can feel they are a part of the total system of furnishing quality products to the ultimate consumer. They have a chance to interact with the marketplace in a small way and thus get a better overall picture of consumer-business relationships than they could from only a narrow departmental viewpoint.

The consumer affairs professional works for business but is specifically charged with representing the consumer and speaking for the consumer to the business. As we mentioned before, the top management of a business is often very well insulated from the consumer. In many companies, however, this insulation is being effectively penetrated by consumer affairs professionals. Many companies have now formed consumer affairs committees, which meet regularly to analyze individual consumer complaints and inquiries and the pattern of these complaints or inquiries. These committees are made up of persons on the working level in the business who can put their heads together and outline corrective actions or at least plans to find and implement corrective actions. In this way, not only is the consumer who originally complained benefited, but all future consumers of the product or service can benefit from the resulting improvements.

There are two types of consumer affairs programs in business. A passive consumer affairs policy consists of responses made as a result of consumer initiated contacts. This involves complaint handling and internal communications. An aggressive consumer affairs policy is the active correction of complaint causes and speaking for the consumer in decision making activities. Both approaches should be included in a successful program.

We feel that a consumer affairs program in business should proceed along at least five avenues.

1. The first action to be taken should concern the consumer himself. If he has a complaint, this complaint should be heard and a fair settlement made without delay. The consumer has already suffered inconvenience because of the unsatisfactory nature of the product or service, and further delay usually adds to this inconvenience. Consumer affairs professionals throughout the country are in general agreement that the vast majority of consumers who contact companies with complaints are not trying to "rip off" the business. Most complaints are legitimate. Admittedly, there are a few who take advantage of businesses and try, sometimes successfully, to gain adjustments to which they are not entitled. These persons represent a very small percentage of consumers, however. A policy of prompt fair adjustment is essential. In the dialogue with the consumer the consumer affairs professional should be open and honest and realize that the consumer is an intelligent human being and should be treated accordingly.

2. The second avenue is that of communication with the rest of the business. Records of complaints must be kept and trends analyzed. The complaints should be investigated beyond settling with the consumer, to determine why the complaint occurred in the first place. These findings then should be communicated to the various operating departments in the company so that the many kinds of expertise available can be brought to bear on the problem. This also allows upper management to know what the consumers are saying and what they consider to be problems with the business. Management commitment to an effective consumer affairs program can then be made with full knowledge of what it involves.

3. Closely following the communication within the company should be the investigation of causes. Not all complaints can be traced to causes within the company, as they sometimes stem from factors occurring after the firm has lost control of the product. Most complaints, however, can be traced to causes that are either directly or indirectly under the company's control.

4. As a result of the communication and investigation, the defined causes of consumer dissatisfaction should then be corrected. This may not be possible in every case, for the state of the art may be

such that absolute perfection cannot be achieved. Attempts should be made, however, to bring all available resources to bear on such problems. Businesses usually hire people because of their talents, and it is often amazing what can be accomplished when these combined talents are applied to problems.

5. Another major area of consumer affairs in business is involvement in the decision making process. Thus far the focus has been on listening to and speaking for the dissatisfied consumer. We need also to consider the consumer who has no complaint.

Almost every activity within a company affects consumers in some way. These areas include design of the product or service, materials that go into a product, people who perform a service, manufacturing of a product, quality control standards, packaging of a product, pricing of products or services, advertising, distribution, labeling, complaint handling, and many more. More and more consumer affairs professionals are taking part in making decisions in these areas, and it is one of the most important parts of their function. This is where the consumer affairs professional can really speak for the consumer and make certain that consumer interests are given careful consideration. When early consideration is given, many potential problems can be avoided without the need for correction and apologies later on.

A little over a year ago, a group of concerned consumer affairs professionals formed an association called the Society of Consumer Affairs Professionals in Business, or SOCAP. The stated purpose of SOCAP is to "foster the integrity of business in its dealings with consumers, promote harmonious relationships between business and government and consumers, and advance the consumer affairs profession." I believe that it helps shed some light on SOCAP if we look at the symbol adopted by the board of directors. This symbol is a Möbius strip, a one-sided surface that is made from a rectangle by keeping one end fixed, rotating the other end 180 degrees, and putting against the first end—like a ribbon that is twisted once, then its ends folded together. This figure has properties that fit in well with the philosophy of SOCAP. First, although it appears to have two sides (like most other things), it actually has only one side. This illustrates the philosophy that business and consumers are not really on opposing sides: when everything is objectively considered, they share many common goals and purposes. Neither can exist without the other, and most adults are both producers and consumers.

The Möbius strip has another interesting property. It can be cut completely in half down the middle but it is still only one piece. This illustrates the philosophy that approaches to consumerism which would try to separate business and consumers into two separate segments of society cannot be successful. Consumers and businesses must work together in cooperation.

Part 2

The Role of the Media: How Effective?

Commentary

SETHI

Although the consumer movement has made significant strides in the past ten years through the efforts of governmental agencies, consumer organizations, and social activist groups such as Ralph Nader's, all that could have been achieved has not been done. Instead of continuing with consumer protection as it is, with its regularity mechanism, judicial process, organized consumer groups, and industry self-regulation, three kinds of balances must be restored between the consumer and the producer: information balance, bargaining power balance, and adjudication and remedy and relief balance.

POLLOCK

In the consumer realm, newspaper editors and television or radio news directors have been something less than crusading. Although they have fought consistently for integrity and protection of sources in news reporting, editors have not looked thoroughly at the full content of their papers or programs. Specifically, editors could substantially improve their service to consumer by scrutinizing the advertisements in their media as closely as the news stories. In addition, most stations and papers could provide better coverage of consumer issues.

KANDEL

Critics of the press have accused it of both being too favorable toward business and advertisers and being too hostile and ignorant of business to treat it competently. The truth probably lies between these extremes, with the print media having done a much better job of covering business news than television or radio. But even newspapers could be much more innovative and aggressive, such as reporting what happened to the person leaving the job when announcing a business promotion—the real story may be the person's leaving rather than the other person's promotion. So although the media's coverage of business has improved in recent years, there is much left to be done.

✳ *Chapter 6*

Emerging Issues in Consumerism

S. Prakash Sethi

The lot of today's consumer is not a happy one. He feels beleaguered, bewildered, and exploited. On one hand, he perceives himself as threatened by hordes of unscrupulous vendors—all using every conceivable means to sell him poorly made, deceptively promoted, and overpriced goods. He finds himself ill equipped to separate accurate information from puffery, to evaluate the relative merits of a product in terms of its price, and to recognize potential dangers associated with product usage.

On the other hand, he has an army of friends, all clamoring to protect his interests and "save" him—whether he wishes to be saved or not—from unsavory and unscrupulous vendors and also from his other "no good" well wishers. These friends come in all political shades and with varying degrees of fervency and institutional clout. They include political leaders, government regulators, self-appointed consumer spokesmen, consumer unions and other organized consumer groups, and last but not least, business firms.

In the case of his so-called enemies, the consumer may think that at least he recognizes them, although he may feel unable to do much about improving his buying situation. But in the case of friends, he may be wary and uncertain because he finds it difficult to distinguish the genuine friend from the fake. There is no uniformity of viewpoint among his friends about from whom he should be saved, from what he should be saved, and how he should be saved. Each one claims to know what his best interests are and constantly warns him to be careful about his other friends. It is small wonder that many consumers today are suspicious in varying degrees of almost all businesses and apathetic toward the efforts of their saviors.

Admittedly, I have presented an exaggerated picture of the current confusion among the ranks of consumers and consumer advocates. However, my point is valid. The consumer movement has made significant strides in the past ten years, and I would not demean the efforts and contributions of various government agencies, consumer organizations, social activist groups like Ralph Nader's, and various business firms. However, their most ardent supporters would be hard pressed to deny that these contributions were not all that could have been achieved or that some of their efforts were ill conceived, poorly planned, and inefficiently executed.

CURRENT APPROACHES TO CONSUMER PROTECTION

Current approaches to consumer protection may be broadly classified as the regulatory mechanism, judicial process, organized consumer groups, and industry self-regulation.

Regulatory Agencies

Most governmental regulatory agencies continue to go their merry way, protecting the industries within their jurisdiction from the vagaries of the marketplace, the ill informed consumers and their vicious, conniving spokesmen, and the well meaning but misguided judiciary and politicians. Notable exceptions to the foregoing are the Federal Trade Commission in its recent change of direction and the newly formed Consumer Product Safety Commission. But, by and large, our regulatory agencies have either misread or misinterpreted their mandate for protecting the public interest.

There is a vast body of evidence pointing out the relative ineffectiveness of the regulatory system in serving what is broadly referred to as consumer interest. Moreover, given the nature of our sociopolitical system, it is doubtful whether substantive improvements in protecting consumer interest can be achieved via the regulatory mechanism. In fact the consumer lobby has recognized this with their support for a bill creating a consumer protection agency. I believe their efforts are misplaced, for the same reason that I consider that the heavy lobbying by business and special interest groups to defeat this bill in Congress was misguided. If experience is any guide, business stood to gain much more by co-opting the effort and molding it in a manner that would provide it with a modus vivendi than by opposing it outright. This idea has caught the imagination of an influential group of people both inside and outside the government and will not "just go away."

Judicial Process

Nor have the judicial processes worked to redress legitimate consumer grievances. As Professor Philip Schrag of Columbia Law School shows so convincingly in his book, *Counsel for the Deceived*, when it comes to litigation, the hapless individual consumer is no match for the corporate defendant, no matter how valid his claim. The game is so rigged that time and money costs put it beyond his reach even before he starts. Class action suits offer one possible avenue and have shown some success, but recent U.S. and California Supreme Court decisions have imposed restrictive eligibility criteria and heavy financial burdens on consumer class action suits.

State and city consumer affairs bureaus, started with great fanfare, have mostly degenerated into window dressing efforts or sops to consumer groups. Even the most effective of them and a model for other agencies, New York City's Office of Consumer Affairs, has fallen upon hard times and is beset by indifference from the new mayor and city officials and internal frustration from lack of effective leadership and accomplishments.

Organized Consumer Groups

Organized consumer groups, while effective in many areas, tend to serve a limited number of needs for their membership, which is generally well educated, middle class, and reasonably well prepared to make intelligent, knowledgeable decisions. These groups have not attempted, or have been unable, to reach the large number of poor and older consumers who need their services most. Similarly, with some notable exceptions, the consumer activists have selected causes for their support, I believe, more on the basis of their visibility and publicity impact than on any long term effect on consumer protection.

Self-Regulation by Industry

The evidence on industry self-regulation and industry-sponsored consumer organizations, such as the Better Business Bureau, is not very encouraging. Industry codes are not stringent enough to provide for consumer safety at the cost of business expense. When violations by member firms are apparent, enforcement has often been weak or nonexistent.

That current approaches to protecting consumer interests have not worked as well as was intended does not mean that they ought to be discarded. There is great scope for improvement in the workings of existing government and private agencies, both business and nonbusiness. However, the point that needs making is that current approaches, even when significantly improved, are not likely to solve the problem. They are in the nature of "patchwork" solutions. We need an integrated approach where the current efforts are incorporated into an overall design to enable the consumer to get a better shake in the marketplace. To this end, I propose the following.

PROPOSALS FOR ACTION

The need for consumer protection has been broadly classified into three categories: (1) right to information, (2) right of choice, and (3) right to hazard-free products. All current activities aimed at consumer protection fit one or more of these categories. The problem of consumer protection, however, has three important dimensions that must be borne in mind in any package of solutions.

1. Generalizations about the needs of the average consumer are likely to prove misleading. The needs of poor, less educated, old, and eve even very young consumers are vastly different from those of other classes of consumers.
2. The issue may often be not quantity of information, selection, or safety, but *what type* of information, selection, or protection from hazards.
3. Under what circumstances should "consumer sovereignty" be restricted or eliminated and the decision as to the availability of a product be made by an outside agency?

The proposals I offer seek to restore three kinds of balance between the consumer and the producer in the marketplace. These are: information balance, bargaining power balance, and adjudication and remedy and relief balance. These proposals differ from the current approaches in two significant aspects: (1) They are of a preventive or proactive nature; they seek to prevent injury to consumers rather than merely help in restitution efforts. (2) Both consumer protection and restitution are automatic and are built into the system; the consumer's role is largely passive. In other words, the consumer receives protection and restitution by right, even when he is unaware that harm has been inflicted or is incapable, for whatever reason, of measuring its impact.

INFORMATION BALANCE

In one sense, there does not seem to be any dearth of information on products and services available to the consumer. Business firms alone spent over $22.3 billion on all forms of advertising in 1973, and advertising by the nonprofit sector was estimated at $2.0 billion. To this should be added information on product labels, articles in the news media, government brochures and bulletins, and activities of the consumer-based organizations. The problem, therefore, is not more but less information. We should provide a balance in the information needed by the consumer to make purchase decisions and be able to evaluate postpurchase effects in terms both of his expectations and the producer's claims.

In the information base I seek is included not only the information for economic criteria but also sociopsychological criteria. "Economic consumer" is no more relevant to our discussion than is "economic man" to a study of the workings of the free enterprise system. This information balance is sought at three levels: the firm, the industry, and the news media.

The Firm

Companies should regularly maintain and publish data on the volume and type of consumer complaints. The information should include the nature of the companies' response to these complaints, and any pending government or industry investigations (or their own research) that might have an adverse effect on the quality or use of their products. To claim that this is proprietary information and should not be disclosed is ludicrous. It is no more radical to publish information concerning consumer complaints than it is to publish information concerning current and projected losses in a firm's financial statements. Consumer satisfaction with a firm's products has a definite effect on a firm's long run prospects and should be an integral part of an analysis of "quality of earnings." It is not too far-fetched to think that astute securities analysts would take such data into account in recommending a firm's stock.

Furthermore, if it is deemed necessary that prospective buyers of a company's stock should know about the company's financial health and future prospects, why should it not be necessary for prospective buyers of a company's products to know about the quality of a company's products as evidenced by a trend analysis of consumer complaints? This is the most urgent task, and I believe business should expect increasing pressure in this direction in the near future from government agencies and consumer groups.

The Industry

At the industry level, there should be efforts to provide uniform standards of performance. This should be done either through industry codes or in association with government agencies and responsible consumer groups. There are some problems associated with this approach which should be borne in mind. These are: the sheer number of products and brands to be dealt with; the question of financing required for such testing and ranking; and the fact that only a limited number of products' attributes can be used and their selection could be tricky.

Also, manufacturers whose brands or models may rank low can simply come up with a new brand or slightly changed model, thus depriving the consumer of the comparability information; and since, for competitive reasons, all brands are likely to perform within a very narrow range of each other on the measured attributes, a manufacturer may heavily emphasize psychological, subtle, or frivolous differences in its advertising campaigns.

These problems are by no means small, but they are not insoluble. Given industry's desire, serious commitment, and the pressure from public and private agencies, significant progress can be made in this direction.

The News Media

Both the print and the broadcast media have been wanting in their obligation to inform the consumer about the possible hazards of products he uses, and about deceptions in pricing, advertising, or other product-related company policies. This was so even when newspapers or broadcast stations themselves carried the deceptive advertising in the first place.

I will confine my proposal to the unique problem associated with the broadcast media and how the imbalance in consumer information might be handled. Airwaves are publicly owned and therefore broadcast media are obligated to devote part of their time to public interest programming and advertising. Also, most heavily advertised products use broadcast media, especially television, as the prime means of reaching their audiences. Therefore, it is equally important that the same media be used to inform the public about other, non-advertised characteristics of these products.

Lest I frighten those in the broadcast industry, let me emphasize that I am not calling for "counteradvertising," in the sense that it is currently understood. I propose the establishment of a national council for consumer information (NCCI), composed of representatives from the broadcast industry, major advertisers, relevant government agencies, consumer groups, and public members. The objective of NCCI would be twofold: to inform the consumer about alternative products or choices that may be available to satisfy his or her particular needs; and to communicate to the consumer information concerning potential hazards of using a given product.

NCCI would not advertise against any specific brand or product but would concentrate on product categories. Examples of its activities: short commercials on the virtues of mass transit, economic and otherwise, compared to the use of personal cars; the convenience element in precooked frozen foods compared with the high prices and the loss of nutrients to the consumer; the pricing of prescription drugs; taste considerations of breakfast cereals compared with their sugar and calorie content.

NCCI would operate much like the National Science Foundation. It would receive from the industry the allocation of a block of time which would bear some relationship to the total paid advertising to be carried out by the broadcast industry, the networks, and individual television and radio stations in a given period of time. NCCI may also be required to distribute this time for communications to consumers as a percentage of total paid advertising in different product categories.

NCCI would appoint ad hoc committees comprised of representatives from various groups, academic scholars, and communication, technical, and marketing specialists. These committees would invite advertising agencies to make presentations to develop advertising campaigns for specified product categories and time periods. The process would be no different from that currently used by advertisers and advertising agencies to develop ad campaigns for private clients. The winning agency could be paid either on a fee or percentage basis. The operating budget of NCCI, which need not be very large, should be covered by grants from government and major advertisers or industry groups.

BARGAINING POWER BALANCE

The conventional dogma of large numbers of buyers and sellers openly competing in the market as the basis of price setting no longer corresponds to reality, except in a few cases. Instead we are faced with an oligopolistic pattern on the supply side, where a handful of firms holds a dominant share of the market. It is easier for the producers to raise prices and also to determine the nature of goods to be produced and the manner in which they are to be sold. This monopoly position is further reinforced by mass advertising aimed at creating consumer loyalty based on brand attributes, which are quite often misrepresented.

The response of the consumer to these pressures is generally unorganized and often ineffective. While strong antitrust and other law enforcement activities are helpful, efforts should be made to educate and inform the consumer to lessen his dependence on brand names as the sole criterion for determining quality and safety. One of the most important activities to meet this need would be the establishment of minimum performance standards, or useful life measures, for various products with a manufacturer's guarantee, perhaps backed by independent insurance. There are indications that some efforts in this direction are already under way. However, a great deal more must be done for it to become meaningful.

Another measure would be the simplification and standardization of manufacturer's warranties to enable the consumer to make use of the coverage provided therein. The seriousness of this problem was highlighted in a recent congressional study which showed that of fifty-one companies, only one offered a guarantee free from catches. The other fifty imposed different types of restrictions that limited the warranty's effectiveness and in many cases made it all but impossible for the consumer to recover his loss from the manufacturer. Congress has recently passed a measure that would set minimum federal standards for consumer product warranties. The measures outlined in the previous section on balance in information should go a long way in meeting this need.

ADJUDICATION, AND REMEDY AND RELIEF BALANCE

The third area of restoring balance between producers and consumers has to do with adjudication of disputes. My proposal calls for a system where the process of redress and restitution is internalized by the firm. What I have in mind could be labelled "internalization of class action suit" process by the firm. Thus, remedy and restitution become an integral part of doing business and are automatically triggered. The following will serve as examples.

Example I.   Suppose a telephone company serves a particular area. Because of the nature of technology, and government regulation, a failure or malfunction rate of 2 percent in the telephone service is considered normal. Let us say that in a given period this rate has risen to 5 percent. Under normal procedures, the phone company would be expected to make refunds only to those customers whose service was actually interrupted. However, in my system we would assume that while there may not have been actual disruption of service in other cases, there was a deterioration in the overall quality of services. Thus the telephone company should be required to refund a portion of the service fee to all the customers in that area. The rate of refund would increase with every increase in the failure or malfunction rate.

Example II. Suppose that in the case of heavy appliances, say dishwashers, the manufacturer's warranty or the industry code specifies a certain useful life and trouble-free service for that appliance. This system also assumes a certain failure rate, say 2 percent, in the first year of purchase. Then if there is an increase in the rate, we would assume this to be evidence of an overall deterioration in the quality of all dishwashers manufactured in a particular model run and the manufacturer would be obliged to make appropriate refunds on the purchase price to all customers who had purchased these dishwashers.

A variant of this approach was used by the Federal Energy Office during the recent oil crisis when it forced some gas stations who had overcharged their customers in a previous period to return a similar amount to the same class of customers in the form of lower prices in the subsequent period.

EPILOGUE

I am sure that most readers will find parts of one or all of these proposals unacceptable, either on the grounds of substance or of detail. However, if they have provoked you to think about them, and perhaps generate your own innovative approaches, they will have served their purpose.

Chapter 7

Who Says the Press Is Free If It Won't Even Tell You Which Supermarkets Are Selling Bad Meat?

Francis Pollock

In the still raging debate over media access, one person whose presence as a participant would seem absolutely necessary and entirely logical has been, by and large, curiously silent: the editor (and his or her broadcast equivalent, the news director). While vital questions about the day-to-day operations of the news media and the role they will play in the future are to a large extent on the verge of being decided now, the editors have generally preferred to step aside and surrogate their roles to their publishers (or station owners).

The most notable exception has been the recently concluded *Tornillo* case. Editors did participate in this one: several filed friend-of-the-court briefs in support of *The Miami Herald* against what they thought was a threat to their abilities to run their newspapers the way they had always done. But the *Tornillo* case, it should be emphasized, related to political coverage and commentary—areas in which the press has often been fiercely independent and vigorous, if not always fair (the thrust of the *Tornillo* case).

It is not entirely surprising, though, that the editors have generally shied away from participation in other areas of the media access debate. If they were to enter the forum, they might well have to respond to some most embarrassing questions about how they currently and traditionally have dispatched their professional responsibilities with regard to the citizen as consumer. And while the same independence and vigor that greeted the *Tornillo* case can occasionally be found when it comes to what might be termed "coverage of the marketplace," most consumer leaders—and an increasing number of consumers—believe that editors have abdicated their professional responsibilities.

Some indication of how citizens perceive their newspapers are dealing with consumer matters is to be found in a study recently conducted by Dr. Samuel Himes, Jr. of the University of Alabama. He surveyed some 1,200 people chosen randomly from the telephone directories of three cities. Eighty-one percent of the respondents felt that newspapers should give stronger editorial support to the consumer than they now do. More than 60 percent believed that articles about consumer problems are "designed not to offend advertisers." A similar percentage said they felt that the accuracy of advertising isn't checked. Many of the respondents said that news reporting in newspapers and on TV is biased in favor of business.

An indictment of the editors' failure to serve the consumer needs of their audiences, and the marketplace itself, might well be constructed along the following lines.

1. *The advertising appearing in the newspaper is no less a communications tool than the news and editorial matter appearing elsewhere in the same package.* That it is not as believable a form of communication as news-editorial matter is beside the point. The fact that the advertiser is willing to pay a substantial sum for space or time is evidence that he believes he can ultimately achieve one or more of the following: sell his product or service profitably; improve his image; get the consumer to keep his name in mind, and favorably so, when the next buying decision is to be made; get the paper to think twice before it prints any unfavorable publicity about the advertiser; get some or all of the above, and get a tax break at the same time (the apparent strategy of several of the oil companies last winter).

2. *Because their newspapers carry advertising that can occasionally (or frequently) misinform, mislead, or even harm consumers— particularly the most gullible—the newspaper itself is a party to the damage that may be done.* It is also beside the point that courts consistently have absolved newspapers of *legal* responsibilities for the claims or actions of their advertisers.

What must be considered here is the professional responsibility of the editor in terms of advertising that is harmful. This is an area not yet formally considered by any of the many editors' associations, although virtually all implicitly or explicitly regard editors as professionally liable for the accuracy of their news and the fairness of their reader access policies. Indeed, in commenting on the issues raised in the *Tornillo* case, many editors strongly argued that the matter would have never become a court case at all had *The Miami Herald* not committed the inexcusable breach of professional responsibility in refusing Tornillo the right to reply, at least in part, to its negative editorial comment about him. That the editor must bear some professional responsibility for harm done by products and services advertised in his paper should be implicit in his role as guardian of the truth.

3. *Professional responsibility for the effects of advertising notwithstanding, editors as a class have studiously ignored the effects on consumers of advertising in their own newspapers. Or they have washed their hands of such responsibility.* An example of how many editors perceive their role in regard to their own advertisements was to be seen in a confrontation two years ago between a consumer activist and the editor of *The Washington Post* at a consumer meeting in Washington. The editor, Benjamin Bradlee, was asked why the *Post* allowed blatantly deceptive advertisements to run in the paper; to support her point, the questioner held up examples of alleged bait-and-switch advertisements that had appeared in the paper. Mr. Bradlee replied that the *Post* did have an advertising code, but that the content of the ads was not his concern. The advertising manager at the *Post* was the person responsible, he said. Most editors in my experience would subscribe to Bradlee's point of view.

4. *Editors have surrendered some of their own journalistic functions to the advertiser.* Nowhere does the editor's failure to the consumer become more apparent than in those areas where he has turned over an apparent news function to his advertisers. The most notable is food price reporting. Turn to the business or financial pages of virtually any American newspaper and you will find prices reported by the thousands: everything from the prices of stocks and bonds to commodities and then some. These prices are accurate and reliable. And they are there because over the years editors have found them to be of great use to the readers of their business or finance sections.

But turn a few pages back to the food section of all but a handful of American newspapers and the only information about retail food prices is to be found in advertisements by the supermarkets, nearly all of these ads hawking in the best carnival fashion that they have the lowest prices anywhere. Such ads, since they almost universally feature loss leaders, are the most imprecise guides possible to food pricing. Yet even today, when food and its price is so vitally important, the editors who deem it their duty to report thousands of prices in their business and financial sections leave this matter to the advertisers.

As absurd as this situation is, editors have been stoking the news columns and editorials in recent years to do the same thing with the prices of prescription drugs. Few consumer stories have been done so frequently in recent years as the ones detailing widespread discrepancies in the prices pharmacies charge for the same prescription drugs. With a good dosage of editorial backup, more and more state legislatures and pharmacy boards have determined that the panacea is . . . price advertising. If the price advertising done by supermarkets is a fair criterion—and it is really the only one to judge by—then the price advertising by drug stores is likely to be just as misleading when it comes. (Parenthetically, while the consumer may be no better off when drug price advertising comes, the editors' papers stand to reap a windfall.)

Although under increasing attack from more responsible editors, the *quid pro quo* of news-editorial space for advertising is still very much a part of American journalism. As innocent as such trade-offs may seem, every inch of them is both an abdication of journalistic responsibility and a deception of the newspaper's readers.

5. *Editors often shortchange their readers by failing to alert them when their own newspapers have been used to mislead, deceive, or harm the public.* There is a host of stories that go virtually untouched by most American newspapers, either because of fear of offending advertisers or because of longstanding tradition that such stories are "just not done" (usually attributable in the first place to the fear of offending advertisers, but long since forgotten). These include accounts of weights and measures violations, credit collection excesses on the part of local merchants, "red-lining" by banks and insurance companies, deceptive sales practices by auto dealers, sanitary violations by supermarkets, questionable or illegal leasing practices by large real estate firms, and so on. All of the above are often attributable to major advertisers and very frequently go unreported.

While it should be noted that more and more papers today are at least printing news about dangerous products (a relatively new phenomenon in American journalism), few if any will go so far as to say that the product had previously been advertised in the paper. While some editors might dismiss this as a hairshirt exercise, the necessity of pointing out to the reader that the product had been advertised in the paper might promote just a measure of greater vigilance by the ad department in the future. By contrast, how frequently do editors remind us that "you read it first in the *Bugle*" when an errant politician is rousted from office after the paper's expose?

While it may be asking too much for editors to report that a dangerous product had previously been advertised in the paper, it is clearly not asking too much that news of such products be reported. Yet many editors still maintain they have no such responsibility. In 1973 the Food and Drug Administration determined that "Pap Chek," a do-it-yourself pap smear kit designed to detect cervical cancer, was dangerous because of the false sense of security it might give to its users. It ordered a recall. Of the magazines that had previously run advertisements for it, only one—*Family Health*—subsequently reported the recall. The others—*McCall's, Ladies' Home Journal, Harper's Bazaar, Woman's Day*—for various reasons did not mention the recall or that they had used the ads.

The vice president of *Ladies' Home Journal* wrote to *Media & Consumer* and said that the magazine had been in touch with the FDA about the matter. "We know the company notified all purchasers of the product that it was deemed unsafe by the FDA and had been withdrawn from the market," he wrote. "Because of this and the fact that a relatively limited number of units were sold, *Ladies' Home Journal* felt no requirement to alert readers editorially, and the FDA shares our point of view." The editor of *Woman's Day* told us she had no jurisdiction over advertising acceptance, placement, or counteradvertising. Then: "Perhaps I should add that our editorial policy forbids brand-name mentions for pharmaceutical and like products, and I have no plan to deviate from this policy."

6. *In summary, the editors have especially failed consumers by their inability, or refusal, to develop appropriate journalistic responses to problems in the marketplace in general and to the advertising that appears in their own papers in particular.* Aside from ad censorship, which is not advocated here and which in any event is more appropriately a publisher's response than an editor's, there are at least four editorial responses to these problems. How adequately editors exercise them may be a useful starting point for evaluating how faithful a news organization is to its consumers.

Reportage. Robust but fair consumer reporting is clearly a prerequisite for undoing some of the harm done by advertisers. Yet as important as the marketplace is, only a few hundred newspapers have even one reporter assigned to consumer matters. Fewer yet have more than one consumer reporter, and only a handful have a consumer editor whose responsibility it is to be the consumer's ombudsman in seeing that the consumer's needs are served by all sections of the paper. *The New York Times* seized the initiative on this matter in 1973 when it appointed a consumer editor and described his responsibilities in part as follows:

> He will be in charge of organizing and directing the coverage of consumer news . . . pull together as best as possible the enormous variety of consumer stories . . . suggest stories across the whole range of consumer affairs to other editors. . . . We all feel that it is extremely important to have one editor-reporter in the area of consumer affairs . . . who will make it his work to follow the developments wherever they may occur, and to act as a stimulant for all the desks.

Critical writing.   Despite a long tradition of criticism in the American press (ranging from politics to sports to the arts), there is little that might be described as consumer oriented criticism. The food pages are bare when it comes to food criticism, there is little to be found in the real estate sections, and rarely is any to be found even on the editorial and op-ed pages. Writing in *Media & Consumer* a year ago, Robert Irvin, the highly respected veteran auto writer of *The Detroit News*, noted that auto writers "are tied to the pattern of reporting routine auto news–auto sales figures, product announcements, and so on—much as White House reporters are tied to Ron Ziegler's announcements." But Irvin acknowledged that some consumer reporters (not the auto writers) have begun to write critical pieces about the auto industry—just as White House reporters eventually began challenging Ron Ziegler. Yet without a high level of consumer oriented criticism, the press only serves as a vehicle for the seller, and thus fails the marketplace.

An editorial policy at least devoted to the public interest in consumer affairs.   There are some who believe that the role of the editorial page in terms of consumer affairs is to side with "the part-time buyer up against a full-time seller," as stated by Colman McCarthy, a *Washington Post* editorial writer. If this be too much of an advocacy position, at least looking at consumer matters in terms of the public interest is certainly a reasonable stance to expect. But because there is often a world of difference between what a paper may say it stands for and what it actually does, there should be abundant evidence that the editorial page tackles consumer matters with the pressing frequency they deserve.

A letters-to-the-editor policy that encourages correspondence a-bout consumer matters. Letters about consumer matters rarely appear on editorial pages, and when they do they often deal in generalities. If the letters-to-the-editor column is to be a genuine readers' forum in terms of consumer matters as well as political affairs, it must encourage and print the tough letters as well.

The journalistic responses called for here are in no way idealistic. They are responses to be found in abundance right now in every edition of virtually every newspaper in the United States—at least in terms of political matters. Few papers, however, have developed them in marketplace matters. And that, coupled with the editor's hands-off policy towards their own advertising as communication, is a major reason why more and more concerned consumers are feeling that their editors are failing both them and the marketplace.

—

✳ *Chapter 8*

How Well Does the Press Cover Business and Finance?

Myron Kandel

Does the press roll over and play dead when it comes to covering business and financial news? Does it allow its objectivity to be clouded, its vanity massaged, even its pocketbook enriched? Some critics of the press say it does.

Is the press biased against business, hostile to its leaders, overly critical about its lack of perfection, and perhaps worst of all, ignorant about how it really operates? Some critics of the press say it is.

How is it possible for honest observers of the same sector of the American press to have two such sharply divergent views? Can there be some truth on both sides of the looking glass? Or are all the distortions in the eyes of the beholders? Writers on the subject of business and the press tend to go to extremes. They either concentrate on the malefactions and omissions of the press—and indeed there are many—or they bewail the damage that a hostile press has done to the image of business in general or even to the very concept of American free enterprise.

But after two dozen years in journalism, more than half of it spent writing and editing business and financial news, it seems to me that the real truth lies very much in between. The American press has turned in a mixed performance in covering this field—frequently very good but more often leaving a great deal to be desired. The blackest spot in the picture is perhaps the most discouraging—the woeful showing of the broadcast media, particularly television news, which despite its ever-increasing popularity, influence, and profits, has largely ignored this most vital area. I say this is most discouraging because television, which has managed to drive many mass circulation magazines out of business, has the resources—although, sadly, apparently neither the desire nor imagination—to make business and finance interesting and relevant to a mass audience. It has not been encumbered by the need to provide masses of statistical material nor has it been tied to long-standing traditions of coverage and placement. But up to now it hasn't risen to the challenge.

Newspapers, meanwhile, have steadily improved their coverage, devoting more space to business news and providing increased and more sophisticated staffs. Even here, however, it sometimes seems that growing tabular demands for space and the increasing complexity of business and financial affairs are making papers run faster just to stay where they are. And despite the progress they have made, only a handful of papers have financial pages that are up to the quality of some of their other sections.

Why this stepchild status for the financial sections? Since newspaper publishing has become big business and publishers are substantial members of their local or even national business communities, one would think that they would be sensitive to the need for more and better business news coverage and would provide sufficient editorial budgets to achieve this. There are several explanations, none of them wholly satisfactory. First, publishers are not known to force upon editors resources they don't ask for, and most top editors of daily papers are abysmally ignorant of business and financial news. At this writing, I can't come up with the name of a single top editor of a major general circulation newspaper who has come up through the ranks of business or financial writing—one key exception in the magazine field being Osborn Elliott, editor of *Newsweek*, who rose just that way. (Both *Newsweek* and *Time*, it should be noted, devote considerable space and effort to economic and business-related coverage.)

Most newspaper editors have usually been content to have business editors and departments that do not give them any headaches. They depend on other parts of the paper to give it distinction. Second, publishers who meddle with the business news coverage of their papers usually do so to tone down some negative news about an important advertiser or other pillar of the business community or to puff him up. Any editor worth his salt resents this kind of interference, and in recent years many editors have been able to get rid of much of it. As a result, many publishers, at least the better ones, have adopted a hands-off attitude. While this generally is to be commended, it does deprive the editorial side of the paper of much-needed objective input from the business world.

It seems to me that most serious shortcoming of newspaper business coverage, given the space and staff limitations, is a lack of initiative and aggressiveness in searching out the real stories behind the stony façades of press releases and public announcements. To cite a small yet nonetheless significant, point of annoyance: publication after publication will run stories, ranging from two- or three-line items to major pieces complete with pictures, about an executive's being named to an important corporate post. But time after time, there's no mention of what happened to the person being replaced. In most cases, of course, a normal retirement, promotion, or departure for a better job somewhere else is involved. But frequently the real story in a personnel appointment is what happened to the predecessor. All too often it's left out, or kissed off with the words "has resigned." An enterprising editor could fill his section with the stories behind the meaning of those two innocuous words. This is a minor point, but it reflects the slothfulness—or is it overwork?—of a large part of the business press, which in general is greatly understaffed considering the volume of news it must cover.

A vigorous critic of the financial press from within its own ranks, Chris Welles, magazine writer and author and onetime business editor of *Life* magazine, accuses the news media of seldom venturing beyond "immediate superficialities" when reporting business and economic stories. He sees a collective self-deception about the realities of business and finance and an acceptance of the view that corporate power "is either largely benign or not at all that extensive anyway, that except for a few unfortunate miscreants businessmen have the public interest at heart and, while garnering deserved profits, are working to build a better America." Overwhelming evidence exists to refute this notion, he says, and he castigates the press for permitting American business to remain largely "shrouded from view."

One of Welles's specific targets was *Fortune* magazine, the weighty and respected business monthly for top corporate management. "Despite its considerable editorial resources and enormous prestige, *Fortune* almost never presents a viewpoint that might unduly upset the sleep of its readership," Welles wrote in the July/August 1973 issue of the *Columbia Journalism Review*. He contended that while 25 recent issues he had studied contained many stories upholding existing standards of corporate behavior and refuting common criticisms, they did not include "a single major critique of a common business practice or accepted ethical precept." He asked: "Must even a powerful and prosperous magazine such as *Fortune* do nothing but docilely uphold the values and common practices of its readers? Has it no higher sense of duty?"

Interestingly, *Fortune* looked at the question of business and the press from the other side of the coin just a year later in an article in its June 1974 issue entitled "Must Business Fight the Press?" The magazine noted that some businessmen wonder how much the press stirs up or overplays the criticism they're getting and, therefore, they tend to be "skeptical, wary and critical of the press, ill at ease and generally defensive in their own encounters with it." However, the article added, "much of what businessmen perceive as bias involves nothing more than a conscientious reporter trying to deal with some large and sensitive issues."

Fortune also noted that many of the businessmen it interviewed seemed ambivalent about what they really wanted from the press. On one hand, they complained that many of the reporters they met were ill informed about the stories they were covering and inaccurate in their reporting; on the other hand, it was not at all clear that they really *want* sophisticated reporting. The article quoted *Los Angeles Times* publisher Otis Chandler as observing: "the better your paper, the more you are in trouble with local businessmen."

Newspaper financial pages usually carry an extra burden in finding sufficient news space, since they are loaded down with figures, statistics, and tables, all of them of intense interest to some segment of a newspaper's readers. I remember when, as the new financial editor of the *New York Herald Tribune*, I went to visit my counterpart on the *New York Times* (my old boss and now competitor) to ask his advice on which pieces of tabular material I could leave out of my pages to free up more space for business and financial news stories. It was a matter he'd thought about many times himself. But he shook his head sadly and told me that whenever he had tried to drop some esoteric-appearing bit of data such as egg prices or the prices on some obscure stock exchange, there had been loud complaints from some special interest area. Over the years, my old paper, his paper, and many others have gone ahead and dropped some limited interest material. In its place, however, have come along some equally space-filling (and undoubtedly important) statistical matter of other kinds.

There even have been some suggestions that papers drop the daily stock market tables and devote the space these now fill to more and better coverage of business news. After all, this reasoning goes, readers who really care about the day-to-day eighth- and quarter-point movements of their stocks can obtain that information by calling their brokers, and would they not prefer in place of the lengthy tables some in-depth reporting that would help them in their business, investment, or personal financial activities? It's an interesting concept, but one, I feel, that goes counter to the recent trend that has seen more and more papers add to their stock tables, rather than reduce them, even in the face of a prolonged bear market.

An encouraging sign in business and financial journalism is the fresh new wind of reexamination that some of its leaders are bringing to long accepted customs and traditions. In May 1974, for example, the ten-year-old Society of American Business Writers, after a good deal of heated discussion, adopted its first code of ethics, believed to be a pioneering effort for a specialized journalistic group. The code, while it may not be the final word on the subject, indicates the kinds of problems business and financial writers and editors are coming to grips with, even if somewhat belatedly. The code reads as follows.

Statement of Purpose: It is not enough that we be incorruptible and act with honest motives. We must conduct all aspects of our lives in a manner that averts even the appearance of conflict of interest or misuse of the power of the press.

A business and financial writer should:

1. Recognize the trust, confidence and responsibility placed in him or her by his publication's readers and do nothing to abuse this obligation. To this end, a clear-cut delineation between advertising and editorial matters should be maintained at all times.

2. Avoid any practice which might compromise or appear to compromise his objectivity or fairness. He or she should not let any personal investments influence what he or she writes. On some occasions, it may be desirable for him or her to disclose his investment positions to a superior.

3. Avoid active trading and other short-term profit-seeking opportunities. Active participation in the markets which such activities require is not compatible with the role of the business and financial journalist as disinterested trustee of the public interest.

4. Not take advantage in his personal investing of any inside information and be sure any relevant information he or she may have is widely disseminated before he buys or sells.

5. Make every effort to insure the confidentiality of information held for publication to keep such information from finding its way to those who might use it for gain before it becomes available to the public.

6. Accept no gift, special treatment, or any other thing of more than token value given in the course of his professional activities. In addition, he or she will accept no out-of-town travel paid for by anyone other than his or her employer for the ostensible purpose of covering or backgrounding news. Free-lance writing opportunities and honoraria for speeches should be examined carefully to assure that they are not in fact disguised gratuities. Food and refreshment of ordinary value may be accepted where necessary during the normal course of business.

7. Encourage the observance of these minimum standards by all business writers.

Other journalistic groups have acted similarly, seeking not only to avert impropriety, but to avoid any possible suggestion of it. For example, the Deadline Club, the New York City chapter of the Society of Professional Journalists, Sigma Delta Chi, had for many years awarded $500 cash prizes for journalistic excellence in a number of categories. The awards were sponsored by various corporations, although the club had sole supervision over the judging and selection of the winners. However, after the society's national convention adopted a strong code of ethics that included provisions on the acceptance of gifts by journalists, the Deadline Club decided to forego the outside sponsorship of its awards. There *is* such a thing as post-Watergate morality, asserted the group's Standards and Ethics Committee (of which this writer was a member), and journalists, along with other segments of American society, should regularly reexamine their practices to achieve more rigorous ethical standards.

It was really only after inflation was publicly identified as the nation's No. 1 enemy that the television networks and many local stations began scurrying around to try to cover economic news on any kind of meaningful basis—as if inflation and other major economic and business problems had developed overnight. In fact, the biggest shot in the arm to public understanding of the deep-seated economic problems of the U.S. was the showing by some public television stations of some of the economic summit meetings in their entirety.

But then public TV, ironically, does a better job on business than the big and highly profitable commercial networks. Its "Wall Street Week" has long been the only regularly scheduled business program seen coast to coast. But despite all the well deserved acclaim that show has received, it has had to scrounge for funds to survive each year and it has never had the resources to do some of the ambitious on-location programming it has on the drawing board. For most of the American viewing public, business and financial news on the home screen consists usually of a quick report of the Dow Jones averages and, when stock prices move sharply up or down, that hackneyed picture of the crowded trading floor of the New York Stock Exchange.

At this writing, the prolonged stock market slump, which has sent prices to a longtime low and decimated the securities industry—not to speak of the investments of countless Americans—has not been deemed worthy of any in-depth news treatment. The casual way in which TV treats business and financial news was pointed up recently when NBC's flagship station in New York launched a new two-hour evening news program. Despite the unusual length of the show, which included special slots for coverage of such matters as entertainment, food, consumerism, and sports, no room was found for business news.

If television—and radio, to a slightly lesser extent—largely ignore the world of business and finance until a crisis that demands coverage erupts, trade papers and magazines sometimes seem to smother their respective fields. Here, too, the picture is mixed. A good part of the trade press is first rate—aggressive, authoritative, accurate, independent. But too much of it thrives on puffery, their editorial material serving merely to fill in around the ads, or even worse, to pay off for them. Some trade papers, it's sad to say, seem to exist primarily to pander to the industries they ostensibly cover. The danger here is that Gresham's law will drive out the really valuable trade publications or diminish their viability. The answer in this case is really up to the businessmen who read the trade press and advertise in it.

In general, the segment of the press that covers business and finance is doing an improving job. Staffs are ever so slowly getting bigger and better trained, more space is being allocated, and management is grudgingly realizing that they must pay more attention to the job being done. On the broadcast side, the picture is gloomier. But perhaps some of the resources being allocated as a result of the fight on inflation will remain once the headlines and top stories deal with other subjects.

In the past, the hope for better broadcast coverage seemed to rest with the prodding of the print media. Maybe now, though, a reawakened interest on the part of TV will spur newspapers and magazines to do an even better job and overcome some of their failings.

Part 3

The Role of the Regulatory Agencies: How Effective?

Commentary

PITTLE

The newest federal regulatory body is the Consumer Product Safety Commission, whose responsibility includes drafting safety standards for a wide variety of household products and home furnishings. In addition to its broad jurisdiction, the Commission has been given some punch—the power to seek court injunctions to keep unsafe products from being marketed and to compel manufacturers to remove hazardous products that already have been placed on sale. This power is not taken lightly by the Commission; only after comprehensive public hearings are safety standards set or legal action taken to require compliance by producers.

KRATTENMAKER

Historically, the Federal Trade Commission has been either neglectful of the consumer or essentially pro-business in its activities. More recently, in the early 1970s, the Commission became more active in making manufacturers back up claims for their products or correct misleading statements about products. To make the FTC a more potent and protective force for consumer interests, several revisions should be made in its functioning. First and most important, appointments to the Commission must be made uniformly to top-quality persons in the field, rather than used for payment of political debts. In addition, the FTC should concentrate on its law revision function, which has the potential for much broader consumer benefit than the settling of individual claims.

ROSENBERG

Standards affect the quality and cost of virtually every product and service. Yet the persons who set standards seldom go beyond the technical aspects of their function to consider the economic and social welfare effects of such standards. The consumer should be represented in standards and certification programs; this could be done by the proposed federal consumer protection agency as well as by strengthening the independent action of the National Bureau of Standards and creating a Bureau of Standards Review.

KATZ

Government regulation of business in the consumer's interest is cumbersome and uneven at best. Industry self-regulation, on the other hand, could provide more effective sanctions at less cost and with less bureaucracy than government regulation now entails. Moreover, self-regulation by industry groups could retain competition within the marketplace while serving broad social needs. The public would retain its right to use the courts to settle specific disputes, but a layer of governmental regulatory bureaucracy would be eliminated.

✳ *Chapter 9*

The Federal Trade Commission and Consumer Protection: An Institutional Overview

Thomas G. Krattenmaker

It is difficult to speak succinctly and persuasively about either the Federal Trade Commission or the present wave of demands for increased protection of American consumers, and certainly impossible to set out a complete overview of both topics in readably brief form. The FTC is one of the oldest of the federal agencies charged with oversight of commercial acts and practices within the national economy; consequently, an enormous body of well reasoned, critical literature concerning the FTC already exists. Moreover, the Commission has demonstrated thus far a remarkable capacity to survive even its most talented and vocal critics so that it continues to be, at least outwardly, the linchpin in the federal establishment's consumer protection program. While comparatively tiny as Washington bureaucracies go, the FTC nevertheless receives annual appropriations in excess of $30 million, employs more than 500 attorneys, and maintains sizable offices in a dozen of our larger metropolitan areas. A full treatment of the successes and failures of the Federal Trade Commission, then, could not responsibly be achieved in the space available. The agency is simply too big, too old, and too much studied to yield to such cursory analysis.

If anything, the consumer movement is an even more amorphous phenomenon. Demands for licensing of persons in certain occupations that deal directly with the public, for removing hazardous products from the marketplace, for better regulation of public utility service and profit levels, or for federally enforced standards of minimally acceptable product performance surely would fit anyone's definition of "consumer protection" suggestions. Yet the FTC deals with none of these problems. This is not to say that the agency is undercommitted or underfunded; only that consumers' cries have echoed, and will continue to do so, far beyond the walls of the FTC.

Finally, any attempt at evaluation of the FTC's performance, or proposals for its reform, tends to lead in two different directions. On one hand the problem arises of what substantive policies the Commission should pursue. Should the agency concentrate on mass media advertising to consumers, or is it more important to police abusive practices of some retailers that bear especially harshly on the poor? Door-to-door selling, credit practices, product packaging and labelling, disclosure of hazards to health and safety that may be associated with the use of certain products, and the operations of travel agencies and vocational schools have all been subjects of consumer concern that have periodically been pressed upon the Commission as matters of utmost urgency that require vigorous and innovative regulatory strategies. And it is both important and sad to note that the FTC's past record in these areas is essentially one of failure and neglect.

On the other hand, an equally important problem is: by what means and processes ought the Commission to carry out those responsibilities it undertakes (or has thrust upon it)? Should private citizens have more or less access to the decision making centers within the agency? What sorts of commissioners, staff, and internal organization are most likely to produce a bureaucracy capable of responding wisely to the dynamic economy it oversees? Those who have studied the Commission's performance in these respects have concluded that the agency has typically been poorly staffed, badly organized, and lacking a sure sense of its mission and priorities.

To be sure, these matters of substance and procedure cannot sensibly be treated as mutually exclusive pigeonholes in which to insert all proposals for reform. As with any system of law, the processes by which consumer and merchant claims are reconciled must be shaped to fit the governing regulatory strategy; and the forms according to which the agency is required to proceed will at least limit the range of plausible proposals for substantive change. Yet the distinction remains viable, if only for the purposes of justifying an attempt to treat such a heroic subject in rather summary form.

Without intending to denigrate in any way the efforts of others to develop comprehensive formulations of the appropriate substantive role of the FTC in the regulatory world of consumer protection, this article seeks to propose some answers to another question: What modifications in the FTC's historical internal modes of operation and self-definition of responsibilities are most likely to produce an institution capable of responding wisely and rapidly to the legitimate complaints and needs of consumers in the American marketplace? At any given moment the utility of the particular substantive policies being pursued by the FTC will undoubtedly appear the central issue. Yet over the long run, in a society and an economy as large, diverse, and dynamic as ours, it is at least arguable that the nature of the institution and its processes will count for more than the policies of that moment. It is doubtful that there lies within us the capacity to delineate immutable principles of business and consumer behavior. Perhaps, however, we can speak with greater assurance about the people, resources, and sense of mission necessary to serve well in the uncertain future.

Of course any discussion of institutional changes that would better enable the Federal Trade Commission to play an effective role in consumer protection must rest upon some understanding both of what is meant by "consumer protection" and of the FTC's historical role in that process. Consequently, these essentially definitional and informational problems will be addressed at the outset.

"CONSUMER PROTECTION": AN ANALYTICAL FRAMEWORK

What is "consumer protection" or "consumerism"? This unavoidable definitional problem consistently plagues those who would discuss the subject. If only because the American nation seems firmly committed to the view that a capitalist, free enterprise system is the best means for organizing society's economic functions, it is appropriate to begin by assuming that, for a federal agency, "consumer protection" must mean governmental activity designed to assure that consumers in fact realize the benefits they should theoretically obtain from their participation in the marketplace.

From that premise it follows that, in one useful sense of the phrase, consumer protection might denominate every governmental effort designed to protect and promote reliance upon the free market as the mechanism for organizing society's economic activities. For while our adherence to the free market model can be explained either as an economic judgment concerning how to produce goods efficiently or as a political conclusion that decision making power ought to be widely dispersed, each of these rationales rests upon the same premise: that the consumer (or individual citizen) is, or should be, sovereign.

In this sense, any official action designed to promote and protect the market mechanism can intelligently be called a consumer protection measure. If an antitrust suit will lower entry barriers in an industry, it will, when combined with the operation of additional natural market forces, ultimately enhance the effectiveness of the consumer's voice in the marketplace. Wise regulation of the profits, prices, and services of a "natural monopoly" such as a public utility will do for the consumer what he, by hypothesis, cannot do for himself. Government procurement policies that stimulate competition and encourage new entrants will ultimately increase consumer satisfaction and lower consumption costs.

For many purposes, employing such a broad definition of consumer protection would be quite helpful. We might, for example, be led to attempt to compare the federal tax dollars annually spent on enforcing the Truth-in-Lending Act with those used to enforce the antitrust laws against corporate mergers. Or private citizens might more easily comprehend the extent to which national tariff policy creates important artificial barriers to entry. Nevertheless, such a broad view of consumer protection is not frequently employed in common parlance—nor is it found in the average bureaucrat's lexicon.

While many governmental policies may enhance or retard the operation of the market system, it is appropriate to define as consumer protection measures those governmental efforts that *directly* preserve consumers' power to voice effectively and articulately their true desires within the marketplace. Such a definition would exclude policies, such as antitrust enforcement or tariff reform, that will benefit consumers only after the further operation of additional market forces and concentrate instead on those policies whose impact is designed to fall precisely upon the consumer's role.

The free enterprise model itself shows that there are three principal areas in which consumers may need such direct intervention, aimed at their level of the economy, by governmental officials to assure the preservation of the system itself. First, as any economic theorist can demonstrate, the market mechanism will not work unless consumers are fully informed. History has shown that it may be necessary for government to adopt policies designed to assure that consumers are neither uninformed nor misinformed about the characteristics of products offered for sale or the legal rights and duties that attend the purchase of consumer goods.

Second, the free market model is both theoretical and egalitarian. That is, it assumes that producers and sellers, relative to consumers, will not enjoy superior bargaining acumen, easier access to the general legal system, or greater knowledge of or protection from existing rules of private law. The free market system will work if many merchants are simply wealthier than individual consumers, but not if consumers as a group are disadvantaged by generally applicable rules of contract law, inability to resort to legal processes, lack of knowledge about the law, or inexperience in the techniques of commercial bargaining. Certain consumers, such as children or the poor, may need special education in the ways of commercial bargaining or straightforward protection from certain practices. Other practices, such as fictitious pricing or bait-and-switch selling, may be too dangerous to permit in any consumer transaction.

Rules of contract law may be unwittingly designed in a manner that permits merchants to take undue advantage of consumers. And if consumers cannot ultimately protect their interests by submitting claims for adjudication, any necessary protections of this sort can be nullified by unscrupulous sellers. In short, consumers cannot effectively vindicate their self-interests in the marketplace if they are ignorant in the ways of commercial dealing or unable to enforce rules of law that fairly govern the consumer-merchant transaction.

Finally, even if consumers are fully informed and able to protect their interests equally with sellers, it is sometimes necessary to put an external "floor" on certain forms of competitive behavior. The same market mechanism that made the horse and buggy obsolete also brought us highway fatalities and air pollution. That is, the use of certain products (or selling techniques) may entail social costs not reflected in the costs of the goods themselves—for example, air pollution. Or risks may seem acceptable to fully informed, intelligent buyers evaluating their own self-interests, but produce unacceptably large social costs when millions of consumers decide to run those risks simultaneously. For example, it may be intelligent for one consumer to take the 1 in 10,000 chance that certain children's sleepwear will catch on fire, but equally intelligent for society to prevent 100 million consumers from running that risk individually and thereby collectively burning 10,000 children. Unless some action is taken to prevent or cure such external consequences of reliance on the market mechanism, some other economic system would have to be adopted to ration goods. By hypothesis, consumers cannot exercise sovereignty over such externalities without extramarket assistance.

In short, then, any government agency that seeks to engage in consumer protection activity needs some sort of normative background against which to measure its responsibilities and potentialities. In America, at least, the model for such action must be the free enterprise ideal. Anything that tends to protect and promote reliance on the market mechanism can rightly be called a consumer protection measure, for both the economic and political justifications for our adherence to this model rest upon a view of the consumer as sovereign, and it follows that measures properly protective of the market mechanism will necessarily enhance ultimate consumer control over the economy.

Nevertheless, for those whose prime concern is with the consumer's role in the marketplace, it is helpful to define as their legitimate goals one or more of the following: (1) assuring that consumers are not misinformed or uninformed about product characteristics or rules of law relevant to a rational purchase decision (hereafter referred to as the information function); (2) enhancing the ability of consumers to protect themselves by redressing unnatural imbalances between merchant and consumer in marketplace acumen or legal protection (hereafter referred to as the protection function); (3) ascertaining that the marketplace exacts from the consumer the true, acceptable costs of the production, distribution, and consumption of various goods offered for sale (hereafter referred to as the function of avoiding externalities). Such a definition both marks out a finite range of subjects for discussion and, more important, provides a policy benchmark—protection of the market mechanism—against which to assess proposals for governmental consumer protection action.

Whether or not it is necessary to the effective and fair operation of the market system that government play a major active role in any or all of these three areas of consumer protection is beyond the scope of this article. What is clear is that government must play *some* role, and that the FTC will be challenged to implement many consumerist proposals in these areas. The focus here is on how the FTC should go about deciding what needs to be done and who should do it. The key to understanding this problem lies in an understanding of how the Commission has responded to such challenges in the past, as well as the powers and resources the agency presently possesses.

THE FTC AND CONSUMER PROTECTION: A BRIEF HISTORICAL OVERVIEW

Creation, Structure, and Powers

Established in 1914, the Federal Trade Commission is the second oldest of the major independent federal regulatory agencies. A product of Woodrow Wilson's "New Freedom" philosophy, which rested principally upon the policies of freeing consumers from monopolies and restoring competition, the primary function of the FTC as originally conceived was to enforce the antitrust laws. However, in addition to empowering the Commission to enforce the new proscriptions on monopolistic practices contained in the Clayton Act, Congress enacted section 5 of the Federal Trade Commission Act to outlaw "unfair methods of competition." Under the rubric of section 5, the new agency soon became involved in consumer protection litigation, while in its antitrust work "by encouraging the formulation of codes of trade practices, [the Commission] entered into something suspiciously like an alliance with the trusts" during the 1920s [1].

In 1931 the FTC's consumer protection authority was sharply circumscribed by a Supreme Court decision holding that section 5 of the FTC Act did not reach practices, no matter how injurious to consumers, that did not injure competitors or the competitive process [2]. Seven years later Congress remedied this deficiency by amending section 5 to reach "unfair or deceptive acts or practices in commerce" and at about the same time the Commission began to show more independence in the enforcement of the antitrust laws. The Supreme Court has within the past decade unquestionably abandoned its earlier restrictive decisions and affirmed that the Commission has virtually unfettered discretion in determining what concrete principles of trade regulation should be fashioned from the rather vague dictates of section 5 of the Act [3]. Over the years Congress has also committed to the FTC responsibility for enforcement of a number of more specialized consumer protection statutes. Chief among these are the Truth-in-Lending Act, the Fair Packaging and Labelling Act, and the Fair Credit Reporting Act.

Structurally, the agency is governed by a Chairman and four other Commissioners. All are appointed for seven-year terms by the president, subject to Senate confirmation. The Commission's operating staff is principally split four ways. The Bureau of Economics, with 181 employees, engages in basic empirical economic research and has no direct responsibility for law enforcement. In addition to its public reports, however, the Bureau of Economics frequently provides extremely useful input into the law enforcement processes of the agency, by detailing the economic consequences of various courses of action. In practice, close to half of this bureau's work directly supports the Commission's antitrust law enforcement efforts. The Bureau of Competition, with a staff of 250, investigates and prosecutes antitrust cases. The Bureau of Consumer Protection, whose work is the focus of this article, employs 303 people (about half of whom are attorneys) in consumer protection law enforcement. Finally, the FTC employs 248 people in twelve regional offices located in large cities throughout the United States and centrally coordinated from the Commission's Washington headquarters. These offices engage principally in law enforcement work, devoting most of their time to consumer protection matters [4].

The FTC establishes substantive standards for business behavior through interpretation of section 5 of the FTC Act, either in the context of individual case adjudication or by promulgation of Trade Regulation Rules, published after hearings at which affected parties may testify and after consideration of that testimony by the Commission [5]. In addition, section 6 of the Act grants the Commission very broad powers to inquire into the practices and records of business enterprises and has enabled the FTC, on occasion, to render public reports containing certain trade practices that may be in need of remedial action [6]. The Commission has also often proceeded by announcing detailed guidelines for behavior in certain industries. These *Guides* lack the force of law but often provide the basis for individual adjudicated complaints.

Individual cases, historically the predominant share of the Commission's work, are brought upon formal complaint issued by the Commission upon recommendation of the staff. Trials are prosecuted by FTC staff attorneys from the appropriate Bureau before Administrative Law Judges, who are employed within the agency. The Commission sits as would an appellate court in reviewing these judges' decisions. Appeal of Commission decisions is available in the federal circuit courts.

For a violation of the FTC Act, the Commission is empowered to issue an order to "cease and desist" from engaging further in the proscribed conduct. No further penalties attach at that time, but violation of a cease and desist order is punishable, principally by a monetary fine, through proceedings commenced in federal district court. While to the layperson the phrase "cease and desist" may carry a suggestion that the FTC's remedial authority is narrowly circumscribed, the lawyer's linguistic ingenuity can generally surmount that apparent obstacle with little effort. Thus, for example, should the Commission decide it is appropriate to require a company to disclose certain information on its product labels, the final order will simply provide that the respondent company must cease and desist from distributing its products without affixing the required disclosure to their package.

On paper, then, the Federal Trade Commission's law making authority is extensive, its remedial powers ample, and its resources by no means negligible. Indeed, it has required truly extraordinary ineptitude and mismanagement to fashion such a woeful history from such promising potential.

Failures and Accomplishments

While this study focuses upon the Commission's processes and essential orientation, a review of the agency's principal activities within the three areas of consumer concerns defined previously is crucial to an understanding of those issues. In recounting the FTC's consumer protection endeavors, it is necessary to employ a rather skewed historical division. On one side lies all the Commission's activity from 1914 until about 1969. It is a very sad story, indeed, and almost uniformly so. On the other side is the period 1970 to 1973. That history, while much briefer, nevertheless is positively heartening. In the difference between the two periods lie some tentative answers to those problems of agency self-definition that have plagued the FTC from its inception and will undoubtedly continue to do so for the foreseeable future.

Decades of Neglect: 1914 to 1969. The earlier and lengthier period was characterized by a number of identifiable tendencies. In performing its information function, the Commission historically concentrated almost entirely on the problem of misinformation or deception. It was vigorous in prosecuting outright lies about product characteristics that came to the agency's attention. However, the FTC did not systematically monitor advertisements disseminated to the public nor did it develop expertise in the sophisticated concepts of mass merchandising and mass media advertising created by larger producers and their ad agencies. Consequently, the Commission's battle against deception was typically waged against localized instances of outright false representations, claims that frequently seemed unlikely to truly deceive those consumers with any sense at all [7].

Equally significant, the FTC appeared largely oblivious to the need for consumers to have accurate, relevant, intelligible information about products that was not being voluntarily disclosed to the public via private advertising campaigns. When the agency sporadically exercised its powers to compel affirmative disclosure, with uncanny consistency it selected as its targets products that did not consume a large part of the consumer's budget or information that seemed essentially irrelevant to a proper evaluation of the product or which consumers could easily discover themselves. Thus, for example, consumers typically received almost no hard, relevant data about the characteristics of automobiles, but the FTC saw to it that they were informed about the length of extension ladders, the size of TV screens, and whether watchbands had been produced in a foreign country [8]. The interests of competitors, rather than consumers, frequently seemed to account for the selection of such targets.

The "old" FTC was both underactive and overly active in pursuing protectionist goals. A number of half-hearted attempts at direct consumer education were undertaken. By any standard of assessment, all failed utterly. Meanwhile, during the 1950s it gradually became clear that a principal obstacle to the ability of consumers to protect themselves was not simply their relative ignorance about marketplace practices, but the legal system itself. Consumers could not force merchants to obey the law because of the costs and practical difficulties of initiating or defending court actions. And lawyers had been successful in creating a number of devices, including the nefarious holder in due course doctrine, which, when applied to consumer transactions, seemed to tilt the law in favor of the unscrupulous merchant [9].

The Commission seemed largely oblivious to these developments in the legal system. Its unconscious response was twofold. First, on a fairly massive scale the agency processed and negotiated the complaints of individual consumers who thought they had been harmed by some merchant's tactics and had the presence of mind to write the FTC about it. Undoubtedly, scores of individual, isolated complaints were settled weekly by the FTC during the 1950s and 1960s but without any broader corrective action being taken against the offending parties. Second, the FTC never grappled directly and seriously with the fact that all these complaints arose against the backdrop of the existing private law systems of the several states; that these complaints largely bore witness to deficiencies in court procedures and the substantive law of contracts and torts that would otherwise have provided some corrective action. Consequently, the Commission never seriously considered whether it might have the power and the responsibility to seek reforms in that legal system, to deal with the causes as well as the effects of unconscionable merchandising practices.

Finally, the pre-1970 FTC took almost no action with respect to the problem of externalities. Occasionally it acted to compel disclosure of information to alert consumers to certain health hazards, most notably when the Commission led the fight to require a health warning on cigarette packages [10]. And, certain that the average consumer was unable to cope with the laws of chance, the FTC waged a never-ending battle against lotteries until well financed and highly respected merchants (such as gasoline stations and supermarkets) started to add lotteries to their bag of tricks. For these sellers, the FTC was content with action that informed consumers of the true risks involved rather than orders that banned the practices outright [11].

Years of Promise: 1970 to 1973. During the period 1970 to 1973 the Commission seemed to behave differently. The immediate cause of this turnabout was President Nixon's choice as chairman of the FTC of Miles Kirkpatrick, a leading member of the antitrust bar. Kirkpatrick had chaired a commission of the American Bar Association that in 1969 issued a comprehensive and scathing indictment of the FTC. One of Kirkpatrick's first official acts was to appoint Robert Pitofsky, an eminent antitrust professor and general counsel of the ABA Commission, to head the Bureau of Consumer Protection. Led principally by these two reformers, the FTC commenced both to explore new fields and to push vigorously to their conclusion a number of promising projects begun in the late 1960s by an agency beleaguered by criticism.

While a full treatment of the measures taken by the Commission during this brief period needs desperately to be compiled, a brief summary must suffice here. In the area of consumer information the FTC continued to wage its war on deception. The agency concentrated, however, on deceptions more widely disseminated and less overt than those usually hit in the past. Additionally, the Commission began to devote substantial resources systematically to programs that would provide information not being generated in the marketplace. Firms that had made false claims were frequently asked not just to stop doing so, but also to disseminate "corrective ads" — that is, statements disabusing consumers of those misconceptions.

The Commission also required members of important consumer goods industries to supply for the public record documentation in support of their advertising claims [13]. Trade regulation rules were promulgated that, for example, required gasoline stations to post octane ratings on the pump and mandated that manufacturers of garments prescribe proper cleaning procedures on the labels [14]. Two major commercial television networks were induced to drop self-imposed bans on commercials that named competitors. The Commission, in short, moved systematically and substantially into the field of noninformation, while tightening the reins on those who would purvey misinformation.

By 1970 the Commission had been largely preempted by other federal agencies from dealing with the externality problem by policing against unsafe products or dealing with the unforeseen social costs of product use. The Food and Drug Administration had been on the scene for decades, the Environmental Protection Agency was alive and apparently well, and the Consumer Product Safety Agency was being conceived on Capitol Hill. Wisely, the FTC's "new breed" shied away from attempting to make up, at that late date, for the agency's historical abstinence from that area.

As for exercise of the protectionist function, the Kirkpatrick record was more mixed. Half-baked, half-hearted attempts at direct consumer protection continued to eat up agency resources, although the program was twice reorganized, redefined, and "reinvigorated." Every day the mailman delivered hundreds of new complaints from aggrieved individuals, and hundreds of FTC attorneys set about to see if the wounds could be salved. On the other hand, a good deal of time and energy was suddenly channeled into what can best be described as reform of the common law. For example, the Commission held hearings on a proposal to abolish the holder in due course rule [15]. A "cooling off" rule for door-to-door sales over $25 was promulgated [16]. (The net effect of this rule is to alter, for one class of commercial transactions, the ancient rule of contract law that an acceptance binds both seller and buyer upon dispatch.)

Further, the Commission announced that it was going to study the desirability of changing the governing rules that determine under what circumstances a merchant, who is contractually committed to deliver services in the future, can retain a consumer's "deposit" where the consumer has determined those future services are no longer desirable [17]. While it is fairly debatable whether any of these reforms ought to be adopted, there is no substantial doubt that each deserves the Commission's careful deliberation. At bottom, each proposal would correct some of the harshness created by the common law courts' traditional inability, or unwillingness, to articulate which rules governing agreements between merchants ought not to apply without qualification to consumer transactions.

From this condensed historical perspective, it appears that at least four themes relevant to the present study underlay the FTC's work during this brief but productive period. First was the emergence of a concern for consumer information equal in intensity to the concern to avoid consumer misinformation. Second, the FTC began to deal with the causes as well as the effects of consumer fraud, and the generally prevailing imbalance of power between consumer and merchant. Third, a sense of the difference between trivial and important consumer concerns emerged. That difference is nowhere better reflected than in the virtual abandonment of efforts to label as such those goods originating outside the U.S. and the concomitant efforts to establish the octane posting rule.

In contrast to the foreign origin cases, the octane rule focuses on information, not otherwise available, which is crucial to a sensible purchase decision on a product that is a main component of most consumers' budgets. Fourth, underlying all the Commission's efforts was a fundamental reorientation in outlook. The Bureau of Consumer Protection was no longer in reality a bureau of competitor protection. The key question to be asked was not are legitimate businesses being harmed by this practice, but do consumers need redress if the market mechanism is to work.

By the fall of 1973, Kirkpatrick, Pitofsky, and Mary Gardiner Jones (a holdover commissioner throughout this period who had consistently been a strong and insightful advocate of consumer interests) had all departed the FTC. Whether the "new, new regime" subsequently installed by President Nixon will carry on the new tradition or succumb to the old one is yet to be seen. And whether the precise policies formulated by the Kirkpatrick Commission were truly wise, or only another flurry of fluff, will not be known for years.

But that the directions, orientations, and themes established by these three leaders of the FTC reflected a more responsible concern with the full measure of legitimate consumer complaints seems beyond serious doubt. While it is necessary to analyze carefully the wisdom of each of these substantive reforms, it is equally imperative to seek to describe what changes or alterations in the basic institutional nature of the Commission hold out some promise that it will continue to play the same themes. It is to this task that we now turn.

THE FTC AND CONSUMER PROTECTION: PROCEDURAL AND ORGANIZATIONAL REFORM

Having some understanding of the nature of consumer protection activity, the legal powers and concrete resources of the Federal Trade Commission, and its historical use and abuse of those powers, it is possible to draw certain conclusions about the institutional nature of the FTC. The reforms suggested below are undoubtedly feasible, although none would be easy to attain. The central inquiry throughout is to discover, principally within the history of the Commission itself, those revisions in institutional form and policy that hold out promise of yielding an agency capable of responding more wisely and sympathetically to the needs of consumers in a dynamic marketplace.

The Appointing Process: Sine Qua Non

First and foremost, the quality of the FTC always has been—and must always be—principally a reflection of the quality of the people who manage it. Relative to other governmental and corporate bureaucracies the FTC is small, blessed with sufficient powers to achieve a wide variety of goals by an incredibly diverse choice of means, and necessarily faced with responsibilities that will change as rapidly as the economy. The central determining factor in the performance of the FTC is, simply, the appointment process. The top priority for one who would create a Federal Trade Commission likely to be a constructive force in the national economy must be top quality commissioners—not money, new legislation, or reorganization. No reform is more obviously necessary; yet its implementation cannot be easy.

The first step toward reaching this goal must be to stop treating the FTC as a political graveyard. Too frequently the Commission has been dominated by third-rate ex-congressmen, scions of wealthy political contributors, worn-out congressional staffers, and FTC attorneys who jump when the White House says "Boo!" While the Commission has by no means been dominated exclusively by dregs from the political garbage pail and has occasionally been populated by some of the finest public servants Washington has produced, it is fair to say that the average run of commissioners has not demonstrated the sort of ability for insightful public administration that the job requires, and that the historical view of the FTC as a place where minor political debts are paid has been largely responsible for that failure.

A second necessary step is to define carefully those qualifications most important for the job. Three distinct ingredients are essential in the makeup of an individual likely to perform admirably in a commissioner's role. One is that quality of training, perception, experience, talent, dedication, and diligence that anyone needs to perform any task well. Another is independence, both financial and intellectual, from those business concerns likely to come before the Commission. A distinct, less frequently discussed, but quite necessary attribute is leadership and decisiveness. It does no good to appoint to the Commission intelligent, independent people who shrink from exercising their responsibility to choose among options and to determine the direction of the institution they nominally head.

As noted previously, a principal shortcoming of the Federal Trade Commission that has persisted almost without exception from its establishment to the present day has been its habitually expressed preference for reaction rather than action, its general sense of overall aimlessness, and its consistent reluctance to state what the Commission expects of the public, the business community, or even its own staff. To remedy this malaise it is necessary that the appointment processes stress not only substantive ability and independence, but equally reward a talent for administration, for collegial decision making, and for resolute determination to accept responsibility.

Perhaps the expression of such views seems trite or a belaboring of the obvious. Surely the observation that institutions primarily reflect the quality of those who run them is no revelatory insight. Yet, for all its obviousness, the point is no less true or important—nothing can substitute for the abilities of those who run the Commission and no other reform can succeed without first accomplishing this one. While the direction such a reform should take is relatively easy to describe—and its importance even easier to document—no simple way exists to bring it about in fact. Higher salaries cannot be the answer. Commissioners are already well paid and it boggles the mind to suggest that people unable or unwilling to work for $40,000 a year are nevertheless the sort of public servants who ought to be attracted to the cause of consumer protection.

There is no neat way to reform effectively the present system of White House nomination or Senate committee interrogation, each of which seems premised on the view that ability is either not measurable or not relevant. It remains particularly enigmatic that senators will toil long and hard to pass what they regard as valuable, insightful legislation and then idly sit by as minimally qualified people are chosen to administer those very statutes. If there are answers to this almost intractable dilemma they must lie in constant exposure of the weaknesses of the appointing process and the men and women it produces by a coalition of informed public interest groups, concerned legislators, and existing commissioners themselves, who ought to display a greater interest in seeing that the quality of the agency is not debased.

Rethinking the FTC's Responsibilities

The triviality and lack of comprehensive, purposeful direction that has pervaded much of the agency's work is not solely the fault of the commissioners. In brief, the FTC has understood that it has been assigned two tasks by the Congress which are, in fact, quite distinct and not substantially compatible. One of these jobs is defining national antitrust and consumer protection policy in a way that comports both with the inevitable changes in the marketplace from day to day and year to year and with the relatively fixed political-economic policies that should constitute the polestars of the FTC's work. Successful pursuit of this goal requires breadth of vision, careful articulation of fundamental policy issues, a sure grasp of the broad economic facts of life, and relatively infrequent—but nevertheless broad-ranging and generally applicable—test case litigation and rule making. It is, in short, a process of continuous law revision that employs litigation principally as a tool for restructuring or reordering substantial commercial practices.

The other task is that of obtaining redress for individual consumers or merchants for harm inflicted upon them by those members of the business community who have failed or refused to conform to the established rules of the game. This process may usefully be denominated as one of complaint resolution. It requires almost exclusively strict and close attention to particularized facts, negotiation with individual respondents, and, because complaints far outnumber resources available to resolve them, some sort of system for determining and enforcing priorities in case selection. Thus, the complaint resolution function necessitates decidedly different skills than the task of law revision.

The FTC engages in complaint resolution essentially for two different reasons. First, without critical reflection, Congress has apparently, though not expressly, demanded it. While neither the FTC Act nor its legislative history suggests that the Commission should act as a clearinghouse for consumer complaints, congressmen today seem to act on the assumption that the FTC is there to clear up their constituents' problems. Additionally, state and federal courts are generally unavailable for resolution of such cases, either because of the high costs of bringing an action founded upon the common law or because they will not enforce private actions arising under the Federal Trade Commission Act [18]. Thus, the FTC frequently steps into the breach, thereby shifting the cost of negotiation and litigation from the persons harmed to taxpayers generally.

A second principal procedural reform of the FTC should be that the Commission concentrate on the law revision function to the almost total exclusion of the complaint resolution process. Bringing what are essentially "private actions" tends to swamp the agency in work that lacks transcendent importance, obscures the need for constant law revision by inducing a sense of complacency about the law as it is and inattention to what it might be, inordinately consumes agency resources, and is a very inefficient and almost invisible method of shifting the costs of private litigation. Superintendence and revision of the law, on the other hand, were the primary reasons for creating the FTC and constitute the sole substantial justification for its continued existence.

In our dynamic economy, law revision is inescapably a continuing necessity. It demands the kind of expertise the Commission is supposed to possess (or acquire)—that of analyzing and determining public policy in a specialized area of economic regulation—not the expertise at fact finding, which no commissioner possesses to any noticeable degree beyond that of the population at large. Indeed, the FTC seems obviously too tiny to be able to undertake any serious commitment to complaint resolution that does not arbitrarily discriminate among the thousands of potential claimants who might seek the Commission's assistance.

In the broad sweep of the development of federal consumer protection law, nothing is as striking as the opportunities the FTC has foregone. Given its broad powers to declare practices unlawful and its elastic remedial authority, there can be no doubt that by appropriate action the Federal Trade Commission could have aborted the necessity for such separate legislation as the Truth-in-Lending Act, the Fair Packaging and Labelling Act, the Consumer Product Safety Commission Act, or the Fair Credit Reporting Act. And it is only because of the inattentiveness of the Commission to consumer needs that Congress, rather than the FTC, is now debating the necessity for a federal warranty bill, a Truth-in-Advertising bill, and establishment of a federal agency that would serve as an advocate for consumer interests before existing federal agencies [19]. While many factors have conspired to produce this truly staggering waste of resources, undoubtedly a principal cause, for the reasons expressed here, has been the Commission's traditional preoccupation with individualized complaint resolution (or "stroking the mailbag," if you will).

Certainly, before withdrawing the Commission's attorneys from this field, it would be preferable to improve individual access to forums capable of redressing harm caused by conduct that violates the FTC Act. For it would be hard to overstate the enormous difficulties presently facing individual consumers who would seek legal redress for business conduct that violates settled FTC Act principles. Were the FTC now to stop suing firms clearly in violation of established rules, the deterrent force behind those rules might be lost. Nevertheless, it seems preferable for the agency to take that risk, in the hopes that others will pick up the slack in the processing of routine matters or that Congress will pass legislation better enabling consumers to sue.

How best to create effective complaint resolution forums is a matter beyond the scope of this article, for the necessary reforms are not within the FTC's statutory competence; but it may be helpful simply to catalog a few promising suggestions. Substantial public funding for free legal services for the poor and subsidized legal services for the lower middle and middle classes are probably essential. Local establishment of accessible, effective small claims courts and arbitration panels would likely do much to improve consumer justice. Moreover, consumers undeniably need a private right of action for violations of the Federal Trade Commission Act. Perhaps such cases should be brought within the agency itself, with the Commission's administrative law judges serving as fact finders and the commissioners themselves providing expert, expeditious appellate review. In any event, legislation would be necessary to facilitate individual consumers' ability to prosecute such cases in the form of class actions.

Adoption of this reorientation of the FTC's view of its responsibilities would obviate the need for certain other institutional reforms often suggested. Were the agency in the law revision rather than complaint resolution business, there would be much less apparent need to seek speedier agency processes. Litigation and rule making at the FTC typically proceed at a snail's pace, but this is not a serious ill if those processes are employed for the grander purposes outlined above. Second, such a reorientation in purpose should make it clear that the FTC is not seriously underfunded or understaffed. Unless the federal government is to wholly displace the typical local, common law processes for resolving consumer complaints, the FTC need not be a giant bureaucracy to occupy an appropriate, important place in the national hierarchy of sources of consumer law and forums for consumer redress.

Thus, concentration on the law revision function would appear to be a preferable alternative both to increased funding and to many suggestions that the processes of adjudication be streamlined. Finally, it may well turn out that such a redefinition of purpose would substantially improve the performance of the commissioners themselves. Certainly the mission of an even tinier Washington institution, the Supreme Court, has typically led men with no superior previous qualifications to attain greater competence than most FTC members have displayed.

Increasing Public Participation in the Agency's Work

As noted previously, some progress has been made during the past five years in increasing the quality of the commissioners and reducing time spent on individual consumer complaints. Yet the fact remains that most appointments to the Commission are greeted with a ringing "Who's he (or she)?" Similarly, it would be difficult to find a dozen nonsupervisory attorneys in the Commission's Bureau of Consumer Protection or Regional Offices who do not typically spend at least eight hours a week answering complaints from businesses or consumers. In a third important procedural area, it is heartening to be able to report greater progress.

Traditionally the processes of federal agencies have remained essentially closed to the public those institutions were purportedly designed to protect. In practical effect, the advent of the much-heralded Freedom of Information Act did little to alter that situation. Thus, at the Federal Trade Commission, members of the public, no matter how great their expertise or how substantial their interest, have not generally been able to participate in agency litigation, find out what investigations were under way within the Commission, discover which industry representatives had access to which commissioners or staff members, or discover information the FTC had compiled but declined to act upon.

Nor could outsiders obtain even the little pieces of information discoverable under the Freedom of Information Act without going through lengthy and laborious procedures before the entire Commission. A few matters have been open to the public for some time. FTC complaints, case settlements, and advisory opinions have been made matters of public record. Proposed settlements have been placed on the public record for 30 days during which public comments were solicited. And *ex parte* communications with commissioners concerning cases then in trial have been forbidden, and, where they occurred by accident, were to be placed on the public record.

In February 1974 the Commission announced a series of further modifications in its traditional closed-door policy [20]. Henceforth the FTC will announce publicly the existence of authorized industry-wide investigations, investigations into acts or practices involving risks to public health and safety, and other investigations that have stopped short of the issuance of a complaint or conclusion of a settlement. Further, proposed settlements will be left open for public comments for 60 days, authority to hand over materials clearly discoverable under the Freedom of Information Act will be delegated to Commission staff, most intraagency memos in files properly closed to the public will be disclosed after a few years; and all members of the Commission staff will be required to maintain, for ultimate public inspection, a record of all outside contacts (including those with members of Congress or the executive branch) "when such contacts relate to investigations or cases." Finally, the commissioners themselves have agreed to maintain records of all contacts with anyone outside the Commission "when such contacts relate to pending investigations or cases."

While it would be easy to quibble with the precise form of some of these rather vague innovations, and while it remains particularly disturbing that the commissioners will disclose only contacts related to specific investigations, these new ground rules ought generally to be praised as far-sighted and appropriate reforms. What remains to be done, particularly in light of the FTC's recent history, is to open the agency law enforcement and reform processes to members of the public with a demonstrated capacity to further the public interest. Those being investigated or sued by the FTC are guaranteed, as they should be, a right to full participation in those processes. Surely we have learned too much to cling to the naive view that the Commission can be expected fully and forthrightly to articulate the countervailing interest of the consumer in all such matters.

The Commission, in many—if not most—instances, is necessarily going to be faced with the task of resolving conflicting definitions of the public interest and necessity put forward by business groups on the one hand and consumer interests on the other. Impartial resolution of the conflicting claims of advocates is, in actual fact, the way of law making as well as of adjudication in this country. It asks too much of the Commission and its staff to charge it, in every case, with the responsibility both for vigorous advocacy of consumer interests and for the wise reconciliation of such claims with those put forward by opposing, fully represented interests.

Accordingly, the FTC should establish formal procedures by which individuals and public interest groups might petition the agency to undertake remedial action that is within the scope of its statutory authority. Such procedures should include the promise of a written statement, from the Commission or its duly authorized delegate, of the reasons for any decision not to act. In the same vein, the agency should establish formal procedures permitting intervention in defined adjudicative proceedings by interested members of the public, and should promulgate standards for determining what showing of interest will be sufficient to gain representation.

The FTC often responds directly to formal requests for action and has occasionally benefited from public interest participation in its proceedings [21]. To date, however, these actions have been taken on an ad hoc basis, without any established ground rules and without any concern for encouraging systematic consumer input into these most vital aspects of the agency's present work. Like the previous proposal for shifting the Commission's orientation away from the specific grievances of individual consumers, this proposal to increase public interest groups' access to the FTC can be accomplished without enactment of new statutes or expenditure of additional funds. All that is required is the will to proceed.

Dramatic evidence of the beneficial impact upon the agency of such improved public access is supplied by the Kirkpatrick-ABA Commission report. In effect, that report is a careful, detailed challenge to improve its performance issued to the FTC by a group of independent, public-spirited expert inquirers. When Kirkpatrick and Pitofsky assumed command of the agency's consumer protection work, they proceeded to put that battle plan into effect, thereby concretely demonstrating the practical utility of the proposals set forth in that report. Unless the FTC is to continue to survive only by successively elevating its critics to the chairmanship, some more permanent, receptive vehicle for public interest input must be devised. The measures advocated in this article should fulfill that purpose.

Reorganizing the Agency's Resources

A fourth proposal for procedural change is ventured with a good deal of reluctance. It is that the Federal Trade Commission undertake a bit of reorganization. Historically, reorganization of administrative agencies has been confused with rejuvenation, and the FTC is no exception to this rule. Move a division, rename a bureau, redelegate some existing authority, and agencies can be instantly revitalized or reawakened in the eyes of too many would-be reformers. The fact is (at least with respect to the FTC) that good people can overcome almost any merely organizational obstacle placed in their way. Playing musical office spaces and inventing new titles for old jobs, unless they are subterfuges for replacing deadwood with talent, are the kinds of agency reform most employed and least successful.

Upon the understanding, then, that they are not offered as panaceas, two specific organizational changes are suggested. First, abolish the Regional Offices. Two things are notable about the Regional Offices. First, they are in fact local, not regional, offices. While the organizational charts of the FTC show that each office is responsible for a multistate sector of America, in fact at any given time all targets of 90 percent of all Regional Office investigations and complaints can be located within the metropolitan area where the office in charge is located. In addition, no Regional Office has brought more than three truly significant cases in its entire history—and none is situated to undertake the sort of consumer protection work urged above. When not dealing with localized consumer fraud, the Regional Offices can typically be found prosecuting firms under the Robinson-Patman Act for illegal price discriminations where the discriminations are wholly confined to one geographic region of the country. Less anticompetitive practices would be hard to invent (although, given time, the history of the Regional Offices suggests that they could do this too). No matter how able the people installed in the Regional Offices, when they are told to stamp out consumer fraud in Kansas City, they are not going to be pursuing those goals or fulfilling those purposes for which the Federal Trade Commission was created.

Second, take the money saved and create a Bureau of Consumer Behavior and Product Engineering. Just as the Commission's Bureau of Economics is its most valuable resource in enabling the FTC to carry out with sophistication and foresight its antitrust responsibilities, so too must the FTC have available the expertise that scientists have been developing concerning the factors that influence consumer behavior, as well as the knowledge engineers and physical scientists can supply concerning the physical properties and potentialities of consumer goods. Presently, many advertisers attempt to ascertain *before* they put the ads on the airwaves precisely how (and how many) consumers will react to them. Yet the Commission comes across such information only by happenstance, if at all. Searching out falsehoods and devising appropriate remedies for them under such conditions is like batting blindfolded against Tom Seaver—it won't work and you could get hurt.

While the FTC under Kirkpatrick undertook a variety of new, substantive programs to deal with the problem of consumer information, none of them was so important as the way in which the FTC at that time altered its method of analyzing the problem. In the past, the Commission typically read ad copy the way lawyers read statutes and predicted the impact of certain practices on consumers by assuming either that all consumers are like all the commissioners or that all consumers are idiots [22]. Under the new regime the Commission's staff set out to learn what advertisers and consumer behavioralists knew about these issues, and to make that knowledge relevant to the adjudication of cases and the definition of the law. Lengthy public hearings on modern advertising practices were held, experts in consumer behavior were hired to analyze the voluminous record compiled, and the facts and theories discovered in the context of the hearings were put to use in the prosecution of cases [23]. Essentially, what is proposed here is that this process of FTC self-education be continued on a wider, more systematic scale. Anyone who has lived through this educational process can attest to its obvious benefits.

The FTC as a Consumer Advocate

Finally, in resolving the conflicting claims of consumer and merchant, the Commission will frequently develop insights that escape those whose decisions have a substantial impact on consumers' interests but who do not have such close and continuous contact with the special problem of the consumer's role in the marketplace. The Federal Trade Commission is thus perfectly situated to serve as an effective lobbying force for consumer interests before the Congress and the other, more specialized federal agencies, as well as state and local consumer protection units. Particularly if combined with the addition of professionals skilled in the analysis of consumer behavior and product performance, such undertakings could be a distinct aid to other agencies, such as the FCC or CAB or FDA, whose activities directly and substantially affect the interests of consumers yet who are almost totally dependent for information upon the identifiable, organized industries they confront. Similarly, members of Congress should benefit from advice on consumer bills that reflects not only the accumulated wisdom of the FTC's efforts at law enforcement, but also the knowledge of consumer behavioral patterns and influences possessed by detached, professional observers of the phenomena.

Again, the Kirkpatrick-Pitofsky record bears witness to the potential of such a program. In 1972 the Commission submitted to the Federal Communications Commission a 22-page document urging the FCC to permit wider access to the broadcast media for public interest groups to respond to issues of product performance and desirability raised by broadcast commercials. That paper carefully and exhaustively surveys the economic role of advertising in the modern marketplace as well as the nature and sources of the FTC's concern for the quality and availability of consumer information concerning product characteristics. The report also thoroughly explores the means by which the FCC can exercise its statutory powers in partnership with the FTC to further legitimate consumer protection goals in this area. The submission to the FCC reflects the sort of solid, informed work which, if carried out on a more systematic basis, ought not only to further the FTC's ability to attain its goals, but more important, attain for consumers an effective voice within many federal agencies where they have not been heard for years.

CONCLUSIONS

If the Federal Trade Commission is to have any chance at all of playing an important role in the nation's consumer protection work, it is imperative that institutional as well as substantive policy changes be made. This article has emphasized the distinction between the two areas and suggested a number of institutional policy changes. These proposals ought to be seen as modest suggestions, for they are offered in the view that only modest institutional reform is necessary.

In another sense, however, these proposals are radical. For they do not repeat, but rather reject, those reformist prescriptions most often advanced. It has been suggested here, for example, that the agency's funding is presently adequate; that speedier litigation and investigation processes are not a matter of high priority; that new legislation is not especially necessary. Additionally, no new proposals are urged for upgrading the quality of the Commission staff because there can be no doubt that a Commission rejuvenated along the lines set out above, would inevitably attract professionals of the highest skill and dedication without any specialized attention to the staff problem as such.

Another plea often voiced, but not directly addressed in this article, is that the FTC needs to add to its staff a well trained, highly motivated, and powerful cadre of policy planners. This suggestion, too, is consciously discarded here. Lack of policy planning, to avoid endless waste of agency resources and to assure that the staff's and commissioners' time is spent on the most promising and valuable alternatives, has indeed been the principal cause of the agency's failures. Those who would remedy this malaise chiefly by institutionalizing a staff unit of planners, however, wholly miss the mark.

The thesis of this article is that the FTC should do policy planning. Traditionally, policy planning has meant a formal planning arrangement to maximize the potential of the agency. Such a reform may eliminate some of the more flagrant shortcomings, such as excessive concern with relatively insignificant problems. But it would preserve the basic orientation and institutional framework of the agency. The institutional analysis of this article argues that such a reform is certainly inadequate, and probably unnecessary.

The policy planning system must consist of able commissioners, properly informed, concentrating on the broad economic issues, with the direct aid of those who will be affected by their deliberations, who adopt a broad concept of the agency's potential responses to felt ills. That is, the fundamental prerequisite is to shape an institution along the lines urged above. With this kind of responsibility exercised at the top, any purely mechanical subsidiary structure of staff assistance and implementation will succeed. Without these prerequisites, any formal planning arrangement at the FTC will fail.

Those who urge the addition of a policy planning cadre to the agency seek an FTC that will exercise its powers with wisdom, a sense of priorities, and a comprehension of what truly counts versus what is mere window dressing. What those reformers fail to see is that these goals cannot be accomplished by a staff appendage, or a bank of computers, or constant admonitions for separate attention to the problem of priorities and effectiveness. Fundamental institutional alterations are essential if the FTC is to realize its potential role in consumer protection. If the changes suggested here do occur, the traditional policy planning problems will also be solved.

NOTES TO CHAPTER 9

1. 2 S.E. Morison and H.S. Commager, *The Growth of the American Republic*, 5th ed., 1962, pp. pp. 532–534.

2, FTC v. Raladam, 283 U.S. 643 (1931).

3. See FTC v. Brown Shoe Co., 384 U.S. 316 (1966) (antitrust); FTC v. Sperry & Hutchinson, 405 U.S. 233 (1972) (consumer protection).

4. The employment statistics were supplied by David Shannon, FTC Director of Personnel, on May 28, 1974. The descriptions of the work of the various bureaus are drawn from personal observation.

5. The FTC's authority to act by rule making was most recently affirmed in Nat'l Petroleum Refiners Assn. v. FTC, 482 F.2d 672 (D.C. Cir. 1973), cert. denied 42 Law Week 3482 (2–26–74).

6. See, e.g., FTC, Economic Report on Installment Credit and Retail Sales Practices of District of Columbia Retailers (March, 1968).

7. See Posner, The Federal Trade Commission, 37 U. Chi. L. Rev. 47, 76–82 (1969).

8. 16 C.F.R. §410 (TV screens); 16 C.F.R. §418 (extension ladders); 16 C.F.R. §13.235–60(c) (foreign origin).

9. See generally C. Katz (ed.), *The Law and the Low Income Consumer* (1968).

10. 16 C.F.R. §408.

11. See Marco Sales Co. v. FTC, 453 F.2d 1 (2d Cir. 1971).

12. See Report of the ABA Commission to Study the Federal Trade Commission (1969).

13. All these actions are described in Pitofsky, "Advertising and the New Consumerism—A Second Look," address delivered at Northwestern University on October 4, 1972. (Copy on file with the author).

14. See FTC, Trade Regulation Rule Concerning Care Labelling of Textile Wearing Apparel (December 9, 1971); FTC, Trade Regulation Rule Concerning Posting Minimum Octane Numbers on Gasoline Dispensing Pumps (December 16, 1971).

15. 36 Fed. Reg. 1211 (1971).

16. See FTC, Trade Regulation Rule Concerning A Cooling-Off Period for Door-to-Door Sales (October 18, 1972).

17. In February 1971 the Commission announced in a press release that it was studying the desirability of adopting a rule providing a mandatory pro-rata refund of deposits made to vocational schools by students who drop out before completing the course.

18. See Holloway v. Bristol-Myers Corp., 485 F.2d 986 (1973).

19. S. 356, 93d Cong., 2d Sess. (1973) (warranty bill); H.R. 21, 93d Cong., 2d Sess. (1973) (consumer advocate); S. 1461, 93d Cong., 2d Sess. (1973) ("Truth in Advertising").

20. The new rules have not, as of this writing, yet been published in the FTC's official compilation of rules and regulations. The most comprehensive source presently available is Engman. Address before the National Press Club, Washington, D.C., Feb. 19, 1974. (Copy on file with the author.)

21. See P. Keeton & M. Shapo, *Products and the Consumer: Deceptive Practices* (1972) pp. 519–525; and the Firestone proceeding discussed therein.

22. See, for example, the cases described in E. Kintner, *A Primer on the Law of Deceptive Practices* (1971), pp. 30–32, 39.

23. Howard & Hulbert, *Advertising and the Public Interest*, A Staff Report to the Federal Trade Commission (1973).

Chapter 10

The Consumer Product Safety Commission: Its Clout, Its Candor, and its Challenge

R. David Pittle

The Consumer Product Safety Commission, one of the newest independent federal regulatory commissions in the country, represents the most current congressional thinking about how to set up and operate a regulatory agency. Prior to 1972, the new federal product safety laws by and large were narrowly drawn to cover specific areas such as flammable fabrics or dangerous refrigerator doors. These laws were clearly inadequate to deal with what was, and still is, a truly monumental national problem.

To see its scope, one need only examine the reports of the National Commission on Product Safety, a government study group which investigated the adequacy of private and public measures to protect consumers against injuries associated with hazardous household products. According to the National Commission, 20 million Americans are injured each year as a result of incidents involving consumer products found around the home. Of the injured, 110,000 are permanently disabled and 30,000 are killed, at an annual cost to the nation in excess of $5.5 billion.

Faced with these awesome statistics and strong consumer lobbying, Congress passed the Consumer Product Safety Act of 1972. This act formally established this Commission as an independent regulatory agency with the task of reducing injuries associated with the thousands of consumer products sold in the United States. Our jurisdiction under the Act covers such products as ladders, seesaws, swings, blenders, televisions, stoves, and similar items commonly thought of as consumer products.

We also have responsibility for some items not readily thought of as consumer products, including structural items found in homes, such as stairs, ramps, landings, windowsills, and retaining walls. Home fixtures, such as doors, architectural glass, and electrical wiring, may be similarly regulated by the Commission. In fact, the only consumer products over which we do not have jurisdiction under the Act are foods, drugs, cosmetics, automobiles, firearms, tobacco, boats, pesticides, and aircraft, all of which are regulated to some extent under other laws.

To insure continuity in the enforcement of existing product safety laws, Congress transferred to us the Flammable Fabrics Act, Hazardous Substances Act, Poison Prevention Packaging Act, and Refrigerator Safety Act. Briefly, the Flammable Fabrics Act established authority to reduce injuries associated with flammability of clothing and certain interior furnishings in homes. The Hazardous Substances Act gives us the authority to require cautionary labeling for most of the toxic, corrosive, irritating, or flammable chemical products found in households and to ban products from commerce in the event that we determine that cautionary labeling cannot adequately protect the public. In addition, amendments to the HSA give the Commission authority to ban hazardous children's toys. The Poison Prevention Packaging Act gives us the authority to require safety closures on packages containing products dangerous to young children who might ingest oral prescription drugs, aspirin, paint cleaners, ethylene glycol, and other poisonous substances.

Where did Congress depart from what one might characterize as the traditional administrative agency format when it set up the CPSC? One welcome change was that they gave us a comprehensive, tough law so that by and large we deal from a position of strength whenever we deal with the industries we regulate. Our law permits us to seek court injunction against the marketing of specific products we decide are unreasonably hazardous, and to enforce compliance with our safety regulations through a broad range of civil and criminal sanctions. Thus, unlike many other government agencies, we have been given full authority to carry out our mission. When we feel the public interest is jeopardized, we do not have to plead for voluntary action from companies. If companies refuse to cooperate voluntarily in removing hazards from the marketplace, we have the means to compel them to do so.

Our effectiveness is not dependent on the benign attitude of the industries we regulate. We do not have to make "deals" with companies to maintain their cooperation in order to protect the public. Therefore, we can avoid compromising the public interest on important regulatory decisions. Although it is helpful to have the kind of statutory power that we do, it is not used to "bully" companies into doing what we want whenever we want. Rather, it has been our intention to try to develop within each company a sense of responsibility for consumer safety that has been absent too often in the past.

In the course of listening to testimony at public hearings, I repeatedly have heard responses from industry representative that have caused me great concern. In particular, the answer to the question, "Did you test for safety before you marketed the product?" has all too often been a dismal "no." This response, I feel, borders on the irresponsible, given the magnitude of the nation's safety problem. Unfortunately, safety has not been a very important consideration of many companies. For example, in a conversation with a motorcycle manufacturer, I was told that a motorbike was being developed for young children. When I expressed concern that injuries were likely to ensue from such a product and asked if they had considered how dangerous this product might be, the response was, "We think that since children can balance bicycles at that age, they can certainly handle a motorcycle—and do you relize what a market there is for this product?" In another case, I asked an importer if he had requested safety information from the foreign manufacturer and was distressed to learn that the answer was "no." "Our main concern was marketability," he said.

I often hear that "It is a free market. Consumers are free to choose whatever they want and the marketplace will force out unsafe products because consumers will not buy them." I have some trouble with that logic. While it might be true that some unsafe products are forced off the shelves, I fear that we also force out some of the consumers after they have been injured. I think that consumers are at a tremendous disadvantage in a marketplace filled with complicated and often dangerous products that they do not fully understand.

Finally, I hear quite often that injuries are usually the fault of consumers because they foolishly misuse products. While this might be true in certain cases, I believe that the emphasis is askew. It is clearly the manufacturer's responsibility, as far as I am concerned, to design products that conform with foreseeable, predictable consumer behavior, rather than to demand that consumers change their normal behavior patterns to match the product. For example, because we can predict that a child is likely to pull the trigger on a gun, it would be irresponsible to give a loaded gun to a child even if we warned the child in advance. Similarly, when epidemiological data demonstrate that consumers foolishly, but consistently, stick their fingers in rotating lawnmowers to clean out the grass, manufacturers should incorporate this knowledge of consumer behavior and design safeguards against this kind of misuse.

One approach to incorporating common use behavior into product design is through safety standards, the "nitty-gritty" feature of our regulatory activities. What is a consumer product safety standard? At the risk of oversimplifying, I would describe it as a set of requirements or rules, issued by the Commission, with which a consumer product must comply to be considered "safe enough" to be sold in the United States. For example, suppose that the Commission, after examining various injury data available to it, concludes that too many people in this country are unnecessarily injured by easily broken widgets. A safety standard could then be written requiring that widgets meet certain stress requirements without breaking. Such a standard thus would elevate the level of safety for consumers because easily broken widgets would no longer be sold.

The ability to set safety standards is not unique to this Commission. What is unique is that the development of safety standards by CPSC is a process in which the public, including consumers and consumer organizations, can play a direct, basic, primary role. Under the CPSA, the Commission is generally prohibited from drafting safety standards by itself. Instead, we must publicly invite interested persons outside the Commission to offer to develop a proposed standard whenever we determine one is needed for a consumer product. Persons who respond to this invitation are called "offerors." The Commission generally accepts one offer (and may accept more than one) to develop a proposed safety standard, assuming we determine that an offeror is competent and will comply with the Commission's conditions for the development of the standard. The important point here is that generally the Commission will not be doing the fundamental development of the standard.

This process is not without its potential pitfalls. Included among those eligible to write safety standards for consumer products are the very companies that make and sell those products. Our experience in standards development, albeit brief, seems to me to indicate that every time we invite offers to develop a standard we will receive one or more offers from an individual manufacturer or group of manufacturers, distributors, or retailers of the product we are trying to regulate.

One does not need a crystal ball to see the potential for abuse inherent in a situation in which an industry has been given authority by the government to develop a safety standard for the product it sells. One might analogize it to the proverbial fox offering to set its own visitation rules to the chicken coop. The Consumer Product Safety Act, however, has safeguards to prevent such abuse. Where the sole offeror accepted by the Commission is a manufacturer, distributor, or retailer of a consumer product proposed for regulation by the safety standard, the Commission may *independently* develop proposals for that standard. More importantly, no offeror is able to develop standards free from public scrutiny and participation.

Under our regulations, each offeror must set forth a comprehensive plan detailing how the offeror intends to involve a broad range of participants (including consumers) in the development of the safety standard. At a minimum, offerors must notify all participants of any working meetings, circulate drafts of the proposed standard to the participants for review, and provide a written evaluation of all criticisms. This, by the way, is a major departure from previous private voluntary standards efforts, which often did not include end-use consumers in the process.

A third, unique feature of the Consumer Product Safety Commission is the extent to which Congress has ensured its independence from control by the executive branch of government. Unlike most other regulatory agencies, commissioners of the CPSC may not be removed by the President on the nebulous ground of "inefficiency." We may be removed only for "neglect of duty" or "malfeasance in office." Also unlike most agencies, the Chairman of the Commission, once designated, is the Chairman of the Commission for the duration of his or her term and may not have the "Chairmanship" removed at the pleasure of the President.

Another unusual provision for independence is that whenever the Commission submits a budget request or legislative recommendations to the President or the Office of Management and Budget (OMB), we must concurrently submit these requests to the Congress. This requirement diminishes the possibility of executive branch interference with or compromise of the Commission's request, because Congress will be aware of our stated needs before the executive branch acts upon them. These points may seem insignificant in the context of this paper—but in the real world of Washington, they are substantial.

I personally believe that Congress went to considerable lengths to create a "model regulatory agency" when it created CPSC. We are well aware of this fact and have attempted to implement this founding spirit wherever possible. We have adopted a policy of candor and openness that we term a "goldfish bowl" policy. Under this policy, all meetings with persons outside the Commission involving substantive matters before the Commission are announced publicly and are open for observation and, hopefully, participation by the public. Written summaries of such meetings must also be submitted by the participants and are available for public inspection. This policy is designed not only to reduce the possibility of impropriety within the Commission (obviously we can never eliminate all possibilities) but also to avoid the appearance of impropriety. Of equal importance, this policy helps us obtain a broad and timely set of competing facts to consider while making regulatory decisions.

This summary of the powers of the Consumer Product Safety Commission may leave many of you shaken. You will argue that by simply describing the Commission's vast authority I have made the most convincing case possible for its immediate abolition. If you do so, you will discover many allies, for the continued existence of federal regulatory agencies is one of the most hotly debated issues in Washington today. Attention to these agencies is long overdue. Some agencies have outlasted their function; others have never performed it. Yet I cannot believe that the solution to the economic problems the United States faces in 1975 lies in simply abolishing regulatory agencies.

Upton Sinclair's *The Jungle* graphically described the conditions under which this country's meat was packed at the turn of the century. The protests of horrified consumers quickly led to the Meat Inspection Act of 1906. Would many of you be ready to let the federal meat inspectors go home and risk a return to that "jungle?"

Although the final report of the National Commission on Product Safety is hardly the literary equivalent of *The Jungle*, it is equally graphic:

> A fourteen-year-old girl testified, "I will be blind in one eye for the rest of my life because of a defective glass bottle."
> A one-year-old toddler in Peoria, Illinois, swallowed about three tablespoons of Old English Furniture & Scratch Cover Polish when his aunt momentarily left the bottle unguarded. He died 40 hours later of chemical pneumonia.
> "The most dangerous years are below age 5," the National Commission reported. "Approximately 7,000 children under 15 die each year in home accidents—a death toll higher than that of cancer and heart disease combined" [1].

The Jungle and the *Final Report* illustrate a basic point that bears repeating. That is, federal regulatory agencies are created in response to problems. Upton Sinclair did not create the Food and Drug Administration—filthy meat packing plants did. Ralph Nader isn't personally responsible for the Consumer Product Safety Commission—it actually was brought to you by those friendly folks who manufacture, import, or sell products that are difficult for the average consumer to use safely.

Critics of the Commission and other regulatory agencies point out that solutions to safety problems cost money. That's certainly true. They also point out that any costs industry incurs in solving safety problems will be passed along to consumers. That's also true. However, I believe that the time has come to debunk a few myths about federal regulatory agencies and the safety standards they set. For example, consider the following charges.

The government never balances the costs of its regulations against the benefits they will bring. Anyone who has ever worked in a regulatory agency is aware that affected industries supply vast amounts of information concerning the economic effects they expect will result from a proposed action. Agencies are legally required to consider and evaluate all comments they receive, including those dealing with economic questions, before they take final action. The Consumer Product Safety Commission in particular is required by Section 9 of the Consumer Product Safety Act to consider the economic impact of any standard it proposes to set. That doesn't mean the Commission's decisions will always please the affected industry, but disagreement with a judgment on probable economic consequences should not be confused with failure to consider it.

Business can solve the problem cheaper and quicker without federal interference. This begs the question somewhat, because if the problem were solved there would be no need for federal action. But two other points are also significant. First, the costs associated with the industry solution may well be the same as the costs of a federal answer. To return for a moment to the widgets, if the government sets a mandatory safety standard for widgets, certain costs will be incurred. These costs include retooling, additional material, new employees, testing, and record keeping. If, on the other hand, the Widget Manufacturers Association (WMA) voluntarily comes up with a safety standard with which 98 percent of the widget manufacturers comply, the same costs are likely to be incurred even if the same level of safety is not reached. Members of the WMA will still have to tool up, buy more material, hire more people, test, keep records of the tests, and destroy or reprocess nonconforming lots.

Second, under certain circumstances the industry solution may actually be more expensive than a federal standard. For example, the widget standard may contain unnecessary requirements that are not technically justified merely because the widget manufacturers who participated in the process could agree to them. Similarly, the standard may unnecessarily restrict widget product design. If the standard does any of these things, it could force smaller businesses out of existence and stifle the entry of new competitors. Limiting competition will eventually result in greater costs to consumers.

The only costs are those directly associated with complying with the standard. This ignores hospital fees, doctor bills, time lost from work, and the pain and suffering that result from injuries. The cost of a judgment or a settlement in a product liability suit will be passed along to future consumers of the product along with any increased costs associated with the manufacturer's liability insurance. If no suit is brought, the cost of the injuries will be paid by the injured consumer, who may in turn be compensated by a health insurance carrier or a government medical assistance program, thus passing along the costs to us all, even those who do not consume the product.

Increased prices to consumers reflect the actual costs of compliance with the federal standard. It is sad but true that some manufacturers may take the opportunity to raise their profits as well as their prices. Others may elect an unnecessarily expensive way of complying with the standard, as has been alleged to be the case with certain kinds of automobile bumpers. And some costs that are being passed on may be attributable to frivolous and time consuming litigation brought by manufacturers to challenge the validity of the standard or delay its effective date.

Finally, an economic slump in an industry may be blamed unfairly on government safety standards in order to divert attention from mistakes in judgment by corporate executives. Are Americans reluctant to buy big Detroit cars because of the costs attributable to safety requirements? Or is the downturn the result of the fact that Detroit cars so equipped cannot compete effectively with smaller, similarly equipped imports? Government safety standards are far from perfect. But their contribution to inflation is greatly overrated. Although cost considerations are not and should not be ignored, all aspects of costs must be examined.

We could be accused of being too tough, but the seriousness of product safety problems in this country calls for strong action. Congress has equipped us well to protect the consumer. The "new" features of the Consumer Product Safety Commission reflect the belief of Congress that many federal regulatory agencies have been co-opted by the industries they regulate, needlessly secretive in their decision making processes, and plagued by delay in their actions. It remains to be seen whether the changes adopted in the setting up of CPSC can effectively prevent these stumbling blocks to adequate regulation for greater product safety. I personally believe they can—especially if the public provides interest and concern in our activities.

NOTES TO CHAPTER 10

1. *Final Report of the National Commission on Product Safety*, Washington, D.C., June 1970, pp. 17, 21, 9.

Chapter 11

Emerging Issues in Standards and Industry Self-Regulation

Ernest S. Rosenberg

Private standards development and certification programs have been studied from the perspective of the participants or users of such programs, from the attorney's vantage point, and from the regulator's perch, but there has been little if any movement toward combining these perspectives to arrive at a comprehensive overview of these programs by those who are responsible for formulating policy in either the public or the private sector.

Standards development and certification programs involve issues of a technical nature that are often unfamiliar to the attorney and the business executive. Consequently, both regulators and industry members have left these incredibly influential activities largely to their employees with technical expertise but without direct access to the policy formulation levels of their institutions. The policy makers' involvement is generally introduced late in the process—when a standard or certification program has resulted in a direct and measurable effect, usually deleterious, either on corporate profits or on the public welfare.

Thus, efforts at reform have generally dealt with symptoms of the deficiencies in standards development and certification programs, rather than with the underlying deficiencies themselves. Similarly, persons involved in the promulgation of standards or the design of certification programs often have largely restricted their attention to the issues with which they are most familiar, that is, the technical considerations, and they have been either unable or unwilling to adequately consider the economic and other social welfare effects of these programs.

The author therefore wishes to begin a dialogue that will lead to a synthesis of these perspectives, based on his experiences as an attorney on the staff of a law enforcement agency charged with the preservation of free competition and protection of the consumer, and as a participant in standards development. The remarks that follow are based more on knowledge acquired through a process of assimilation than on hard research. They are largely addressed to those who are either unfamiliar with the more technical aspects of the law, or with standards development processes, or both.

Standards affect the quality (the appearance, performance, and composition) and the cost of virtually every structure and product and for many services, bought, sold, and used at every level of commerce. They are unquestionably essential tools for the conduct of commerce, from the recovery of raw materials through the delivery of a product or building to the ultimate consumer. However, standards may also have deleterious effects upon competition, the quality, safety, and cost of products and buildings, and upon the consumer who uses them.

It has been estimated that there are over 20,000 industry standards in effect in the United States in addition to more than 36,000 government standards in use (primarily in the form of purchase specifications) [1]. More than 400 organizations have been estimated to be at work in this country developing, revising, and reviewing standards [2]. From an antitrust viewpoint, private standards development and certification programs are risky enterprises, since these activities ordinarily involve competitors agreeing with one another as to how certain aspects of their commercial activities will be conducted. Every standard has the potential for circumscribing some facet of commercial operation. This potential may never be realized, but it may be realized in extraordinarily profound ways.

The impact of standards, real or potential, must therefore be directed in socially acceptable channels, to facilitate the workings of commerce, to lower prices, to improve the quality and safety of goods, to lower cost, and so forth. Simultaneously, the potential for diminished competition, for impeding innovation, or for other economic or consumer injury must be eliminated where possible, or at the very least, severely limited.

Based on the author's experience as well as instances that have been brought to light in litigation [3], the potential for abuse in standards programs is greatest during the development and promulation stages. Consequently, these stages must be most closely scrutinized, and these stages in the process are most in need of reform. Fortunately, they are most susceptible to reform and control because these stages precede the dispersion of standards and their effects throughout industry and the marketplace. Prior to making the tentative suggestions for reform incorporated in this article it is first necessary to explain what standards are, how they operate, and how they are written.

STANDARDS AND CERTIFICATION

For the purposes of this discussion, *standards* are sets of conditions or requirements, prescribed and either formally adopted or widely recognized and accepted, whether promulgated by government agencies or merely established by custom or agreement, among buyers, sellers, or other governmental or commercial units. They may operate to prescribe methods of constructing, evaluating, or using products, delineate acceptable or preferred conduct, or facilitate communication among those in business. *Certification* is the process of assuring compliance with a standard by various instrumentalities, such as the seller of a product, a government agency, or some other party.

Quite often, when the role of standards in commerce is discussed, the word "standard" is prefixed with the word "industry." Some standards are indeed purely industry standards, that is, they are written by and for commercial entities with relatively narrow interests and with little or no government or other public involvement or scrutiny. But some standards are developed and promulgated through organizations that attempt to balance the commercial or other institutional biases (as opposed to private biases) of the technical experts who actually do the drafting. Some of these organizations even provide for the inclusion of consumer, academic, and government representatives in the drafting and promulgation processes.

Many standards are also promulgated by various governmental groups. In a sense, every government regulation is a standard. Some are standards in the ordinary sense, such as purchase specifications; others are standards of conduct. However, government promulgation is no assurance of a standard's freedom from defect. As noted by the Federal Trade Commission's Task Force on Industry Self-Regulation in April 1972:

> Government procurement agencies at both the federal and state-local levels have elected to use, in developing their purchasing specifications, the various "voluntary" standards promulgated by the selling industry groups, thus incorporating into government purchasing programs whatever restraints of trade have been built into the standardization-certification programs of the private sector [4].

In the United States, the National Bureau of Standards (NBS) does considerable basic research for and development of standards in an advisory capacity; it has no regulatory authority and cannot mandate standards. Other agencies are advised by NBS, but they often generate their own standards to address their specialized needs.

In spite of considerable government activity in this area, the overwhelming majority of the standards used in commerce in the United States originate in the private sector, although many of these standards ultimately find their way into government regulations and specifications. These private standards are initiated, developed, or promulgated by a variety of organizations ranging from third parties such as independent laboratories, the National Safety Council, and the National Fire Protection Association, to certifiers such as Underwriters' Laboratories, to technical and engineering societies such as the American Society for Testing and Materials and the American Society of Mechanical Engineers. To a somewhat lesser extent, these activities are also conducted directly by the trade associations of interested industries.

The vast majority of all of these organizations involved in standards writing belong to the American National Standards Institute (ANSI), a private organization (albeit with government employees and organizations in its membership) which generally acts as a standards clearinghouse. ANSI is intended to act as a starting point for anyone who perceives the need for a new standard. It refers such parties to the standards-writing organization most appropriate for the task and, if the standard is referred to it for ballot after promulgation, it may certify a standard as an "American National Standard." Although American National Standards are strictly voluntary, unless adopted or referenced by governmental authorities, the designation carries a great deal of weight and may in effect become mandatory via virtually universal acceptance.

ANSI also performs two other extremely significant functions. It certifies the procedures of some standards-writing organizations and it acts as the United States representative to the various international standards-writing organizations through committees ordinarily chosen from its membership. It thus performs functions that are quasigovernmental and that are, in fact, conducted by government agencies in other countries.

The most widely respected process of standards development in the United States is generally referred to as the "consensus standards system"; that is, all interested parties are permitted to participate or review standards and to vote on them. Only after a consensus is reached are the standards "approved." (That, at least, is the theory.)

A true consensus standard goes through several stages. Generally, a technically competent committee begins the work by splitting into subcommittees and task groups. Once a draft is prepared at the task group level it goes through a series of ballots. If negative votes are cast, the draft is sent back down in the chain of approval for resolution of the negative votes.

Resolution of negative votes may take several forms. The draft may be amended to satisfy the objections noted in the negative note; the negative may be found technically incompetent, irrelevant, or frivolous, or the negative vote may be overridden. Thus, "consensus" is not necessarily synonymous with "unanimity." Precisely how large a majority is needed to override a negative vote varies from one organization to another. So consensus cannot be defined more precisely than something less than unanimity but something more than a simple majority.

In practice, the consensus reached in the balloting may be a consensus in form only. The original drafting of standards documents, even in the most procedurally enlightened organizations, is done by task groups that are not balanced between producers, sellers, consumers, and general interest representatives. Often it is at this stage that special interests prevail and questionable provisions are inserted into draft standards.

Although there is always the opportunity to cast a negative vote further up the ladder of approval, deficiencies in draft standards are often subtle and difficult to detect unless one has taken part in the original deliberations at the task group level. This problem is compounded by the fact that final approval of many standards may be based on the most superficial review of the draft submitted for ballot, even though the draft may have been prepared by highly interested parties without input from, or accord of due process protections to, other highly interested parties. In spite of this, there is a prevailing presumption that drafts emerging from expert organizations, committees, or task groups are technically competent and free of partisan commercial taint. This presumption can often lead to the most perfunctory approval of questionable documents.

The abuses attributable, at least in part, to the use of such procedures range from deception of the consumer, because of reliance on data generated by inadequate tests, to restraints of trade and to the sale of dangerous products certified as safe. However, the type of abuse, the degree of deleterious effect, and the potential for abuse varies with the type of standard involved. The distinctions between the various types of standards in this regard are discussed below.

Perhaps the most common misconception about standards, particularly among attorneys, is that they are all alike in terms of their impact upon their subject products, competition, and the consumer. This misconception is largely attributable to a lack of familiarity with the many different types of standards that affect commerce in widely varying ways and to greatly varying degrees. Persons who are familiar with standards categorize them in several different ways; however, all the common classifications essentially resolve to the following: (1) standard definitions, nomenclature, and classifications; (2) standard methods of testing; (3) performance specifications; and (4) design or construction specifications. Each class of standards has purposes and benefits peculiar to it, and each presents certain distinct hazards, but the degree and nature of the hazard in each instance varies significantly.

Standard definitions, nomenclature, and classifications are often needed to facilitate communication among sellers, buyers, and third parties. Often these standards are prerequisites to the development of the other classes of standards discussed below, since terms that might be considered to be generally understood are subject to widely varying interpretations. These elementary standards are needed to organize and proscribe the work of technical committees involved in standards development. When they operate properly, standards of this type eliminate semantic roadblocks to efficient standards development and can greatly facilitate the task of the drafters. As essential as these standards are, however, they can have the effect of rigidifying or channeling thinking and thus creating a barrier to truly innovative thought. Definitions of terms may be adopted which are organizationally "neat," but which depart markedly from the way a lay person might understand the terms.

Classifications at variance with the way lay persons group items may lead to the adoption of different standards for products that are ordinarily or potentially in competition with one another. The subjection of the items to different tests, because of their classification in different categories, may create a situation in which they cannot be compared to one another and thus do not compete with one another. For example, assume that performance tests are drafted for vacuum cleaners but that different tests are designed for cannister models than for uprights. The test results for one type might not be comparable to the test results for the other. Consequently, some consumers might be misled as to the relative performance of a given cannister and a given upright, while those who understood that different tests were involved would still be left without a basis for comparison.

Standard methods of testing to measure various properties of products or materials are essential for the generation of data adequate to enable comparisons between products or materials. Moreover, most performance, design, or construction specifications include prescribed test methods to be used for verification of compliance with the specification. But deficiencies or dangers often arise in the design and application of test methods.

Test procedures designed to predict the performance of products under actual use conditions may improperly rank products as to the feature tested, may give an unrealistic rating as to safety, or may distort the degree of variation between products. Test results based on such deficient test procedures can mislead the consumer and injure competition by concealing or distorting competitive advantages of either specific products, or groups of products, by the inclusion of biases in the procedure, whether or not such inclusion is inadvertent.

The most common source of such test design deficiency is the failure to properly account for all the variables that will be encountered under actual use conditions. If variables are excluded or given improper weight in a test, the advantages or disadvantages of a product's performance or design can either be concealed or unfairly accentuated. Standard test procedures can also be misapplied or their results misrepresented. This is often beyond the control of the body that promulgated the test procedure, but proper design of the standard and the inclusion of appropriate caveats in the document can somewhat reduce the potential for later abuses.

In a recent case before the Federal Trade Commission, test procedures were at issue which allegedly exhibited design deficiencies and which were allegedly misapplied [5]. Many plastics manufacturers were charged with advertising certain types of foam plastics used in construction as nonflammable based on test results arrived at through test procedures approved by a well respected technical society. These same procedures had also been adopted by virtually every building code authority. However, the plastics in question do burn and present a serious hazard when improperly used. The problem involved resulted from the use of test procedures written by a task group that, it was alleged, was "captured" by the very manufacturers whose products would be tested. The test did not account for environmental factors that would be encountered in real installations and, although the tests were small scale laboratory tests, their results were represented as establishing the safety of the products in large scale installations.

One final area of concern with standard methods of testing is that they can operate as performance, design, or construction specifications while appearing to be test procedures that only generate data.

This results either when a test is designed in such a way as to preclude or bias testing or products designed in particular ways or made of particular materials, or when the data generated have an inherent value, that is, when those relying on the test results have preconceived values for certain levels of performance on the test. When a test procedure operates as a specification, it may have the unfortunate effects associated with specifications, as discussed below. However, this potential is more insidious in the case of a test method, since it appears to be less than it actually is.

Of the various types of specifications, performance specifications present the fewest potential problems. Nevertheless, they are hazardous. These standards ordinarily incorporate test procedures, but rather than simply involving the generation of data, performance specifications assign a value to the results of the standard test involved. A given result may be set as "minimal" in the case of a minimum performance standard, or test results may be categorized in various ways (such as "bad, good, better, best") in the case of grading standards.

Thus in the case of a performance specification, value judgments have been made about various levels of performance, unlike mere test procedures, which only yield data about which everyone is free to make his own value judgment. As noted above, however, test procedures alone can *operate* as performance specifications. For example, if an automobile is tested pursuant to a standard procedure and is found to get five miles per gallon, it will be perceived as a poor performer without any value judgment being made by the testing agency or the developers of the test procedure.

Under circumstances in which certain levels of performance can clearly be identified as necessary for the accomplishment of a task or for the safety of the user of a product, performance specifications can perform a valuable and even indispensible function. Since the *means of achieving* various levels of performance are not specified, those wishing to comply with the standard have some latitude as to how to build their product. In this respect, performance specifications are preferable to design or construction specifications.

Nevertheless, performance specifications can have unfortunate effects. Minimum performance standards may set a level of performance so high that less expensive, albeit inferior products are excluded from the marketplace. In the instance of a safety standard, this may be desirable; in other cases a purchaser with modest needs may be forced to buy a product that exceeds his needs. Thus he is forced to pay for capacity which, in his case, may be wasted. Conversely, if the level of performance in a safety performance standard is set too low, and products are certified as meeting that standard, the public can be exposed to unreasonably dangerous products—and worse still, may be lulled into a false sense of safety that may tend to actually increase the danger.

Grading specifications also may have socially undesirable effects. If the parameters of the grades established are unreasonable, people relying on the ratings may be deceived. Obvious examples would be grading schemes in which a product is rated "good" when in fact many consumers would find that level of performance unacceptable or at least disappointing. Similarly, a grading specification that was too strict might rate too many products as "poor" when in fact many consumers would find them acceptable. Nevertheless, the ratings would result in sales losses for the "poor" products that would force those manufacturers either to withdraw those products or to redesign them to improve their rating. In all likelihood this would mean unjustifiably higher prices and the loss of an area in which consumers should have a choice.

Grading standards and minimum performance specifications may also impose uniformity on a product. Unless a means is provided by which manufacturers can demonstrate superiority over competing products in the same grade, there is likely to be competitive pressure just to achieve the minimum level of performance for that grade, particularly if cutting performance results in a cost savings. Thus it is often better to express performance on a continuous scale rather than to break the scale into grades, whether the number of grades is two, as in the case of a minimum performance standard (pass or fail), or more, as in the case of a grading specification.

Naturally, if the units in which performance is expressed are incomprehensible to purchasers, it may be necessary to assign grades to various points on the scale. This is particularly true if small variations in test results do not reflect appreciable variations in performance. In other words, if test results must be translated or if they must be related to the purchaser's value system, grading may be necessary. The deficiencies of performance specifications discussed previously may exist even if the test procedure on which they are based is perfectly acceptable. Naturally, if the test procedure itself is deficient, the potential for economic or consumer injury is compounded.

The types of standards discussed to this point have been dealt with in order of increasing potential for abuse or deleterious effect. The last class of standard—design or construction specifications—is by far more dangerous than those discussed previously. In developing such specifications, a judgment has been made not only as to a desired level of performance, but also as to how that level of performance must be achieved.

The most common forms of design or construction specifications are the building codes. Rather than specifying how strong a building must be, as measured by a specified test, building codes set forth what materials may be used and how they are to be used. In the case of building codes, this is probably necessary since it greatly facilitates inspection for compliance. In other areas, it is not justifiable to use such specifications unless there is no other feasible way to address the problem. Obviously, design specifications may be necessary for components of products to fit together or for products that must be used together to be compatible—e.g., wall receptacles and electrical plugs. Generally, though, these specifications should not be used since their effects are so drastic.

Just as a minimum performance standard may remove any incentive for improving a product, design and construction specifications remove any incentive for improving performance or developing better or cheaper ways for achieving performance. These standards freeze products as to the design, construction, or materials used. This precludes competition on these points and, perhaps even worse, creates deterrents for research and development as to the features covered by the specification.

These dangers were recognized by the Federal Trade Commission when it advised a standards organization that "Construction or specification standards should not be used except in exceptional circumstances *and never when performance standards can be developed* [6] (emphasis added). Even in the area of safety, Congress has expressed a similar distaste for design specifications. In enacting the Consumer Product Safety Act [7], Congress authorized the Consumer Product Safety Commission to issue safety standards, including specifications for "performance, composition, contents, design, construction, finish, or packaging of a consumer product" [8]. But Congress also specified that "The requirements of such a standard . . . shall, whenever feasible, be expressed in terms of performance requirements" [9].

Although this discussion of standards and the standards development process must seem somewhat complex and abstract, it nevertheless touches only superficially upon a highly complex and influential area of commercial activity. It is hoped that at least the following points have been communicated:

- Standards are essential for the operation of a sophisticated and complex economy.

- There are different types of standards, each of which serves a different function and each of which presents its own dangers.
- The abuses attributable to standards, potential and realized, are a function of both the standards themselves and the standards development process.
- These abuses can result in reduced competition, higher prices, consumer deception, reduced product quality, and physical injury to product users.

The following sections of this paper will be concerned with various attempts that various law enforcement agencies have made to cope with the deficiencies of the standards development process and the deleterious effects of standards, the potential for reform through consumer participation in preparation and approval of standards, and tentative recommendations for additional reforms.

STANDARDS AND GOVERNMENT

Given the importance of standards to the operation of the economy and the impact they have on competition and the consumer, it is not surprising that standards and standardization and certification activities have often been the subject of legal proceedings. Because of the limitations of space, past legal activities in this area will be summarized rather briefly.

Many areas of government at all levels employ standards to carry out their functions, from procurement to trade regulation. But governmental scrutiny of the deficiencies of standardization and certification activities has been limited and generally has been directed toward the more obvious effects of specific programs rather than the structural deficiencies of standardization generally. This approach has ignored certain problems completely and has failed to provide clear guidance to those involved in such programs in many important respects.

At the federal level, reform of standards activities has been primarily accomplished through enforcement of the Sherman Act [10] and the Federal Trade Commission Act [11]. However, these activities generally have been directed against commercial entities in interstate commerce who have employed standards or certification in an anticompetitive, unfair, or deceptive manner, rather than against the standard involved or the activity that preceded promulgation of the standard or certification scheme.

Standards and certification programs that have been used to fix prices [12], exclude competitors [13], or control production [14], have been found to be illegal, since any agreement toward these ends is per se a violation of the antitrust laws. In other areas, however, the courts have employed a "rule of reason" approach to situations in which no *concerted* effort has taken place to privately *enforce* deficient standards or where procedural inadequacies were significant but not egregious enough to constitute conspiracy. In doing so, the courts have looked to certain factors as dispositive of the legality of a program that results in a restraint of trade. In an often quoted opinion, Justice Brandeis capsulized these factors in the following manner:

> ... the court must ordinarily consider the facts peculiar to the business to which the restraint is applied; its condition before and after the restraint was imposed; the nature of the restraint and its effect, actual or probable. The history of the restraint, the evil believed to exist, the reason for adopting the particular remedy, the purpose or end sought to be attained, are all relevant facts [15].

In 1971 the Federal Trade Commission summarized the law, based on cases and its interpretation of the Federal Trade Commission Act, in its response to a request for approval of a certification program [16]. The minimal criteria set forth by the Commission were directed toward the three types of restraint of trade *effects* of standards programs noted previously, deficiencies in standards themselves and in the development process, and the necessary prerequisites for certification programs. As to standards themselves, the Commission noted that design and construction specifications may be used only in extraordinary circumstances and only if performance specifications cannot be developed instead. This, however, was the only point at which the Commission addressed the issue of deficiency in a standard because of its class and design.

In addressing standards development programs, the Commission noted that provision must be made to ensure that standards reflect existing technology and that they be reviewed and revised in light of technological innovation. In both standardization and certification programs, fees charged must be reasonable and related to the costs of the program; membership in organizations involved in such programs must be open to all competitors; "due process" must be accorded to all parties either interested in or affected by such programs; and the validation of standards should include a determination by some party independent of those directly interested that the criteria incorporated in the standard are "meaningful and relevant."

Participants in these programs were advised that representations relating to standards must be truthful and that private standards may not be mandatory. Naturally, private standards adopted by government bodies with proper authority can be mandated. This is, in fact, the manner in which abuses in private standards have been effectuated as a result of inadequate review of private standards by the promulgating government agency.

Several of the provisions in the Commission's response were specifically directed toward certification programs. Denial of certification cannot be based on nonmembership in any association or organization, the fact that the applicant is a foreign competitor, or the applicant's inability to pay a fee. Furthermore, granting or denial of certification should be determined "by an appropriate organization independent of those immediately affected by such programs." Finally, certification programs should, where possible, be based on grading specifications rather than minimum performance (pass/fail) specifications. The Commission also expressed the opinion that, when a standard is challenged, "the burden of proof respecting reasonableness is upon those who develop and enforce standards."

These guidelines set forth the manner in which individual companies and organizations can best assure avoidance of litigation, but because of the format in which they were presented and the way these points were drafted, they did not reach many of the more subtle structural deficiencies in standards development and certification. Terms such as "due process" and "reasonable" must be more closely defined and related directly to specific deficiencies in such programs. Moreover, it appears that additional specific, affirmative requirements are needed, although current law may be adequate with regard to prohibitions.

In 1972 the Commission appointed a staff Task Force on Industry Self-Regulation and released a precis of the staff's preliminary findings [17]. In addition to the deficiencies addressed by the Commission in its 1971 summary of the law, the Task Force noted the following deficiencies:

Lack of procedural safeguards to insure consideration of the viewpoints of all groups affected; in particular, failure to notify persons likely to be affected by a proposed standard early enough in the proceedings and to provide them with sufficient background information to allow them to participate meaningfully;

Lack of consumer participation at the very basic level of standards-writing where most decisions are made;

Insufficient voting power given to consumers to allow them to block unsatisfactory standards;

Domination by larger industry members at all levels of the standards-writing process;

Financial dependence of standards organizations upon contributions of larger industry members;

Unnecessary financial barriers to participation in standards programs by smaller firms and consumers in the form of listing fees, travel requirements to attend meetings and votes, protracted proceedings, etc.;

Use of the "consensus" principle to reduce standards to the lowest common denominator or to override a valid minority position;

Poor format of ballots, which provides insufficient information to cast an informed vote on the proposed standard;

Inadequate provisions for appeal to a disinterested party;

Failure even to follow existing procedures;

Consistent reliance on design and construction, as opposed to performance standards;

Failure of safety standards to address themselves to all significant foreseeable hazards;

Poor format of the standards themselves, which often makes revision cumbersome and isolation of important factors like safety difficult;

Frequent deceptiveness of certification both as to the underlying criteria upon which the certification is based and the competence of the certifying body;

Failure of certification labels to separate various aspects of safety and performance so as to provide maximum consumer product information;

Certification on the basis of testing of an inadequate sampling of products [18].

Few, if any, standards or certification bodies or programs exhibit all or even most of these deficiencies. However, virtually every organization and program exhibits some of them, usually with the unfortunate effects that one might expect.

The concerns expressed in the two documents noted congealed and ripened with the *Plastics Case* [19], and the Commission has now announced the initiation of an investigation of standards setting and product certification activities [20]. Hopefully, this investigation will result in staff recommendations for a trade regulation rule that will address the structural deficiencies now evidenced in both standardization and certification.

The types of reforms which might be forthcoming from such a proceeding, and some reforms which may arguably lie outside of current FTC authority, are discussed in the concluding sections of this paper.

STANDARDS AND THE CONSUMER

It was noted earlier that the stage of standards development during which the potential for abuse is highest, and the stage that is most subject to reform, is the initial drafting process. During this first stage, the rationale for each provision in a standard, options available, trade-offs (safety versus cost, for example), and problems are discussed. The insights gained from participation in such discussions cannot be readily communicated to someone who only has a draft to review. Many of the subtleties of these discussions are not reported in minutes of such meetings, when minutes are even kept.

Thus, the key to reforming standards is somehow to monitor and police the first stage of drafting by initiating participation by a broad range of interests. One way to achieve this would be to insert consumers into the process at this point with adequate voting power to ensure that the consumer voice is not only heard, but heeded as well. Questions arise, however: Who will represent the consumer? Where will enough consumer representatives willing and able to cope with technical issues be found? Who will pay for their participation? How will consumer participation affect the drafting process?

One attempt to accomplish this has been undertaken by the Consumer Product Safety Commission (CPSC). This agency has issued criteria for development of safety standards under section 7 the Consumer Product Safety Act [21], which includes a requirement that consumers be given the opportunity to participate [22]. In order to make compliance with these criteria feasible, CPSC has solicited and received offers from members of the public to participate in the development of safety standards. This list of volunteers is provided to organizations who are involved in safety standards development and CPSC will pay for the expenses of such volunteers in appropriate circumstances.

This is a new experiment and it is not yet clear whether it will bear fruit. Generally, though, it appears that the obstacles to genuine consumer participation in the hundreds of meetings of committees writing standards for consumer products are too great to hope that this will provide a long term solution. Although safety standards evoke immediate public interest, most other standards are generally perceived as boring. Even to persons with keen interest in a standard under development, the meetings are tedious. Attendance at meetings is costly and, except in the area of safety standards, consumers now have to bear the cost of travel and lodgings themselves. Finally, there simply are not enough technically knowledgeable people available to attend all of these meetings.

This is not to say that standards development can be allowed to continue without introduction of the consumer viewpoint at the earliest stages of drafting. To some extent this can be accomplished by the presence of consumer representatives, but consumer participation must be supplemented by increased government involvement and scrutiny. Yet, this involvement need not take the form of regulation.

The probelm at the drafting stage is not ordinarily venality on the part of the industry representatives; it is a problem of limited perspective. Everyone serving on standards-writing committees is "biased." This is said without intent to malign the good faith of such participants, but no one is able to see a problem from every perspective. In the past, technical committees were comprised of technical experts who essentially spoke the same language and who shared an understanding of one another because of relatively homogeneous backgrounds, either educational or commercial, or both.

Commercial producers and users may have very different needs and objectives, but they have a common understanding of and feeling for commercial pressures. They have a common ground for judging actions, the bottom line on an account sheet. End-use consumers do not share this commonalty of perspective with users, producers, or with each other. Nor do consumers comprise a homogeneous group. They buy identical products for varying reasons and uses, often unforeseen by either the producer or the seller of the product. They judge products by a myriad of criteria, only some of which relate to cost factors. Often they do not speak the same language with engineers or with businessmen.

Even goverment and academic representatives have some common basis for dealing with one another. Either they are engineers or scientists who share a technical competence with the members of committees representing commercial interests, or they are educated by continuing face-to-face contacts with the commercial interests or even the individuals involved. These shared backgrounds and contacts facilitate communication in a manner available to most consumers.

Thus, consumers have a different perspective on a given standard, but this perspective is difficult to translate into a standard because of communications barriers between consumers and the technical experts on drafting committees. What is needed, then, is a group of experts, comfortable with technical issues, who can bring a synthesis of consumer oriented perspectives to the committee table and who can supplement participation by "pure" consumers. This and other proposals are discussed in the following sections.

TENTATIVE PROPOSALS FOR REFORM

The proposals set forth in the following discussion are not suggested under any claim of expertise. The author has simply been fortunate to have participated in standards development and to have brought to that participation his training as an attorney, his experience in antitrust and consumer protection, and his consumerist predisposition. As noted earlier, however, no one can adequately represent or understand all perspectives. Consequently, these proposals are tentative and admittedly incomplete; and their refinement should be undertaken after more study, accumulation of experience, and more expert input.

Agency for Consumer Advocacy

Unfortunately, legislation that would have created an agency to represent the consumer failed in the 93rd Congress. Before the 94th Congress considers the creation of such an agency, the legislation should provide for participation by the agency in standards development as well as administrative proceedings.

Participants in standards development from such an agency should be people with a firm understanding of the antitrust laws and a clear mandate to represent the consumer. They must not only understand the law, but also be comfortable with technical issues. Engineers with legal training or lawyers with an engineering background would be ideal, but all that would be necessary is the ability to read whatever is required to develop an understanding of what a product does and how it does it, as well as a familiarity with both legal issues and technical jargon.

The representatives of the Agency for Consumer Advocacy would not function as lawyers or engineers on the committee. Rather, they would function as consumer representatives knowledgeable enough to see and understand technical issues as well as the potential competitive effects of a standard. They would not have veto power; they would not subvert or supplant the voluntary standards system, only contribute to it.

National Bureau of Standards

The National Bureau of Standards (NBS) is an arm of the Department of Commerce. Yet, standards do not serve industry alone, but the economy as a whole, including consumers. Consequently, NBS should be made an independent agency charged with basic research, coordination of standards activities, liaison with international standardization organizations, certification of standards-writing procedures, and fostering of consumer participation in standards writing.

The functions of the American National Standards Institute would largely be taken over by the government under this plan. This would assure that no standard with the prestige and influence of an "American National Standard" could be issued unless the criteria set by

NBS were followed. This plan would also contemplate payment of consumer expenses for participation in standards-writing activities from a fund that NBS would administer. However, experts employed by NBS would not be precluded from participating themselves.

Finally, under this plan concerted activity by competitors in the standards area could only be carried out within organizations accredited by NBS. Other standards activities would be rendered violations of the antitrust laws through rules issued by the Federal Trade Commission.

Bureau of Standards Review

A Bureau of Standards Review should be created within the Federal Trade Commission. This bureau would advise NBS in its preparation of criteria for standards development procedures as well as advising other agencies of the competitive effects of standards developed or adopted by them. The bureau would also review all design or construction specifications to assure that performance specifications were not feasible and it would investigate claims that given test methods or performance specifications are in fact clandestine design or construction specifications. Finally, the bureau would provide arbitration in cases in which any party feels unfairly prejudiced by a certification or standardization activity.

CONCLUSIONS

The voluntary consensus standards development system is essential to the smooth operation of commerce. If the system did not exist, dominant firms could dictate the design of products in their industries. Producers of superior products would have difficulty penetrating new markets by demonstrating the superiority of their products, since standard test methods either would not exist or the generally accepted test would be the test used by the industry leader. Such a test could be designed to show the industry leader's product in an unduly favorable light and its competitors' product in an unfairly poor one.

The potential for abuse under a system in which one company or a few companies could dictate an industry's standards is mind boggling. Clearly, voluntary consensus standards developed with broad participation are to be preferred. Nor would the author suggest that the government supplant the voluntary standards-writing organizations; this would be too costly and inefficient. But some mechanism must be developed to prevent abuses while minimizing the interference and delay that is typical of bureaucracy. It is hoped that some contribution has been herein made to begin the process of developing solutions.

NOTES TO CHAPTER 11

1. Federal Trade Commission, *Preliminary Staff Study (Precis): Self-Regulation—Product Standardization, Certification and Seals of Approval*, Washington, D.C., April 1972), at 1; (hereinafter cited as Precis).

2. *Ibid.*, at 2.

3. See, for example, *In re Society of the Plastics Industry, et al.*, file number 732 3040, consent orders provisionally accepted, 1974 (hereinafter cited as the *Plastics Case*).

4. Precis, supra at 16.

5. *Plastics Case.*

6. 38 Fed. Reg. 28276 (October 12, 1973).

7. 15 U.S.C. § 2051 *et seq.*

8. 15 U.S.C. § 2056.

9. *Ibid.*

10. 15 U.S.C. § 1, *et seq.*

11. 15 U.S.C. § 41, *et seq.*

12. C-O-Two Fire Equipment Co. v. United States, 197 F.2d 489 (9th Cir.), cert denied, 344 U.S. 892 (1952); Bond Crown & Cork Co. v. FTC., 176 F.2d (4th Cir. 1949); Fort Howard Paper Co. v. FTC., 156 F.2d 899 (7th Cir. 1946); Milk and Ice Cream Can Institute v. FTC., 152 F.2d 478 (7th Cir. 1946).

13. Radiant Burners, Inc. v. Peoples Gas Light & Coke Co., 364 U.S. 656 (1961); Fashion Originators Guild v. FTC., 312 U.S. 457 (1941); Eastern States Lumber Ass'n. v. United States, 234 U.S. 600 (1914).

14. National Macaroni Manufacturers Ass'n. v. FTC., 345 F.2d 421 (7th Cir. 1965).

15. Chicago Board of Trade v. United States, 246 U.S. 231, 238 (1918).

16. 38 Fed. Reg. 28276 (October 12, 1974).

17. Precis.

18. *Ibid.*, at 19, 20.

19. *Ibid.*

20. FTC Order Settles Proceeding Involving Marketing of Plastics Presenting Fire Hazards; Rule Making Proceeding Instituted," FTC Press Release (July 29, 1974).

21. 15 U.S.C. § 2056.

22. 39 Fed. Reg. 16206, 16215 (May 7, 1974).

Chapter 12

Industry Self-Regulation: A Viable Alternative to Government Regulation

Robert N. Katz

At various times a broader use of industry self-regulation has been proposed or tried. Frequently self-regulation is proposed by an industry to forestall government regulation or control [1]. At other times it is proposed in the public interest because of general economic problems. The passage of the National Recovery Act is a good example of this since it was believed that industry could ease economic problems during a depression [2]. While current economic conditions may justify new evaluation of industry self-regulation, an additional impetus is generated by the demand for increased social awareness from the business entity [3].

Self-regulation conjures up different responses from different people. Some are reminded of the thought expressed by students describing the honor system: "The school has the honor and we have the system." Others liken it to asking foxes to guard chickens; they feel that entry into an industry can be restricted, that giants of industry can dominate a regulator's scheme, and that the public interest can be subverted. The resolution to these objections can be found by ensuring that when a fox guards the chickens an eagle watches the fox—a self-regulation program overseen by government surveillance can provide an effective regulatory scheme in the public interest.

Because of the growth and complexity of our economic system, because of the demand for social response from business, and because of the lack of efficacy of government regulation standing alone as a protector or insurer of the public interest, it is appropriate to evaluate the feasibility of expanded industry self-regulation programs. I would submit that, if for no other reason than the less-than-total success of government regulatory programs [4], self-regulation under certain conditions is indeed feasible. And there are other reasons, of course.

Those other justifications, which will be discussed in more detail later, include that the cost of self-regulation rests directly upon those directly affected, namely the industry involved and the consumers of that industry; that industry self-regulation operates more speedily than government regulation; that industry is more knowledgeable about violations that occur (and the profit in such violations, if unpunished); and that industry is more motivated to enforcement. In 1969 former Attorney General Ramsey Clark pointed out that antitrust violators are, to established companies in the same industries, ". . . sharks swimming in these guys' waters" [5].

BACKGROUND

Although business collaboration in the public interest is a relatively new phenomenon, the history of business collaboration in the self-interest of business is of course quite long. Early examples of this collaboration are found in the history of the insurance industry. For instance, companies joining together to share the risk of one company's ship not coming in did result in some benefit for broad sectors of society. Merchants did not have to charge as much for products that arrived to cover the contingency of products being lost at sea.

Guilds provide an additional example of early collaboration. As the prevailing form of business organization shifted from sole proprietorship and partnership to corporations, and as the trust mechanism became utilized (with its attendant abuses), business collaboration was frowned upon. This eventually led to enactment of the antitrust laws, although even under common law, relief from predators' conspiracy could be obtained.

The antitrust laws, both federal and state, render it risky for the business entity to engage in any form of collaborative activity with competitors. Practically every corporate counsel will advise the client to be very wary of trade association activities [6]. Yet despite the risks of possible antitrust violation, trade association activity abounds. And there have been numerous cases involving antitrust violations growing out of trade association activity. The area of greatest risk occurs in dealing with industry codes and product standardization [7] —the very areas that most proponents of industry self-regulation advocate as having the greatest potential benefit for the public interest from industry self-regulation. Illegality is clearly present when there are collective actions that set prices or allocate markets.

DISCUSSION

Industry codes of fair practice are not uncommon [8]. Indeed, some of these have the blessing of goverment. In most instances, however, the collaborative effort is for the self-interest of the industry involved. But the type of industry self-regulation that I envision as an alternative to government regulation goes beyond guides and voluntary codes [9]. An industry self-regulation program based on voluntarism without sanctions is little more than a PR pep talk for the industry. The failure of voluntarism can be seen in many instances in which government relied on moral suasion. An excellent example is the attempts at voluntary restraint in direct foreign investment by U.S. companies in the mid sixties, when businessmen were concerned that competitors would not exercise restraint [10]. We can conclude, as does M.J. Rossant, that over time any voluntary program will spring leaks.

Yet when coercion is involved, antitrust violation is present. Therefore, exemptions from antitrust laws must be provided. This is not a new suggestion; our antitrust laws are already riddled with exemptions. Some exemptions have resulted in virtual freedom from any regulation, while others have provided for regulatory overseeing by specific government agencies [11]. Agriculture, labor, foreign trade export associations, transportation, the securities industry, and professional baseball provide examples. Some exemptions are statutory; others are a result of case law. This is not to advocate exemption from antitrust laws for industry self-regulatory programs without the interposition of some continuous government surveillance and supervision. Rather, what is suggested is that exemption with supervision be extended to virtually all industry, as it now exists in the transportation and securities industries.

The Maloney Act and Webb-Pomerene Act provide models from which we may start. There are many who would oppose any extensions of such exemption, even in special circumstances. For example, Richard W. McLaren, Assistant Attorney General, Antitrust Division in 1971 [12], did not look favorably upon pooling of research activity in pollution control areas, arguing that pooling of capabilities had not been shown to be necessary. Such an approach, I submit, helps the big stay big and the small stay small. Moreover, the advantages of exemption, within limits, outweigh the risks.

Any industry association desiring to engage in a self-regulating program should be permitted to do so upon filing application and registration with the Federal Trade Commission. Pursuant to rules issued by the FTC all agreements, procedures, and policies of the association should be implemented only after approval by the Commission, with hearings when requested by interested parties according to the Administrative Procedures Act [13]. Decisions of the industry self-regulating body could be appealed to the commission and then to the courts.

Any self-regulatory program submitted for approval by the Commission should include certain provisions. First, there should be insurance of fairness and impartiality; second, there should be provision for open membership and participation; and third, there should be provision for full disclosure of all activities of the self-regulating body. The incentives for a company to participate could be economic, moral, and legal. As a participant the company would have access to certain shared data, would have a "seal of approval," would be assured of certainty of legality of approved acts and practices, and could be freed from filing certain reports with multitudinous government agencies.

SOME INDUSTRY EXAMPLES

The Maloney Act of 1938 added section 15A to the Securities Exchange Act. That section provided for the formation of national securities associations to supervise their membership with overseeing by the Securities Exchange Commission. The associations had certain requirements in order to be registered with the SEC, among which were (1) fair procedures for discipline and denial of membership; (2) fair representation in operation of the association; (3) fair dues structure; and (4) open membership (with qualification).

Policing and Discipline

An organization whose procedures for dealing with disciplinary matters have been filed with the SEC is the National Association of Securities Dealers. District Business Conduct Committees consider action on complaints involving violation of NASD Rules of Fair Practice or SEC regulations. The National Business Conduct Committee reviews all district disciplinary actions and, on appeals or on its own, holds hearings and drafts recommendations to the board of governors. The board, in turn, renders the final decision, appeallable to the SEC and then to the courts. The SEC cannot increase the penalties, though it can reduce them. Thus the vast majority of disciplinary activity is within the organization.

In providing for policing, some steamship conferences have utilized a "neutral body" concept, choosing an independent accounting firm to conduct rate violation inquiries [14]. The Air Transport

Association agreement with travel agents provides for arbitration. Regardless of the method or procedure, "fairness" is demanded [15], although the Supreme Court has recognized that "fairness" is an "elusive concept" [16].

The NASD proceedings are kept private until appealed to the SEC, except that after the period of internal review has expired a summary statement is issued giving names, violations found, and sanctions imposed. This serves to protect parties from injury when unfounded (or at least unprovable) complaints are made. The NASD is quite active in disciplinary proceedings. Prior to 1959 over 1,200 complaints had been filed with the NASD [17]. In 1961, 486 complaints were filed [18]; in 1972 there were 374 formal complaints and 94 summary complaints filed. Few of these reach review by the SEC. An SEC staff study noted that while NASD proceedings are relatively informal, there is a trend toward more formality [19]. A survey of securities dealers indicated that the leaders overwhelmingly felt that the NASD was fair and reasonable in its procedures.

Large Firm Domination

Criticisms received were primarily that the NASD tended to favor the larger firms and deal more severely with smaller firms and that there was not consistency between district and national policies. The former criticism was voiced frequently in the survey, with additional comment that actually the industry is dominated by the "private club" of the New York Stock Exchange. It might be concluded that self-regulation by the exchanges has not been effective and has come about only with prodding from the SEC [20]. Responses to the survey, the Special Study report, and Robinson & Bartell, supra, indicate that neither the NYSE nor the NASD get involved in long range and major policy issues, although the NYSE does so more than that NASD. These criticisms are worthy of concern by the NASD board and staff.

They are not unique to the NASD, however, nor are they indictments of self-regulation as opposed to the government regulation. In practically all trade associations small members fear the domination of the association by large members. Proper rules, approved by the overseeing government agency, can ensure freedom from domination by the large members. A strong and independent executive and staff are also essential so that director and staff are free from undue pressure. It might be added that although most self-regulating bodies select chief executives from within the industry, a good argument could be made for going outside the industry. (It is interesting to note the reasons for selection of Judge Kennesaw Mountain Landis in

1920 as Chairman of the National Baseball Commission [21] —prominent beyond suspicion, not connected with the industry.)

Furthermore, domination by large members of the industry is not confined to self-regulatory programs. Many observers have pointed out that large companies are able to forestall government regulation, while small ones are not, and that large companies can invoke delaying tactics. The fear that self-regulation would result in a lack of uniformity of policy may be a valid one, but so far the government has had failings in this respect that would suggest that government regulation is not the solution to the problem.

Membership

Open membership for qualified industry members is mandatory for success of a self-regulatory program. Present statutes require that membership not be arbitrarily denied, and antitrust policy further supports this. This policy would also be necessary for any trade association [22]. A more difficult issue, however, is ensuring that there be broad participation in self-regulation programs. Although membership in the NASD is voluntary for over-the-counter brokers, virtually all are members because of the economic realities and advantages.

There have at times been suggestions that membership be compulsory [23], but in view of the broadly based membership, this would appear unnecessary. It is noteworthy that the over-the-counter industry wanted some form of self-regulation with government surveillance (the exchanges have resisted such supervision) [24]. A program will falter if there is not broad industry participation. The erosion of efficacy of the motion picture industry codes attest to this. The activities of the Motion Picture Association of America have done little to forestall censorship, on the local level at least [25].

Full Disclosure

I would submit that any self-regulatory program should provide for full disclosure of all association activities to the overseeing government agency. On occasion the SEC inspects operations of the NASD, or one of its offices. To ensure protection of the public interest I would argue that industry self-regulation associations should submit periodic (monthly or quarterly) reports of their activities to the overseeing government commission. In addition, transcripts of proceedings of all association membership meetings and board or committee meetings should be maintained for inspection by the commission. While such a requirement would not eliminate anticompetitive activity that is not in the public interest, it would render such activity less convenient for industry.

Ensuring Public Interest

The commission, in ensuring that the industry self-regulating body is not subverting the public interest, could take the following steps:

1. Grant exemption for limited periods of time only; for example, three-year terms subject to hearings or renewal.
2. Compare price movement in the specific industry with price indices generally.
3. Examine consumer complaints filed with various agencies, as well as litigation that is filed in courts.
4. Review complaint proceedings conducted by the self-regulating body as well as review complaints that are disposed of without hearing.

These actions, among others, could ensure that abuses of the public interest antitrust policy are minimized. Benny Kass, counsel of the National Advertising Review Board, has suggested that industry self-regulating bodies include on their boards of directors public members who are not connected with the industry. (This has apparently worked well with the National Advertising Review Board.) Such public members bring an additional perspective to the deliberation of the self-regulating board.

SELF-REGULATION: SOME MAJOR ADVANTAGES

Given the existence of a program for industry self-regulation along the foregoing lines, could such a program work better than government regulation without industry self-regulation? I submit that such a program of industry self-regulation would be more effective than government regulation. After thirty-five years of securities industry self-regulation, observers have mixed feelings about its effectiveness. However, the Special Study concluded that self-regulation was effective and should be continued [26]. Professor Jennings appears to be hopeful but ambivalent [27]. Professor Loss is clearly of the opinion that self-regulation is a force for the public good, though there is room for improvement [28].

The NASD has been diligent, especially when compared to the SEC with respect to inspections. In 1968 and 1972 the NASD conducted examinations of offices, books, and records of about 45 percent of its membership [29]. On the other hand, the SEC in 1969 examined only about 5½ percent of the "nonmember" broker/dealers [30]. The SEC is charged with providing regulation of nonmembers comparable to that provided by NASD for its members.

Psychological Factors

Desire of the industry members to be self-policed is not unique to the over-the-counter securities industry. It has been proposed often by leaders in numerous industries. A survey of California manufacturers concerning methods of pollution control indicated that 71 percent favored policing by an industry committee; only 37 percent favored policing by a government agency. Although the questionnaire did not provide a space for respondents to indicate "both government and industry regulation," 9 percent suggested both. Furthermore, it is significant that 68 percent of the respondents indicated a willingness to serve on such an industry committee.

Industry self-regulation can thus be more effective because of the psychological factors involved. Government regulation is carried out in an adversary proceeding in most situations, with government (and supposedly the public interest) on one side, and the individual company (and sometimes the industry) on the other. Under a system of self-regulation, when policing is involved the industry is most often seeking to serve a regulatory purpose for the common good, and thus, arguably, allies itself with the angels. When the industry acts unjustly, the overseeing government agency and court review ensure ultimate fairness.

Punitive Action

Sanctions imposed by the industry are in most instances more stringent than those imposed by government. NASD sanctions have ranged from fines of $100 to $50,000 to removal from membership (forty-four members were suspended in 1972), which is tantamount to closing one's business. On the other hand, the Federal Maritime Commission would, not infrequently, grant or renew licenses to freight forwarders who had violated acts administered by the FMC. The Commission thereafter would refer the violations to the Department of Justice, but that agency would decline prosecution on the reasonable theory that by granting or renewing a license, the Commission had in effect granted a pardon, and imposing of criminal action would be refused by the courts.

In other situations we see that government agencies drop proceedings when the respondents agree to a consent decree and cease and desist order. The rationale for this is that if the respondent agreed to stop doing what it never had admitted doing, the regulatory purpose has been served; the role of government, after all, is not to be punitive or seek retribution. This gives perpetrators one free violation—until caught a second time. Not so with industry self-regulation! The policing body, to quote Ramsey Clark's comment above, doesn't want sharks swimming in its water. Furthermore, the industry policing body is more knowledgeable about how infractions occur and the profit therein. Thus it is not surprising that industry sanctions have appeared to be more stringent.

Time Lag

The speed (and relative low cost as a result) of enforcement by industry is an additional advantage found in self-regulation. Because industry proceedings are less formal, investigation and resolution are more prompt. It is not rare for an FTC matter to consume more than six years before final determination in court. Such a time lag is far more rare under industry self-regulation.

Shared Problems

Doubtless there are potential dangers that will be voiced about industry self-regulation. These dangers or fears, however, are actually present even in the absence of industry self-regulation. The fear of control by those dominant in the industry has been discussed. The fears that standards established by an industry self-regulatory body would produce anticompetitive results because of increasing costs to marginal producers are identical to the fears of marginal companies faced with stricter pollution control laws and such acts as the Wholesome Meat Act of 1967. And it is true that such fears are justified. The answer, however, lies in the fact that unjustified standards promulgated by a self-policing body may be challenged before the overseeing government agency, with ultimate resolution by the courts.

Another objection to self-regulation is that the encouragement of collaborative activity makes it easier to engage in anticompetitive activity that violates antitrust laws. The fact is, though, that if companies or individuals of bad faith wish to conspire, they will do so—self-regulation or not. Further, it is important to note that a self-regulatory program does not totally exempt a company from the antitrust laws. When parties or a segment of an industry engage in an unapproved self-regulatory program that is restrictive of competition, or engage in actions outside the scope of an approved program, the parties would still be subject to civil or criminal prosecution under the antitrust laws [31]. Increased industry self-regulation, with a resultant reduced "day-to-day" role for government regulatory agencies, is not in total conflict with those who would urge deregulation of industry and stricter enforcement of the antitrust laws [32].

Safeguarding the Public

Industry self-regulation systems, with safeguards, could be of public benefit in a number of industries—tire, furniture, food processing, and pharmaceuticals, for example. In these industries the self-regulating body could establish standards (subject to review of the overseeing agency) for manufacturing processes, test procedures, and products. Some observers have opined that the Food and Drug Administration's cleanliness standards for some food products are too low, but that industry now has no incentive to upgrade these standards.

Further, it is interesting to speculate whether, had there been an industry watchdog committee, the prescription drug MER-29, which proved to have dangerous side effects, would have been on the market so long. Apparently competitors of the William S. Merrell Co., the drug's manufacturer, had been aware of the dangers of MER-29, [33] but there was no industry association similar to NASD to which the matter could have been brought. The court did assess the maximum fine against Merrell, in the sum of $60,000, and the individuals involved received sentences up to six months on probation. It is interesting to compare the gravity of the complaints here and the laxity of the sanctions with the relatively less serious complaints (involving finance, not life) before the NASD and the more severe sanctions imposed there.

CONCLUSIONS

Industry self-regulation would thus provide for self-policing and self-enforcing by the industry or subunit involved. The elimination of some adversary aspects could reduce costs and provide society with less detailed government regulation but broader general regulatory policy.

The late Eli Goldston pointed out that socially responsible response from the corporation could come only when that response does not operate to the competitive disadvantage of the corporation [34]. Milton Friedman has stated that a corporation that can boast of its social program should be scrutinized by the Department of Justice, for that company would surely be in a dominant anti-competitive situation [35]. A supervised industry self-regulation program could offer a competition situation that would provide for corporate social response consistent with the broad public interest more quickly and more economically than is present with the government regulation of today.

NOTES TO CHAPTER 12

1. "A Free and Responsible Press," Commission on Freedom of the Press, Chicago: University of Chicago Press, 1973 (c. 1947).

2. National Industry Recovery Act, 48 Stat. 195 (1933).

3. Harvey J. Levin, "The Limits of Self-Regulation," *Columbia Law Review* (April 1967): 603–644.

4. Louis Kohlmeier, *The Regulators*, New York: Harper & Row, 1969; Mark J. Green (ed.), *The Monopoly Makers*, New York: Grossman, 1973; and Mark J. Green, *The Closed Enterprise System*, New York: Grossman, 1972.

5. Ramsey Clark, former Attorney General of the U.S., in a speech delivered in May 1969.

6. George P. Lamb and Sumner S. Kittelle, *Trade Association Law and Practice*, Boston: Little, Brown, 1956.

7. *Ibid.*

8. Levin, *loc. cit.*

9. Jerold Van Cise, "Regulation—By Business or Government?" *Harvard Business Review* (March-April 1966).

10. M.J. Rossant, "Tipping the Balance," *New York Times*, February 11, 1965, 57:6; and Robert Frost, "Executive Mood Shifty," *New York Times*, February 12, 1965, 37:2.

11. Earl W. Kintner, *An Antitrust Primer* (2nd ed.), New York: Macmillan, 1973, p. 124ff.

12. Richard W. McLaren, speech, April 1, 1971, Antitrust Division, American Bar Association, Washington, D.C.

13. Administrative Procedures Act. 5 U.S.C. 551 et. seq.

14. States Marine Lines, Inc. v. Federal Maritime Comm. 376F2d 230 (1967).

15. Silver v. New York Stock Exchange 373 U.S. 341 (1963).

16. Hannah v. Larch 360 US420 at 442 (1960).

17. Louis Loss, *Securities Regulation* (2nd ed.), Boston: Little, Brown, 1961.

18. NASD Report to Members, 1961.

19. Securities and Exchange Commission, Report of Special Study of Securities Markets. 4 R Doc. No. 95, 88th Cong., 1st Sess. 1963.

20. Robinson & Bartell, "Uneasy Partnership: SEC/NYSE," *Harvard Business Review*, January-February, 1965.

21. *New York Times*, October 2, 1920, 1:1; and *ibid.*, November 13, 1920, 1:3.

22. American Federation of Tobacco Growers v. Neal 138 F2d 869 CA 4th (1950). See also Ch. 14 Lamb v. Kittelle, op. cit.

23. Special Study.

24. Richard W. Jennings, "Self-Regulation in the Securities Industry: The Role of the Securities and Exchange Commission," *Law and Contemporary Problems*, (Summer 1964): 663–690.

25. Dilemmas of Filam Classification: Freedom of Information Center Report No. 122, School of Journalism, University of Missouri, December 1967.

26. Special Study.

27. Jennings, *op. cit.*

28. Loss, *op. cit.*

29. NASD, Report to Members, 1968.

30. 35th Annual Report, SEC.

31. Carnation Co. v. Pacific Westbound Conference et al. 383 US213 (1966).

32. See Richard Posner, "Natural Monopoly and Its Regulation," *Stanford Law Review*, 21, (1966):548.

33. Robert Heilbroner, et al., *In The Name of Profit*, New York: Doubleday, 1972, p. 113.

34. *Business Lawyer*, March 19, 1973, Proceedings of ABA National Institute.

35. Milton Friedman, speech at "Business Tomorrow II" conference (Chicago: November 20, 1973).

※ Part 4

The Role of the Courts

Commentary

KASS

The rise of the consumer activist has brought necessary government and business recognition of consumer issues. His tactics may take any of several forms: use of an "Action Line" service of the media, influence or introduction of legislation, initiation of court action (individual, class action, or even antitrust). In short, the consumer activist is quite often seeking full disclosure and free market competition from all areas of business. Ironically, these were also the original objectives of the business he seeks to reform.

BARTON

The consumer movement has brought political reforms and a general sense that consumers have certain basic rights that must be protected by government. Principal among these rights is that of relief—usually through litigation. Among the methods for consumers to seek redress are the class action lawsuit (which recent court rulings have made more difficult to pursue); a suit filed by a public agency on behalf of one or more consumers; and small claims court. Other means of settling consumer claims without going to court are offered by agencies that provide mediation for disputing parties, such as tenants' organizations and the Better Business Bureau.

PHILLIPS

An important facet of consumerism, law reform is offered by several "legal services backup centers" throughout the nation. Each of these centers focuses on a special area of legal services, including housing, welfare, consumers, education, migrant problems, the elderly, health and the environment, employment, and native American rights. Specifically, the housing law center has worked to organize the urban poor, to see that low cost housing is replaced after urban renewal projects have razed inner city residential areas, and to influence housing legislation that will assist consumers in purchasing or rebuilding homes. Similarly, the strategic orientation of these backup centers could benefit consumers by providing research, advocacy, and technical assistance in many areas of contemporary life.

✳ *Chapter 13*

Consumer Activist

Benny L. Kass

The consumer movement today gives me a deep sense of both frustration and relief. Relief because many of the issues and concerns to be expressed in this paper have been crying out to be put on the table. Frustration because so much has happened and yet, in reality, so little has happened. Even as this article is being written, the Senate of the United States for the fourth time has rejected creating a Department of Consumer Affairs.

Over the many years that the consumer activist has been plying his trade, there have been successes and there have been defeats. Perhaps the most significant success was the recognition of consumerism by government and industry. Perhaps the most significant defeat was the failure of government and industry to implement and enforce their recognition of consumerism. Even at this time, the President of the United States largely ignores the consumer input as the government considers its "war on inflation."

Yet at the same time, the consumer must also share some of the responsibility. Consumers—all of us—are caught in a most dichotomous dilemma. For example, we want the luxuries of a supermarket, where we can fill up our grocery cart once a week and bring all the food home to our freezers and our big refrigerators. And yet we are unwilling to accept the preservatives that must go into our milk and other products to give these foods longer shelf life. We want the thrill of a fast car, but we deplore their lack of adequate safety features. We use the television as nothing more than a free baby-sitting service, especially on Saturday mornings, and yet we cry out loud about the garbage that is being shown our children on television. And we express deep interest and concern over a wide range of consumer legislation, but we fail to flex our voting muscles at the election booth.

To add to this mixed feeling of frustration and relief, there is the additional element of political in-fighting among consumer organizations. Rather than recognizing that in unity there is not only strength but the possibility of success in Washington, the various consumer persons and organizations are a divided house. Each tries to grab on to a particular issue, ride it for a while, and drop it like a hot potato when a new issue springs forward. Furthermore, rather than recognize that political compromise is still very much part of the legislative process, we see consumers and their spokesmen urging an all-or-nothing fight on the various issues pending before legislative bodies. It is thus a most difficult task to attempt an answer to the question, "Who speaks for the consumer?" And yet, before one can even tackle that question, a basic definition of who *is* the consumer must be presented.

One often hears the generality that "all of us are consumers" and thus every piece of legislation or regulatory action affects all of us as consumers. This has been used—all too often—by the business community in an effort to deflate the thrust of the consumer position. How many times have we heard the question: "Who speaks for the consumer; who do you represent?" This question is a fair one, deserving of an answer. But, like most lawyers, I answer with my own question first, namely, "Who speaks for the business community?"

In the recent fight for the consumer advocate agency, Marcor spoke for the consumer, and yet the grocery manufacturers spoke for the businessmen. It is a topsy-turvy world in Washington nowadays, and such strange alliances are more or less taken as commonplace. It is suggested that the question of who speaks for the consumer is clearly out of date. Does it really matter any more? Does it matter whether one consumer advocate represents five people, fifty people, or five million people on a given subject? Must we have a numbers racket within the consumer arena?

It is proposed that the real issue goes to what the consumer is saying, and what is attempted to be accomplished? After all, in the final analysis, neither the consumer nor his advocate makes the decision. It is either a court of law, a legislative body, a governmental agency, or a corporation that makes the final decision. All the consumer is asking is that his voice be raised and then heard by the decision makers.

Turning now to the role of the consumer activist, it is submitted that there are at least five avenues (or perhaps strategies is a better word) for the consumer to take when he feels he has been wronged. First, the so-called "do-nothing" strategy. Here, the consumer decides not to fight a wrong, but rather to write it off to bad experience and just ignore it. This syndrome has variously been referred to as the "you can't fight City Hall" approach. It is to be noted with great interest that this first strategy is becoming a way of the past.

The second avenue for redress is the so-called "miscellaneous" area. Here, the consumer is frustrated and angry, but knows not where to turn. As a result he reaches out for any available assistance, often grasping at straws, and often these straws are not even the right pillars. The history of the "Action Line" columns in our daily newspapers, of the action programs on local television, and of the various ombudsmen around the states signifies that this factor is something to be reckoned with. The consumer hopes—if not expects—that an agency such as Action Line will get a rapid resolution of his frustrating problems.

Clearly, the one drawback of such agencies or complaint centers goes is funding. There is no guarantee that any such agency will remain ongoing; nor is there any assurance that these miscellaneous, ad hoc organizations will have either the permanence or the clout needed to accomplish the stated objectives of consumer redress.

The third strategy that the consumer activist has undertaken lies in the legislative area. Here, working with the various state legislatures or with the appropriate committees of Congress, the consumer advocate has sought enactment of consumer oriented legislation in such areas as product safety, credit, housing, and food and economic pricing.

Unfortunately, the history of legislation at both the state and federal levels leaves a lot to be desired with respect to the consumer. Legislation is watered down by industry-sponsored legislators, just enough so that those covered industries can "live" with the legislation. Or the law is made sufficiently vague so that the enforcement agency is mandated to draft implementation regulations. It is at this level that the consumer rarely, if ever, has representation or even support.

Using Washington as an example, there are very few consumer advocates before the Civil Aeronautics Board or the Federal Trade Commission; there are none before the Interstate Commerce Commission. And if this is so in Washington, how much less "activism" is there at the state and local levels? Thus, matters that sound like good consumer legislation in reality become meaningless legislative enactments. We have already alluded to the defeat in the Senate of the consumer advocacy agency, whereas in the 1960s, at least there were a sizable number of consumer bills signed by Presidents Kennedy and Johnson.

Without meaning to become political, the Nixon-Ford administration has shown no sympathy, no support, and no understanding of the consumer. In fact, we have often witnessed in Washington diverse positions being taken by Mrs. Knauer, the president's special assistant for consumer affairs, and the administration. How many of us can remember those days when Mrs. Knauer fully supported class action legislation, only to find the Justice Department testifying against her? Recently, while Mrs. Knauer was speaking forcefully in favor of the Department of Consumer Advocacy, the White House was leading the opposition. Thus, many consumer advocates have become frustrated with the legislative process and have turned to other avenues of reform.

The fourth area of interest to the consumer activist is litigation. Perhaps the advent of the Neighborhood Legal Services Program created a greater understanding of the power of our courts. During the late 1960s, as the OEO funded Neighborhood Service programs and their various backup centers brought lawsuit after lawsuit, reforms were developed in many of the traditional areas of the law. We know that the Supreme Court of the United States has prohibited taking of property without due process of law. Recent cases have determined that property includes wages, so that garnishments cannot be had, for example, without a fair hearing.

We have seen the development of a brand new area of landlord-tenant law, developed primarily by the agressive, young poverty lawyer who was frustrated with existing statutes but unable to change them in the legislatures. The list is extensive, and the accomplishments even greater. Perhaps the clearest recognition of the impact of the Neighborhood Legal Services Program on the consumer revolution was the fact that Congress recently prohibited federal funds from sustaining any backup legal center to support the newly created Neighborhood Legal Service Corporation.

But poverty law was not the only area in which the consumer activist found success in the courts. Middle class Americans were finding that the courts were sympathetic to truth-in-lending lawsuits, warranty habitability lawsuits, and other areas that affected the middle class pocketbook. The procedural device of a class action became a successful means of providing restitution to all consumers who were affected by a corporate practice. In fact, the Supreme Court was so concerned with the success of class actions that it recently attempted to curtail their impact. It is extremely ironic, however, that in recent months those corporate defendants and their lawyers who have been violently opposed to consumer class actions have themselves become plaintiffs in consumer class actions to recover the monies they lost in oil and wine schemes. Perhaps Charles Ponzi will become the ultimate savior of the consumer class action.

But class actions are not the ultimate in consumer reform; there has been greater reliance on private antitrust actions; and there have been successful challenges in the housing market. One of the most significant court decisions was in New Jersey, for example, when the Court found a mortgage lender—as well as the seller—responsible for breach of the warranty of habitability and fitness of a new house. (California has seen a similar decision.) In every area affecting consumers, the imaginative and resourceful lawyer has found that our legal system, albeit slow, is perhaps the most effective way of creating consumer reform. Yet the slowness of the courts has forced consumers to direct their energies into new and imaginative arenas. The small claims court, which for years was a collection agency for the creditor, has in many parts of the country become a highly successful method of resolving the one-to-one small dispute. The Better Business Bureau and the American Arbitration Association have been developing consumer arbitration programs, whereby the consumer obtains rapid and inexpensive resolution of his controversy.

It must be pointed out that there still should be no substitute for the advocacy function, which perhaps does not always find its way to the arbitrator's table. Of equal concern with respect to arbitration is the fact that the arbitrator can only decide the individual consumer's problem. If, for example, a homeowner in a 200-unit development arbitrates his wet basement problem with the developer, were the arbitrator to find in favor of the consumer, 199 other homeowners would not get the benefit of any relief—unless they too sought arbitration. These, of course, are details that will be worked out. The fact remains that today great emphasis is being placed on developing mechanisms to resolve consumer disputes, and resolve them short of the courthouse.

But let us look momentarily to the future and to some of the consumer goals. As a lawyer, I want to start with my own profession, for I am not pleased with what I see. Our fees are exorbitant, our ethics are questionable, and our abilities are shallow. We make every effort to maintain our profession as a closed society. How many nonlawyers can understand the legalism in a contract, or a lease, or an option to purchase, for example? And yet when serious efforts are made to enact reform, our lawyers become defensive of their own livelihood, such as in the no-fault insurance debate.

It is submitted that two basic reforms must take place within our legal profession. The first involves putting public members on the boards, both in the Ethics Committee and in the Admission and Disbarment Committee. The second deals with the question of advertising. While I recognize that lawyers should not advertise their services as Proctor and Gamble sells soap, the fact remains that our services are really no different from any other object for sale. And there is no question in my mind that proper advertising will result in competitive pricing.

The ramifications that are suggested for the legal profession, of course, are equally applicable to every profession. Our country is receiving inadequate and expensive professional services, in every area of life. Whether it be the doctors or the optometrists, the undertakers or the accountants—all these professionals must be accountable to the public they serve. There has been a recent, though quiet, revolution with respect to pricing of prescription drugs. Many lawsuits around the country have determined that any prohibition on such advertising is not only unconstitutional but a deprivation of the public's right to know. It is submitted that all professions will, in the near future, be required to drop their restrictions on price advertising.

Turning to another topic, it is predicted that the traditional area of public interest law is on its way out. Recently, the Ford Foundation made it very clear that it can no longer fund certain public interest law firms in Washington. Those lawyers engaged in public interest law are finding clients hard to come by, at least the paying clients. Thus, the public interest lawyer will venture into new areas, one of these being group legal services. There is presently a very vocal debate within the American Bar Association as to the scope of group legal—or prepaid legal—services. But this debate is merely a last gasp effort by some of the members of our bar to stall for time. There is no question that group legal services' time has come.

What is significant to me, at least, more so than the availability of low cost legal services, is the potential for *preventive* law. If we stop and think about it for a moment, we realize that the role of the lawyer is to get us out of a jam once we are in it. But who is watching to keep us out of trouble? Our brothers in the field of medicine at least require an annual physical. Why not an annual "legical?" Why is it that in my own private practice my clients call me up and say: "Mr. Kass, I have just signed a contract to buy a house. Can you represent me?" Needless to say, I usually represent those individuals, but the temptation is so strong to say, "Sorry, it's too late!" Thus, the group legal services program should see a rapid rise in the very near future.

One other area of interest to me is in the field of voluntary self-regulation. Although the time for analysis is still too short, there has been a significant trend in industry created self-regulatory bodies, whether in the advertising area, the major appliance industry, or the automobile repair companies. Granted, a lot of this is an effort to negate legislative efforts; but, in my opinion, regardless of the original motive, it does appear that some of these self-regulatory bodies are having an impact on their own industries.

One final—and novel—solution must be discussed. There is on the horizon a corporation known as Public Equity Corporation. It is a Delaware corporation, which will very shortly file its prospectus before the Securities and Exchange Commission. Why is this unique? Because Public Equity Corporation is, by its own definition, an anticorporation corporation. The business of General Motors, for example, is making and selling automobiles. The business of Kodak Corporation is in the photographic arena. The business of PEC will be to create a climate of consumer reform within American Industry.

How will it accomplish this objective? First, it intends to fund consumer litigation and to sue on its own behalf when the Executive Committee, authorized by the Board of Directors, and ultimately the stockholders, give their okay. Second, it will generate and sell consumer information and education materials, to be distributed widely on a profit basis. And finally, it expects to be an umbrella for group legal service programs in selected cities throughout the nation.

Thus, we have seen a significant change in the basic strategies of the consumer activist. The activist has gone from the traditional to the imaginative, and now indeed there is a return to the traditional. It is quite ironic that the goals and objectives of the consumer activist are embodied in the laissez faire spirit of capitalism and competition. Granted, the consumer relies on government agencies and the courts to prod and spur on such competition, but its ultimate objectives are a free, competitive marketplace. This irony cannot be forgotten, and its message must be told.

Chapter 14

Private Recourse for Consumers: Redress or Rape?

Babette B. Barton

What's good for General Motors is reputedly good for the nation, so then do laws that champion consumer rights run counter to the higher public interest? The fact is that with a healthy business climate and satisfaction of consumer demands so interdependent, temperate awards can foster mutual rewards; inadequate or excessive relief may bring helpless victims and hapless victors. The purpose of this article is to explore the policies underlying the private law of consumer protection. What the study will undertake to show is how, in regulating and resolving conflicts between commercial and consumer interests, the law serves in a dual capacity of referee and handicapper—how rival interests are weighted and undue imbalances compensated, and why compromise must often emerge as the catalyst to sustained competition.

This study begins with a brief examination of the social, political, and economic influences that have helped shape the modern-day private law of consumer protection. Subsequently, particular forms of privately enforceable regulations are discussed in the context of describing the interests that the law seeks to further; and the legal mechanisms for obtaining private recourse for consumers are the subject of our final consideration.

THE EVOLUTION OF THE PRIVATE LAW
OF CONSUMER RIGHTS

The campaign by the modern-day consumer movement to crown the consumer king had its forebears in those revolutionary forces that formed, not from the ranks of a populist uprising, but out of pressures of the industrial revolution. The once sovereign doctrine of caveat emptor (let the buyer beware) [1] dissipated as a natural waste product of industrialization. Abandoning the buyer to his own risk "per caveat emptor" may have suited the exigencies of preindustrial times when, in face-to-face bartering over simple products designed to meet simple needs, the consumer could be expected to choose his own cracker wisely as he delved by hand into the cracker barrel—and guard himself against danger and deception through personal inquiry and inspection [2]. But as advances in marketing techniques and technology outstripped the consumer's expertise, a free and unregulated market could no longer be counted on to achieve the economically "efficient" solution of resources being optimally allocated to their most highly valued use [3]. Consumers simply became unable to select and judge what products and quantities were best [4].

Ironically, the business community has played a significant role as a coalescent of the consumer movement. The marvel and multitude of products spawned by its technological genius has bewildered consumers and brought forth calls for regulators to intervene [5]. Then too, businesses themselves, feeling threatened by the realities of industrialization in which unfair and monopolistic practices flourished, demanded self-protection through legal curbs on anticompetitive practices that have proved to be precursors of basic modern consumer protective legislation [6]. Furthermore, by failure to keep its own house in order, industry created a vulnerable host environment for such highly publicized exposés as the critical attack on Chicago's meat packing industry by Upton Sinclair in his book *The Jungle*, which in turn prompted the Pure Food and Drug Act and other inspection laws that were ancestors to still other modern enactments [7].

It was not until the 1960s, however, that the force of consumerism assumed its electrifying shape. What fused the giant reaction, from a political scientist's perspective [8], was a mounting tension of public concern built by the woes and wooing of unrelated heroes and events: Senator Estes Kefauver's drug hearings, morbidly punctuated by the Thalidomide tragedy; Ralph Nader's David and Goliath tilt with General Motors and the auto industry; politicians eager to divert public attention to the domestic scene from the unpopular entanglement in Vietnam; and muckrackers who wrote convincingly of the dangers of an unregulated market—Rachel Carson [9], John Kenneth Galbraith [10], Ralph Nader [11], and Vance Packard [12], to name but a few.

In 1962, President Kennedy managed to capture the spirit of the newborn movement and embody its tenets in his widely noted presidential proclamation of a Consumer Bill of Rights [13]. According to the presidential message, the consumer was said to possess four unchallengeable rights: the right to be informed, to choose, to be heard, and the right to safety. Despite their overt simplicity, so comprehensive was their thrust that the four spanned all causes of relief that the consumers have since or perhaps are ever likely to demand [14].

The right to be informed meant not merely that the consumer be given adequate information essential to an enlightened and intelligent choice, but also an assurance of freedom from false and deceptive tactics. The right to choose was a call to provide consumers with access to a variety of competitive offerings competitively priced, or, in the case of natural monopolies such as utilities, the right to obtain satisfactory quality and service at fair and carefully regulated rates. The right to be heard sought both an assurance that consumer interests would receive full and sympathetic consideration in the formulation of government policy, and fair and expeditious treatment in the tribunals. The right to safety encompassed nothing more (and nothing less) than a right to be protected from dangerous and defective products hazardous to health and life.

In essence, the Consumer Bill of Rights was a bill of principles rather than a blueprint for practice. None of the four enumerated rights was self-executing dogma. Yet the proclamation set forth a comprehensive, albeit generalized, platform of consumer rights and demands that now had been legitimated by presidential announcement. Lawmakers were thus faced with the challenge to design equitable formulas for safeguarding and enforcing the now acknowledged rights.

Emerging Statutory Standards on the Federal and Local Scenes

The decade of the 1960s marked the beginning of modern-day efforts by Congress on behalf of each of the consumer's four rights [15]. On the whole, the congressional enactments had a public law orientation that stressed the reform of industry and business practices enforceable by public agencies rather than private individual action. The characteristic feature of the laws—and indeed of those enacted in the earlier part of the century as well [16]—was their ad hoc political response to tragic events and personalities of the times [17]. The same was true in each of the four areas of consumer interest; laws were shepherded to victory by appealing protagonists able to capture public attention and mobilize it into effective pressure for reform.

Legislative examples from the right to safety are perhaps the best known. In addition to the earlier cited Thalidomide tragedy, which spotlighted Senator Kefauver's largely unnoticed drug hearings and resulted in the 1962 Kefauver-Harris amendments to the Pure Food and Drug Act [18] —and Nader's now legendary fracas with the czars of the auto industry, which culminated in the National Traffic and Motor Vehicle Safety Act [19] —the reported tragedies from flammable fabrics and inadequate child safety protection inspired passage of other safety acts [20]. Even a new meat inspection law became legislative fact after Nader's charges against the industry's marketing practices became immortalized as the "four D's": the dead, dying, disabled, and diseased animals sent to slaughter for human consumption [21].

The other consumer rights had their effective popular spokesmen too. Spearheading reform on the right to be informed were Senator Paul Douglas, whose crusade to disclose the cost of borrowing ultimately materialized after his tenure in Congress in a Truth-in-Lending Law [22]; and Senator Philip Hart, whose Truth-in-Packaging law [23] won enactment despite, or perhaps because of, his personal ridicule and belittlement by industry spokesmen who denied that consumers suffered from deceptive packaging and inadequate information on contents [24].

Appealing advocates also aroused legislative attention to the right to be heard, for testimony by individuals victimized by the evils of big-brothering in the credit reporting industry [25], with its secret dossiers built on unreliable gossip, rumors, even mistaken identity, successfully lobbied the enactment of a Fair Credit and Reporting Act [26] to restrict the contents and use of credit files and allow consumers to introduce counterbalancing truths. And in the fourth area of the right to choose, which depends upon vigorous regulation of unfair and anticompetitive practices that undercut meaningful choice, critical attacks by crusading groups such as Nader's Raiders on the FTC [27] aroused a chorus of demands on Congress to overhaul and revitalize the watchdogging activities of that and other federal administrative agencies.

But despite the flurry of congressional activity in response to political pressures of the sixties, advances in private consumer interests were limited at best. The heated controversy embroiling each campaign resulted in bills being agonizingly debated, then either compromisingly legislated [28] or relegated to endless filibuster and frustration. The laws that were enacted contained critical shortcomings that slowed if not stymied the drafters' hopes: gaps in coverage through oversight or compromise that sometimes left the consumer little better off than before [29]; delays in promulgating regulations, divided responsibilities, and inadequate funding that undercut hopes for effective enforcement [30]. Yet measures to upgrade protection by bringing private pressure to bear—bills to authorize consumers to institute private federal class actions [31] and to create a federal ombudsman to advance individual interests and rights [32] —repeatedly bowed to defeat based on industry's fears of harrassment and of unwarranted claims.

At least one clear lesson was to emerge from the federal experience of the sixties: the need for advance study and deliberate legislative action to supplant knee-jerk reflexes to public pressure that neither assuage fears of business nor complaints of consumers. Apparently the lesson has not been lost on Congress. Its recently enacted Consumer Product Safety Act [33] embraces a new and promising model. Eschewing the piecemeal approach, the Act creates an omnibus agency endowed with a comprehensive range of powers, the need for which was overwhelmingly documented in extensive hearings and thoughtful studies by a predecessor product safety commission [34]. Based on the same model of empirical study as a prelude to legislation, efforts such as the Senate Commerce Committee's recent co-sponsorship of a study of actual class action litigation [35] may break the stubborn stalemate that, based on undocumented fears, has heretofore prevented passage of bills containing the machinery that could create meaningful private relief.

Paralleling the federal legislative experience of recent years has been a profusion of activity at the state and local levels. Whereas state and local administrative agencies have significantly upgraded their levels of responsibility in monitoring white collar crime, the major emphasis locally has been on individualized rather than governmental institutional arrangements to implement the consumer's range of rights. An expansion, if not explosion, of actions has been authorized that consumers could themselves enforce. The subject of the enactments has been far ranging: from regulations affecting entire industires—for instance, the credit industry, including retail installment sales [36], to regulation of particular types of business, including vocational schools [37], health and dance studios [38], television [39], auto [40], and other service establishments.

Particularized business practices and terms of contract also have become the objects of attention: uniform rules to govern commercial transactions became a reality with adoption by the states of the Uniform Commercial Code, whereas the once commonly enacted

Printers' Ink Laws [41], containing criminal sanctions for false and misleading advertising with intent to deceive that law enforcement agencies had well nigh ignored [42], were replaced with broad ranging legislation to curtail deceptive and anticompetitive practices that individual consumers could themselves enforce [43]. The substance of these and such other recent consumer measures as antideficiency and cooling off legislation will be examined in more detail below.

Judicially Recognized Consumer Rights to Relief

As the increased political awareness and responsiveness to consumerism began to be manifest in legislative and administrative branches, coincidentally a startling series of developments was unfolding in the courts. Reported decisions disclosed a marked shift in favor of consumers; precedents were abandoned by courts traditionally hamstrung by the constraints of stare decisis and its dictate that established rules hold sway.

The most dramatic of the judicial advances occurred in the area of product safety, with a revolutionary explosion of developments to which economic theory holds the key [44]. As the data on the costs and incidents of product injury mounted [44a], new principles of tort law developed to provide remedies for the loss. No longer did courts feel bound by time-tested limits on the doctrine of negligence, which had once restricted recovery in tort to actions by an innocent buyer against his seller for injuries from a defective product that had been negligently supplied.

After first expanding the realm of liability to hold a manufacturer responsible for personal injuries to a consumer, notwithstanding the lack of privity of contract between them, in cases involving a defective product negligently produced [45], the later cases engrafted a doctrine of strict liability to permit the buyer of a dangerously defective product to gain recourse from the manufacturer for personal injury regardless of fault [46]. Basic to the expanded theories of recovery justifying "enterprise liability" was the rationale of the superior ability of the commercial sector to monitor product defects and to absorb the often catastrophic costs of injury to a single consumer by spreading the loss to the consuming public at large [47].

In the area of contract law as well, as discussed further below, courts began to evidence a growing sympathy for safeguarding consumers against the superior expertise and economic strength of business. Standardized form contracts, to the printed terms of which the consumer seemed to have no option but to adhere (so-called "adhesion contracts") [48] became vulnerable to judicial invalidation [49], as did "unconscionable" clauses and contracts [50] that were found to shock the conscience [51]. And finally, the Constitution, with its admonition against deprivation of property without due process of law [52], became the touchstone of decisions that foreclosed creditors' overzealous and premature enforcement of their rights against debtor-consumers who had not had an opportunity to protect their properties against seizure, by requiring due notice and fair hearing in court [53].

Balancing Interests in Developing Consumer Protections

Given the burgeoning endowment of private rights for consumers by the rush of events of modern times, how much longer would the best interests of consumers stay apace? Indeed, not even the developments to this point have met with uniform acclaim [54]. For laudable and rational as their wellsprings may be, protective measures inevitably entail some sacrifices and costs.

Take the enterprise theory of liability, for example, which is based on the premise that the damages to recompense one consumer's injuries will be absorbed as a business expense to be passed on to others. The impact of this on consumers is not that the cost of injury is eliminated, but merely shared. And even if the expense were not so directly deflected, the impact for consumers might still be adverse if, for instance, the affected business were forced out of the market and the prevailing level of competition thereby reduced [55]. This same propensity for good and harm is true of nearly any protective measure, for given the kaleidoscope of consumer interests, some inevitably collide.

A person's own self-contradictory desires can create ambivalence and aversion to protection. Consider a few simple illustrations. While the consumer insists on safety in the products he buys, he refuses to abide such warnings as the buzzers on unfastened seat belts or the Surgeon General's incontrovertible findings on the dangers of cigarette smoking. While the consumer demands the right to choose among competitors from products that are competitively priced, he balks at the removal of interest ceilings that would allow rates to be fixed by free market forces, distrusting the efficacy of competition in this context. His insistence on a right to be heard and to his own day in court may be compromised by support of "no-fault" programs that are premised on automatic settlements to obviate the high costs of litigation. Or, despite demands for information so as to make the wisest choice, consumers continue to indulge in sprees of impulse buying, ignoring objective data such as the costs of borrowing and contents of packaging in favor of their own ganglia of perception.

A further complication in determining the appropriate scope of regulation is how best to reconcile the diversity of interests throughout society. Should we impose a fail-safe system despite the resulting costs and regardless of benefiting only a few, perhaps those most vulnerable or gullible or with the highest thresholds of risk aversion? Or, rather than insisting on absolute safety, can we continue to market automobiles, Salk vaccine, and other purveyors of injury if satisfied that the product does not create an "unreasonable risk" [56]; and, if unreasonable risk is to be the test, how is this criterion to be applied? [57].

Experts disagree on the best form of regulation and the proper scope of private rights. Among economists, distinct and contradictory schools of thought exist as to when "efficiency" (the use of resources where their value is greatest) is best achieved through governmental regulation that might, for example, ameliorate transaction costs that detract from efficient allocation [58]. There are also differences of opinion on the normative goals that regulation should seek and the premises as to optimum patterns of distribution: should everyone's interests be judged on a principle of equal yet diminishing marginal utilities, or according to the Rawlsian theory of justice that calls for maximizing the relative lot of the least well off in society. Or should the distribution strive for Pareto optimality, that peak of equilibrium achieved by increasing of satisfactions through redistributions that make one person better off without reducing the lot of another? [59].

Lawyers, too, are divided over what regulations qualify as equitable and wise. Is it fair, for example, to insist on ceilings on interest for the benefit of the general public although this may drive necessitous high risk borrowers from the legitimate market into the hands of high rate loan sharks [60], or paternalistically preclude them from ostensible luxuries that are essential to their psychic or other needs? [61]. And, ask other social scientists, do we in fact know enough of motivation and consumer needs to justify regulation of business behavior and particular forms of preventive relief? [62].

If, as is apparent, not all protections are sound panaceas, how are the merits of a regulation to be judged? Consider the wisdom of banning a product or service, whether acupuncture, a contraceptive, or even a motorcycle equipped with wings. The curb could protect, but at what price? Psychological and economic benefits from self-determination are forsaken, and perhaps even physical health, particularly if the regulation should force a consumer to a substitute, perhaps black marketed product, posing even greater danger. For society at large, even if the regulation were to induce relative savings in revenues and man hours of productivity that might otherwise have been lost from product or service related injury or death, they may be outweighed by the toll exacted from alternative conduct.

There are also costs of enforcing not only the primary regulation but also the black marketing or other substitute arrangements to which the consumer will turn. And not to be discounted is the possibility that the regulation will deter research into and marketing of products that would be beneficial in upgrading public good. In sum, the desirability of regulation is a function of projected immediate and long term benefits balanced against correlative costs, tempered by due regard to enforcement costs and probable alternative behavior were regulation to be imposed. A conscious choice of values must be made in deciding how to weight each factor, including the primacy of individual or societal interests, and who in particular should bear the brunt or benefits of regulation.

Competition among interests is reflected in the patterns of regulation discussed below. The precise form and scope of regulation represents an accommodation of diverse interests. How well the balance has been struck is left for the reader to decide.

FORMS OF PRIVATE RELIEF

Preventive Measures

As the foregoing discussion suggests, the law may consciously tolerate a risk of injury to consumers by refusing to impose a ban despite the prospect of individualized danger. The same is as true of economic as of physical harm. Thus, for example, the "buy now, pay later" pied-piper refrain is not legally silenced (albeit censored by Truth-in-Lending), for although it may curry individual financial disaster, lenient credit is the backbone of our affluent society [63], considered necessary to support the economy from collapse. Assuming, however, that a cost-benefit analysis argues for some type of preventative measure, compliance can be effected through either the public or private sector. Each has relative merits. Regulation at the hands of public agencies provides centralized enforcement, hence consistent policy that eases burdens of compliance and that fits the resolution of each case into the entire regulatory scheme [64].

Private enforcement adds other dimensions of costs—the time consuming, expensive, and often frustrating nature of case-to-case resolution, plus potential harassment of the defendant by frivolous or holdup claims [65]. Moreover, the very form of regulation may necessitate public action, as with a regulation calling for confiscation of a dangerous product. And yet, because of an individual's high stake in his own case and his superior knowledge of the pertinent facts, private enforcement can be the more effective and efficient regulatory approach, with deterrent and remedial effects producing benefits that outweigh its costs [66].

Whatever the reasons for selecting a private law in lieu of or to supplement a public preventative regulation, the interests sought to be furthered are of the type discussed below.

Illegal Contract Terms and Tactics

In determining what rules should govern the conduct of parties to a contract, private law of contracts is based on a free enterprise philosophy that, in general, assumes that the greatest good will comes from deferring to each party a freedom to contract in his own best interests [67]. Whereas the task of courts is to insure certainty and orderly, peaceable implementation, the substance of the contract is a matter generally left to the parties' bargain. The consumer himself is expected to avoid merchants who peddle products and practices that appear unsatisfactory; in that way, resources will be allocated to satisfy competitively determined wants.

Nonetheless, certain terms and tactics so frustrate the principles underlying freedom of contract as to be singled out for restraint. The prototype is fraud (or deceit), which, by classic definition, is the false representation of a material fact with an intent to deceive that becomes actionable if justifiably relied on to the injury of the defrauded party [68]. Not only does fraud offend a lawyer's notion of justice by its attempt to benefit one party over another by deceit, but if left unregulated it could so frustrate expectations as to impede the willingness of individuals to enter into voluntary undertakings. Furthermore, in economic terms fraud creates inefficiencies in the market, since the consequence of the deception is to skew resources away from their most highly valued uses [69]. Also, the legitimate business enterprise may be unfairly penalized by the opprobrium of those who suffered at the hands of the unscrupulous actor.

The reasons for imposing protections are less one-sided when applied to other false or misleading practices that fall short of fraud as classically defined. If, for example, deception occurred because of a seller's exaggerated and enthusiastic exclamations of quality, the law is hesitant to characterize this unequivocally as a legitimate cause of complaint for fear that regulation of what is known as "puffing" could create unwarranted reliance by one on the opinions of another, or tempt consumers to inflate claims of opinion unduly to the status of imagined warranties [70].

How individualized the test of misrepresentation should be is troublesome as well. Should variations in gullibility and naivete of consumers be relevant to the outcome, or would that exact too high a standard of caution and restraint in business conduct? [71]. And, should lack of scienter be material, or are there certain practices so inherently deceptive as to warrant the prophylactic of a ban? [72].

The wisdom of spelling out what types of deceptive acts constitute proscribed and actionable forms of conduct, contrasted with imposing a generalized ban, has been actively debated in state legislatures [73]. The Federal Trade Commission has taken a position favoring "small FTC Acts" in the states modeled on Section 5A of the FTC Act that would enjoin and create causes of action for the violation of any "unfair or deceptive acts or practices" [74]. Consumers generally are sympathetic to that position, fearing that the specification of a defined list of proscribed practices tacitly invites the commission of other unfair acts that had not been specifically banned [75].

The business community, on the other hand, has resisted such efforts out of fear that the category of "unfair and deceptive practices" would generate liability for a whole range of activities that could not be effectively monitored against, or might lead to overzealous interpretations by the judiciary in behalf of undeserving consumers who were either not misled or whose own shortcomings, rather than the seller's overreaching, caused the complained-of injury. What, for example, should be the result of marketing large packages, clearly marked as to weight, that are priced higher per unit of weight than a smaller package of the same product?

Despite the still live debate over what tactics can rightly be said to fall within the general rubric of an unfair and deceptive practice, there are certain specific egregious acts and contractual provisions that have won near unanimity of condemnation as beyond the pale of what is tolerable in the legitimate marketplace today [76]. One is the well known "referral sale" [77], which holds out the enticement of a promised rebate or commission to the consumer on any future sales made to persons referred to the seller by that buyer. The basic evil of the referral sale is its covertly deceptive nature, for the enticed participants could not realistically expect to earn commissions in view of the pyramiding effect of referrals by the seller's original customers, together with referrals by those who are themselves referred, which would entail an upward spiralling chain involving thousands of referrals in order not to overlap with prior contacts [78]. In addition, entering into contract in the hopes of making profits on future referrals has been condemned as an illegal gambling contract [79].

Another inherently deceptive practice is the "bait and switch" campaign, which attempts to lure a customer into an establishment by bait of an attractive advertisement or offer that the seller has no intent of honoring, planning instead to switch to a product that would result in a more profitable sale. The most common form, unfortunately too familiar, is the ad for a nationally known product at bargain prices, with the advertiser planning to disparage that product or to disclose its previously disguised flaws once the consumer bites and enters the store [80]. Here again, disguised deception is the intolerable vice.

Closely related is the ostensible "free gimmick" or "bargain sale" device, whereby the consumer is falsely led to believe that a product will be given to him free or at minimal cost if he will agree to pay what in actuality is an exorbitant price either for "handling" (for instance, a 30-year magazine or encyclopedia subscription), or for an essential accessory (such as the expensive case for a "free" sewing machine), or for educational fees to acquire needed skills for a supposedly windfall job [81].

Certain types of contract terms also have fallen into disrepute because of their propensity for unfair surprise or their deprivation of a consumer's opportunity for fair vindication of his rights. One type is the so-called "balloon payment" [82], the description for a disproportionately excessive payment that follows a series of smaller installments and that tends to take a consumer unfairly by surprise, either because of its size or because the consumer might have realized he could not have afforded to enter the contract had the sum been spread more evenly among all the payments.

Another increasingly invalid provision is the clause in a contract calling for confession of judgment [83], by which covenant the consumer is barred from contesting his liability in the event that he defaults in payment. Offsetting the savings in litigation costs from this expeditious procedure is the injustice that would result were the consumer to agree to such a term and thus be denied his day in court to vindicate his cause, often against such disreputable tactics as the referral sale or bait and switch [84]. For similar reasons, the ability to cut off a consumer's potential defenses by assignment of the consumer's contract or negotiable instrument to another has also fallen into growing discredit [85].

Traditionally, the law has looked with favor on a "holder in due course" [86] who, in good faith and without knowledge of defenses, purchased the right to collect the consumer's contractual undertaking. In the interests of removing impediments to negotiability in the marketing of commercial paper, the law compelled a buyer to honor his original promises regardless of any rightful defenses he might have had against the original seller [87].

But appropriate as this rule may have been in resolving the competing interests of commercial antagonists, it has fallen harshly on unsophisticated consumers who lack the expertise to protect themselves against unsatisfactory performance by their sellers. Therefore, rather than requiring the consumer to satisfy the assignee's claims and then hope to be made whole by bringing suit against the seller, the trend is to allow the consumer to assert his defenses against the third party financier [88]. Hence, the risk of protecting against unsatisfactory performance is shifted, making the assignee responsible to take such necessary precautions as the monitoring of the seller's performance prior to the assignment or the securing of a right of recourse against the seller should valid consumer defenses be asserted [89]. Ultimately, of course, the cost of the protection must be borne by others [90].

Besides the prohibition of specific contractual terms and tactics that tend to deny the consumer full enforcement of his contractual expectations, there are other weapons that the courts have used to prevent hardship on consumers from obligations undertaken other than by free choice. Thus, courts have at times refused to enforce the terms of so-called "adhesion contracts"—printed standardized forms to which a consumer has felt forced to adhere because of his relatively weak bargaining position in contrast to that of the seller's[91].

Although standardized forms may be ideally suited to the parties' wants, and may even produce savings in transaction costs that can be passed on to other consumers, such arrangements nonetheless could be economically unsound as well as unfair if the terms were coerced or otherwise not a fair reflection of what the consumer desires [92]. Analogously, contracts may be revised by courts under the theory of "unconscionability," when a great disparity in bargaining position is detected coupled with an element of unfair surprise [93]. In both cases, the law allows for ad hoc monitoring to assure that the policies underlying freedom of contract prevail.

Disclosure Legislation

In the view of some knowledgeable observers [94], the impersonality of the marketplace and resulting breakdowns and imperfections in information flow have so exacerbated consumers as to constitute the greatest single cause of the consumer movement. Certainly information is an essential complement to the fight against fraud and deceptive practices, as well as basic to the vision of optimum allocation of resources by free market forces. Furthermore, to require producers or manufacturers to furnish information on mass produced goods could give rise to significant savings in transaction costs compared to the otherwise atomized and repetitious acts that might be entailed were consumers individually to obtain comparable information. Yet, beyond regulation of half-truths, misrepresentation, and other false and deceptive practices [95], or the growing trend toward requiring "as is" labelling when a product fails to satisfy an implied warranty of merchantability [96], the law is surprisingly silent as to which facts that a consumer can enforceably demand.

While pressures for information to permit quality comparisons have materialized in limited forms of disclosure legislation, even these laws seem little more meaningful than empty window dressings. Ongoing efforts to secure unit pricing (to help overcome what Representative Benjamin Rosenthal has characterized as the "peril of the shrinking package"), open dating, grading and quality comparisons, and technological advances to bring computerized information to the point of purchase [97], taken in conjunction with the disappointing reported results of shopping tests [98], are all testimonials to the inadequacies of the Truth-in-Packaging law to satisfy consumer needs.

Furthermore, skepticism voiced by antagonists as to the uselessness of information on the cost of credit [99] has been confirmed by empirical studies. Since low income and unsophisticated consumers rarely engage in comparative shopping, disclosure has been found to be meaningless for them [100]. Even middle class, educated buyers demonstrate an insensitivity to what is required to be told them as to the cost of credit in auto purchases, preferring instead to patronize on the basis of subjective, nonpecuniary criteria [101].

The conclusion may be inescapable that what little information the law requires to be furnished to consumers is as irrelevant as a red/green warning signal for the color blind. What is needed if there is to be meaningful protection is creation of disclosure laws that take account of behaviorists' studies of the factors that motivate consumers to buy [102].

"Cooling-Off" Statutes

To prevent unwise and unwanted contracts, particularly by consumers who may have succumbed to the high pressure and debilitating tactics of the door-to-door salesman, cooling-off statutes (as the name implies) grant consumers a grace period of decompression during which to reflect objectively on the wisdom of having entered into contract [103]. Typically, the consumer is given an escape hatch of three days to a week to decide whether to be bound by the terms of a home solicitation sale. The purpose is to combat the evils of magazine, encyclopedia, and other itinerant vendors whose prey are the vulnerable—the low income and uneducated who do not venture out to shop [104], consumers in their homes who have not sought such a purchase and hence have their defenses down and who are captive audiences for the tenacious salesman who refuses to leave until the contract is signed [105].

However, since the applicable scope of cooling-off statutes is limited, so too are their protections. Typically, the statutory terms are restricted to cover only credit sales or cash sales in excess of a stated floor, since these have the greatest potential to cause the trauma of overcommitment or regret. And yet the excluded cash transaction could represent a huge outlay in the budget of a low income consumer, as well as encourage a fast-talking peddler to work to part his victims from their cash. The typical statutory exception for services or goods provided for an emergency—a self-evident exception to prevent an otherwise calamitous delay—allows the unscrupulous itinerant home improvement contractor to perform his qualityless craftsmanship on house sidings, roofing, and heater replacements in defiance of a consumer's ability to renege [106].

Similarly, the shoddy or otherwise unsatisfactory product that arrives days after the order is placed cannot be disclaimed by the once pressured, now disillusioned consumer who is dumped to the earth of reality long after the cooling-off period has expired. Finally, the common statutory authorization of a cancellation premium, ostensibly to compensate for costs the seller may have incurred in processing the contract, may itself dissuade the less-than-satisfied consumer from exercising the right to cancel.

Given these statutory limitations, it is small wonder that an empirical study has found that cooling-off legislation is of only minimal value to consumers [107]. The trickster and fly-by-night are virtually unaffected, whereas the legitimate and established entreprenuer normally values an untarnished reputation and customer good will enough to extend customers the right to change their minds even when pressure selling has not forced an unwanted contract.

Restraints on Creditors' Remedies and Rights

In an effort to stem harrassing, tortious, and other overreaching tactics in the collection process, a significant trend in recent years has moved in the direction of limiting the available remedies of creditors that tend to take unfair advantage of inexperienced consumers as vulnerable prey [108]. Many of these developments were referred to earlier, including legislative restrictions on confession of judgment and waiver of defenses and the judiciary's refusals to enforce unconscionable and adhesion contracts as well as its recognition of constitutional limits on prejudgment garnishments and attachments.

Other notable examples are the increasingly legislated curbs on repossession and resale, as well as deficiency judgments. The goal of these is to prevent unjust enrichment of a creditor at the expense of a defaulting debtor who may have succumbed to overcommitment by pressures of easy credit. One approach has been to preclude such unfair tactics as the repossession of an article, followed first by a prearranged resale at an artificially low price and later by a suit against the debtor for the deficiency on the debt. After the dust settled the debtor would find himself stripped of the property that had been repossessed, yet accountable for nearly all that had formerly been owing (all but the artificially small amount collected at the contrived foreclosure sale)—an amount often in excess of the original debt [109].

One antidote has been to require that foreclosure sales be advertised and open so as to maximize the amounts that they bring [110], the costs of advertising the sale thus becoming the major price tag for this protection. Another approach has been through antideficiency legislation that permits a creditor's repossession but not his collection of the balance of the debt. The price of this protection is far greater, for if the article has significantly depreciated in value—as is typical of automobiles and household furnishings—repossession will not make the creditor whole. Hence, if risk of default is shifted to the creditor, any loss may eventually find its way to other consumers [111]. Therefore, as a compromise between ameliorating undue harshness to the debtor and loss to the creditor, some antideficiency statutes or proposals circumscribe the type of goods and amounts of money to which the relief measure will apply [112].

Miscellaneous Preventative Measures

The foregoing discussion was intended as a selective illustration of the most significant interests that have accounted for the development of private preventive measures. The same or similar policies underlie the many other common and material types of restrictions that form the private law of consumer protection. For example, in the interest of deterring fraud, statutes frequently prohibit blank spaces in contracts that could otherwise be unscrupulously completed or require delivery of a completed copy of the contract to the buyer on signing to forestall improper alteration of terms. Legislation to guard against unfair deprivation of an unwary consumer's rights may take the form of requiring contracts to contain paragraphs appraising the buyer of his rights, or venue restrictions on where to bring suit to assure a convenient forum for the consumer.

Restrictions on wage garnishments or on what properties may be subject to liens, including, in the case of add-on sales, protections against loss of purchased property earlier when default in payment fails to cover later added-on purchases, all are to lessen the hardships from overcommitment by assuring that a debtor will not be stripped of all former possessions or necessaries for future livelihood and support. And, to deter unjust enrichment of creditors at the expense of consumers, laws may restrict the definition of what constitutes a default or limit loading charges, including credit life insurance, and otherwise regulate chargeable rates.

There are, of course, costs generated by the protections. In varying degrees, they hamper self-determination in business conduct, tend to curtail consummation of contracts or lenient extensions of credit and to augment operating expenses that somehow must be borne. Obviously, some of the restrictions may be more easily justified than others. Again, the reader is left the choice.

Remedial Measures

While preventive measures function to mitigate the occurrence of consumer injury, supplementary remedial relief is also essential to a well balanced protective scheme. Preventative measures, after all, are often designed to tolerate a calculated risk of individual harm— which, if and when materialized, can be dealt with by appropriate remedies after the fact. For example, a promising wonder drug may be given clearance for the market, notwithstanding evidence of its capacity for harm, based upon the rationale that if an individual patient to whom it is administered suffers an adverse reaction, the injury will either be compensated automatically or at least upon a finding of negligence in the prescription or production [113]. Furthermore, without a program of remedial sanctions to give teeth to preventive measures, defiance could too easily replace compliance. Legislative bans on products and practices could otherwise amount to no more than paper shields against the mettle of determination by an unscrupulous profiteer. In other words, prevention as a cure is workable only for the pure.

This is not to say that every injury is a wrong that should create an offsetting right to relief. Perhaps consumers may be forced to assume a noncompensable risk of harm to encourage new products to reach the market [114]. Or the consumer's own actions may forfeit his right to recompense; for, to take an illustration, why make others share the cost of a consumer's dereliction by permitting application of the theory of enterprise liability to insure a consumer against risk by spreading his damages as an operating expense to others, if the consumer could have avoided his injury by reasonable means of self-protection? [115].

Assuming that some quantum of relief is warranted, however, other variables complicate the appropriate scope. First, recovery might either be limited to out-of-pocket expenses caused by breach of contract and product injury or be extended to include compensation for economic losses in the nature of lost profits as well. The choice is relatively simple, given the principles of freedom of contract, in cases in which the defendant chose to warrant against the plaintiff's lost benefit of his bargain; even a remote manufacturer would be responsible for the economic loss [116] covered by the manufacturer's own express warranty [117].

But in the absence of a warranty on the subject, do the justifications for enterprise liability in the realm of product injury—the superior ability of the business sector to monitor against product defects and insure against their risks—argue for imposing liability for economic loss in addition to physical harm, or would this assess too great a responsibility to expect the business community to absorb or against which to insure? [118]. A similar issue is involved in determining the equitable limits on liability by a financier to whom a consumer contract is assigned. Should the assignee merely be subject to consumer defenses against the assignor-dealer for out-of-pocket losses, but not be responsible for defenses based on liability of the dealer for product or personal injury from defective products? [119]. Second, the culpability of the defendant could be another factor affecting not merely the right of recovery [120] but also its amount [121].

Awards of extraordinary or punitive damages for certain types of misconduct [122] such as false and deceptive practices, or the knowing merchandizing of an unsafe product [123], could be justified both as a necessary stimulant to encourage consumer actions and as a deterrent to otherwise improper conduct for which the probability of detection and successful prosecution seem otherwise remote [124]. Without the threat of punitive damages, a merchant may willingly continue to practice his outlawed tactics, gambling on what past history shows to be dismally low odds as to the probability of detection and successful prosecution for egregious consumer wrongs [125].

Attorneys Fees

Another, perhaps more potent alternative to punitive damages for stimulating consumers to seek judicial relief [126] is to award attorneys fees to the consumer for the successful prosecution of his case. The historic rule of law requiring both parties to absorb their own costs of litigation has fallen most harshly on consumers. For whereas business has been able to absorb the costs of house counsel and litigation as an overhead expense of operations, an individual consumer has had to shoulder his own entire expense or else be deterred from seeking court recovery for what was often justly due.

The modern approach compromises the past rule by allowing attorneys fees—but only to a victorious consumer [127]. In that way the disincentive to court action is reduced without correlative encouragement of frivolous claims. In addition, since the consumer's claim may involve relatively meager sums, the trend is toward authorization of fees commensurate with the time spent on the litigation, rather than merely proportional to the damages at stake [128], so as to encourage adequate and willing representation for mounting a first rate attack.

Repair, Replacement, and Other Specific Forms of Relief

While monetary relief in the form of damages and attorney fees may be the most satisfactory answer for remedying product injury after the fact, it is little solace for a beleaguered consumer's common everyday headache of defective products that simply won't work, or at least not as they should. If a consumer believes that he has purchased a product that will perform, that is what he wants—performance, not refund.

Unfortunately, the purchase of a product with guarantee or warranty attached is not a sure method for avoiding the trauma of breakdown. The guarantee itself may be nothing more than an elaborate device for putting the consumer on notice of defects that he must assume. Whereas the original purpose of warranties under the law was to protect the consumer by a promise of a product's quality of performance [129], over the years disclaimer of quality often became the thrust and substance of a warranty's fine print [130]. Today, the prevailing rule under the Uniform Commercial Code requires a warranty of fitness or quality before a consumer can be heard to complain that the product he purchased does not satisfy the particular uses for which he bought it [131]; thus, an electric saw need not turn out a finished edge unless the saw was warranted to satisfy the demands of a carpenter's art.

Even the implied warranty of merchantability that a product is fit for its obvious task [132] —that a saw is capable of cutting wood— can be negated by proper forms of disclaimer that put the buyer on notice of a probable deformity in the product [133]. To be sure, recent decisions in the area of product liability have somewhat ameliorated the hardships and frustrations to consumers from disclaimer provisions by granting at least limited recoveries notwithstanding terms of disclaimer [134]. And, on occasion, in view of the particular facts before them, courts have refused to enforce the disclaimer provisions of adhesion or unconscionable contracts, reforming the contract to eliminate these and other unfair provisions or granting rescission of the entire contract because of its unconscionable terms [135]. But such relief is only sporadic and normally restricted to cases of great disparity between the sophistication and bargaining power of the buyer and the seller.

Second, even the warranties that purport to give unlimited guarantees are often more honored by breach than by observance, for which no one factor is inevitably to blame. Inadequate facilities for repair or replacement, poor compensation for warranty service, unskilled repairmen, and low public esteem or prestige for their callings, all contribute to the problem of the unsatisfied customer [136]. Not to be discounted, either, is the consumer's own contribution to the problem by carelessness, misuse, and general failure to heed operating instructions [137].

Given the multifaceted causes, it may be too simplistic to demand that the unsatisfied consumer be mollified automatically by cost-free replacement or servicing of a product about which he complains [138]. Yet the inequities of our current hit-or-miss approach are documented in a fairly recent, already classic study of servicing and warranties in the automotive industries and support a strong case for enterprise liability without regard to fault [139]. According to the findings, the customers who received the best warranty and repair service were those most highly valued by the service establishment, with little correlation to who or what was at fault in the auto's state of disrepair. The less valued are presumably left to decorate their cars to resemble giant lemons, then to burn or bury or hatchet them to oblivion amidst rites of publicity-seeking sensation.

A novel and more democratic step toward solving complaints of inadequate product performance was recently enacted by the California legislature in the Song-Beverly Warranty Act [140]. Beyond providing that the implied warranties of merchantability and fitness can be disclaimed only if no express warranties are given [141], and only on condition that the product is clearly affixed with a warning label of its defective condition [142], the Act additionally imposes an affirmative requirement that repair facilities for all but certain excepted products must be provided within the state by anyone—manufacturer, distributor, or retailer—making express warranties for the product [143]. Although the consumer may be required to bear certain costs of repair, such as by purchase of an insurance contract for service [144], the product must be repaired within a designated time (normally 30 days) or otherwise its cost (less that attributable to use of the product by the buyer) must be reimbursed [145]. Willful failure to comply with these requirements gives rise to treble damages plus reasonable attorney fees [146]. The legislative solution thus furnishes a compromised solution in lieu of prolonged battles in which no one wins.

FORUMS FOR PRIVATE RELIEF

Judicial Actions
The quest for justice for consumers through the traditional forum of private litigation has had a relatively poor track record to date. When victimized by a fraudulent trickster, the consumer may be either unwilling or ignorant of the right to bring suit, or unable to marshall the legal mechanisms to assert his claim before his wrongdoer has fled the jurisdiction or squandered the ill gains. Then too, if the consumer manages to press suit, he faces the unattractive prospects of prolonged litigation, requiring exacting burdens of proof to establish the adversary's default or malfeasance and to negate the consumer's contributory negligence or assumption of risk. And too often the typical complaint, although high in frustration value, is too slight in monetary terms to warrant the time and expense of court action.

The highly publicized class action technique has been both heralded and villified as a possible answer to the dilemma [147]. Proponents argue that by authorizing the banding together of a class of consumers having common interests—those who have suffered similar injuries at the hands of the defendant arising out of a similar set of facts and whose relief would be readily divisible if awarded in lump sum to the class—the class action would inspire suit by those whose claims seemed otherwise too insignificant individually to pursue; would represent significant savings in litigation costs; free court calendars from current overcongestion; and incidentally, as a by-product of the numbers involved, give publicity to wrongful practices to put others on guard against similar abuse.

But for many of these same reasons the business community has feared the spectre of class action suits; the likelihood of harrassment by the undeserving who now have little to lose by bringing suit; the danger of blackmailing the defendant into settlement because the threatened adverse precipitous publicity on filing the action would not be erased from the public's mind even were the defendant ultimately vindicated in court.

The circumstances in which class actions are appropriate maneuvers are still being refined by legislatures and courts. Several variations of bills have been bottled up before Congress [148], the more restrictive variety requiring a triggering mechanism of approval by some designated federal agency as a condition precedent to the consumer class suit, but even this version has not mollified the concerns of the business community over the possibility of frivolous suits. At the state level, other experimental restraints have been proposed or adopted: carefully supervised pretrial hearings before a judge to demonstrate the good faith nature of the case and to allow for pretrial settlement through appropriate correction, repair, replacement, or other remedy by the merchant [149]; limitations on the amount and type of damages allowable in a class suit [150]. Still other local laws leave enforcement primarily to a consumer spokesman whose responsibilities are clarified in model legislation [151].

Whereas some state courts have taken a liberal view of the rights of consumers to band together to press their rights [152], the United States Supreme Court has issued two decisions that will seriously impede such future efforts: *Snyder v. Harris* [153], refusing to allow aggregation of consumer claims in determining whether the $10,000 jurisdictional limit in diversity cases has been satisfied; and the recent *Eisen* case [154], which interprets Federal Rule 23(c)(2) as requiring that a person bringing a class action give individual notice to every member of the class who can be identified with reasonable effort (here 2.5 million persons), regardless of the cost of notification.

The limited experience with class actions to this time makes it difficult to assess to what degree they can and will produce meaningful protections for consumers without exposing business to undue suits. Important empirical studies on class actions in selected jurisdictions have recently published preliminary results [155] that may confirm the disillusioning individual experience reported by Schrag [156] of endless delays, sparring over preliminaries, a host of dilatory tactics by defendants to wear down the fund of patience and money available to press the consumer's cause.

Few class actions in the recent surveys have been concluded successfully for the consumer, but too many are yet pending to warrant a definitive judgment at this point. What conclusion does seem safe, based on numerous reported interviews with counsel for defendants, is that the fears of blackmail or harrassment by worthless claims have proved virtually groundless.

Public Suits—Agency Actions

A variation of the class action device of a private individual undertaking suit as a representative of others in the class is the action by a public agency that seeks private redress for individuals as a supplement to the injunction or other public relief sought by the suit [157]. The procedure has advantages as well as deficiencies. Whereas the business community may view the governmental agency as more trustworthy than individual consumers not to bring frivolous or unwarranted suits, the consumer may fear that the remote agency will not be as effective or tenacious as the individual in pressing for redress [158].

On the other hand, there are some grievances that would otherwise go totally unredressed without agency intervention—those where the defendant is outside the aggrieved's jurisdiction, or has committed an offense for which either no authority or no prospect of private litigation exists [159]. At any rate, the use of government to secure private relief has been quite circumscribed to date, the courts tending to disallow this unless the enabling legislation seems clearly to authorize such action—a limitation that may well be wise given the relative merits of private over public suit and the political reality of limited agency budgets that should be spent in the most economic fashion to push for public goods [160].

Small Claims Courts

In theory, the institution of small claims courts appears to be an optimum solution to the mountain of costs and delays that often dissuades the consumer from seeking to remedy his grievance in court. The small claims court is designed for expeditious, relatively inexpensive resolution of small matters by its jurisdictional limits on the amounts and form of recovery (such as California's $500 maximum and no injunctive or other specific equitable forms of relief), and its barring of attorneys from appearing in representative capacities.

Despite its even-handed design, in practice the typical consumer finds himself at serious disadvantage [161]. His sporadic or once-in-a-lifetime venture into court may be matched against a professional representative of business who is in court on such causes on a regular basis, who is paid to make such appearances, and need not fear (as might the consumer) a loss of employment for spending his working hours in court rather than on his job [162]. Deadlines for appearance or response may go unheeded by the consumer, or he may be so awed by the legal jargon and pretension as to be tongue-tied when called on to present his case. Not so his learned adversary.

Aware of the failings that in practice have kept the small claims court from fulfilling its promise, recent innovations have been introduced in an effort to restore the balance. Legal aid experts sitting in the wings have offered counsel, short of court appearance, to the consumer. And in court, judges have sometimes undertaken responsibility to see that justice is done, asking for mockups or other evidence to substantiate a case against the consumer before default judgment may be taken. Night court has been instituted to accommodate the individual who is not free to attend during working hours, and the legalese has been reduced to more understandable versions.

Yet for all these reforms, there are still significant numbers and groups in the land, particularly those who are undereducated and in the lower socioeconomic class, who refuse to seek help in the courts, believing, for obvious reasons, that the systemized establishment is not their friend [163]. For those many who are intimidated or insufficiently motivated to proceed to court, the answer may rest in neighborhood conciliation or mediation centers [164]. Obviously, there may be shortcomings—inequalities in the level of sophistication of the parties, a defect already developed in Small Claims Courts [165]; the dangers of nonadherence to an adverse decision or of results that yield one-sided justice.

To date, the experiments are too young to judge. Yet the hopeful experiences of Better Business Bureaus, Chambers of Commerce, and businesses' own internal complaint centers in bringing about customer satisfaction by ventures at conciliation suggest that mediation too can succeed in voluntary dispute resolution. After all, the consumer's only remaining alternative may be the extrajudicial pressure of picketing and boycotts, and this for business could spell the ultimate private sanction—loss of customer good will.

NOTES TO CHAPTER 14

1. For an interesting historical treatment of the doctrine's bastard origin and reign, see generally Hamilton, "The Ancient Maxim Caveat Emptor," 40 *Yale Law Journal* 1133 (1931).

2. See Henningsen v. Bloomfield Motors Inc., 32 N.J. 358, 161 A.2d 69 (1960). See also Seavey, "Caveat Emptor As of 1960," 38 *Texas Law Review* 439, 441 [1960]:

Medieval England was a land of farms and small towns. Most of the trading was between neighbors who were familiar with each other; the dealing with strangers was largely done at fairs which were held periodically at the larger towns. To these fairs came traveling merchants with their ideas of business morality derived from the Oriental bazaars in which no trust was given or expected—a point of view thoroughly understood by the courts of Pei Poudre in which disputes between the merchants were settled. It is not strange that the phrase caveat emptor was accepted as indicating the standard, nor that the Kings' courts refused to grant a remedy to a deceived buyer in a transaction in which the seller had not expressly warranted his statement to be true.

But the finding of a warranty would entitle the buyer to relief. Compare Chandelor v. Lopus, 79 Eng. Rep. 3 (Ex. 1603), with Storrs v. Emerson, 72 Iowa 390, 34 N.W. 176 (1887).

3. See S. Oppenheim & G. Weston, *Unfair Trade Practices and Consumer Protection* 1–2 (3d ed. 1974).

4. *Ibid.* See also Barber, "Government and the Consumer," 64 *Michigan Law Review* 1203, 1226 (1966): "To sum up, modern consumer markets are a long way removed from those that classical economics presupposed. Sellers are few and confine their rivalry to nonprice factors. Products, though fungible, are differentiated through advertising, packaging, and other tricks of contemporary merchandising. Price data are often vague or misleading. Finally, the growing impersonality of retailing makes the situation worse. If the consumer, now drifting aimlessly on a great sea of irrelevant information, is to be placed in a position where he can make informed purchase decisions, governmental action is essential." But see R. Posner, *Economic Analysis of Law* § 3.6 (1973).

5. "The new drive for consumer protection began in the late 1920s and early 1930s with the publication of several popular books on the abuses of advertising and the sale of adulterated products. When Stuart Chase and F.J. Schlink published *Your Money's Worth* in 1927, it became an immediate bestseller. It pictured the consumer as an Alice in Wonderland of conflicting product claims and bright promises and pleaded for impartial product-testing agencies." Gaedke, "The Movement for Consumer Protection: A Century of Mixed Accomplishments," *University of Washington Business Review* (Spring 1970), pp. 31–35.

6. Farmers, in particular, were the impetus for much of the early regulation. See M. Nadel, *The Politics of Consumer Protection*, pp. 6–9, 28–29 (1971).

7. Ibid., pp. 11–12; Gaedke, pp. 32–33.

8. *See, e.g.*, Nadel, chapter 2; *cf.* Aaker and Day, "Introduction: A Guide to Consumerism," in *Consumerism: Search for the Consumer Interest* (1971).

9. R. Carson, *Silent Spring* (1962).

10. J.K. Galbraith, *The Affluent Society* (1958).

11. R. Nader, *Unsafe at any Speed* (1965).

12. V. Packard, *The Hidden Persuaders* (1957) and *The Waste Makers* (1960).

13. President John F. Kennedy, Special Message on Protecting the Consumer Interest (March 15, 1962).

14. For an elaboration of the four rights covered by the presidential message, see Executive Office of the President, Consumer Advisory Council, First Report (U.S. Government Printing Office, October 1963).

15. For brief discussions of the highlights of the legislative activity, with acknowledgements that the outburst of legislation did not mean the millenium had come, See W. Magnuson and J. Carper, *The Dark Side of the Marketplace* Intro. (Prism ed., 1972); Aaker and Day, op. cit.

16. See Gaedke, op. cit.; Nadel, op. cit.

17. See for example, Nadel, pp. 28–29.

18. PUB. L. No. 87–781 (October 10). The background to passage and shift in focus of the hearings in response to the tragedy is fully discussed in Nadel, pp. 121–30.

19. PUB. L. No. 89–563 (Sept. 9, 1966), discussed in Nadel, pp. 137–43.

20. See Magnuson and Carper, chapter 5.

21. Nadel, p. 183; Bishop and Hubbard, "Danger," in *Consumerism*, pp. 297–303. Equally provacative was the jingle published by *The Evening Post* during the era of Upton Sinclair's exposé of the Chicago meat packing industry:
"Mary had a little lamb
And when she saw it sicken
She shipped it off to Packingtown
And now it's labeled 'chicken'." Ibid., p. 297.

22. Consumer Credit Protection Act, 15 U.S.C.A. § 1601 ff. The background to passage is examined as a case study in Nadel, pp. 130–37.

23. Fair Packaging and Labeling Act, 15 U.S.C.A. § 1451 ff.

24. Some of the struggles that Senator Hart encountered in securing enactment of the law are detailed in Hart, "Can Federal Legislation Affecting Consumers' Economic Interests Be Enacted?", 64 *Michigan Law Review* 1255 (1966).

25. See 115 CONG. REC. 2410 (1969) (remarks of Senator Proxmire).

26. 15 U.S.C.A. § 1681 ff.

27. Cox, Fellmeth, and Schulz: *The "Nader Report" on the Federal Trade Commission* (New York: Baron, 1969). See also ABA, Report of the Commission to Study the Federal Trade Commission (1969).

28. For example: "As originally conceived and introduced, the purpose of the [Truth in Packaging] bill was to facilitate price and quantity comparison of retail grocery items by shoppers—in short, to introduce price competition in the supermarket. It was to accomplish these objectives by package size standardization which would allow a simple price comparison. This provision was eliminated from the bill and the substitute version merely allowed for voluntary limitation of a number of package sizes plus such minor features as prohibiting the use of qualifying adjectives before statements of quantity (e.g., ten jumbo ounces). Again, the result reflected the intensity of industry opposition." Nadel, p. 229. See generally Forte, "The Fair Packaging and Labeling Act: Its Legislative History, Content, and Future, *Vanderbilt Law Review* 761 (1968).

29. Thus, results proved nearly equivalent in shopping tests conducted before and after enactment of the Truth in Packaging Law, as reported in "What's Happened to Truth in Packaging?" *Consumer Reports* 24 (January 1969).

30. "For example, there is evidence that the truth-in-lending bill will not achieve the original goals, partly because of lack of understanding of the problem and partly because of inadequacies and confusion in the enacted legislation. Similarly, it is dismaying that after two years of experience with the truth-in-packaging bill it is being referred to as 'one of the best non-laws in the book.' In this particular situation the problem seems to lie with the interest and ability of the various regulatory agencies to implement the law." Asker and Day, *supra* note 8, pp. 16–17.

31. See Oppenheim and Weston, p. 751.

32. *Ibid.*

33. Consumer Product Safety Act, 15 U.S.C.A. § 2051 ff.

34. National Commission on Product Safety, *Final Report* (1970).

35. Senate Comm. on Commerce, 93d Cong., 2d Sess., *Class Action Study* (Comm. Print June 1974).

36. See Uniform Consumer Credit Code. See generally B. Curran, *Trends in Consumer Financing* (1965).

37. See CAL. EDUC. CODE § 29035 (West Supp. 1974).

38. See CAL. CIV. CODE § 1812.51 ff.; 1812.81 ff. (West, 1973).

39. CAL. BUS. & PROF. CODE § 9800 ff. (West Supp. 1974).

40. Ibid. See Note, "Regulation of Automative Repair Services," 56 *Cornell Law Review* 1010 (1971).

41. See Oppenheim Weston, pp. 543–44.

42. Ibid.; accord, Magnuson and Carper, pp. 31–33.

43. See text at notes 67–81 *infra.*

44. See Keeton, "Products Liability—Liability Without Fault and The Requirement of a Defect," 41 *Texas Law Review* 855 (1963); Prosser, "The Assault Upon the Citadel (Strict Liability to the Consumer)," 69 *Yale Law Journal* 1099 (1960), and "The Fall of the Citadel (Strict Liability to the Consumer)," 50 *Minnesota Law Review* 791 (1966).

44a. For some statistical compilations, see Bishop & Hubbard, pp. 283–303. See also the reported studies of the National Commission on Product Safety.

45. The leading case in the early assault on the citadel of privity was MacPherson v. Buick Motor Co., 217 N.Y. 382, 111 N.E. 1050 (1916).

46. The next giant onslaught against the citadel came with the leading case of Henningsen v. Bloomfield Motors, Inc., 32 N.J. 358, 161 A.2d 69 (1960).

47. See Greenman v. Yuba Power Products, 59 Cal.2d 57, 27 Cal. Rptr. 697, 377 P.2d 897 (1963) (opinion by Chief Justice Traynor). See generally Morris, "Enterprise Liability and the Actuarial Process—The Insignificance of Foresight," 70 *Yale Law Journal* 554 (1961).

Another related rationale for enterprise liability is that such allocation of loss, without regard to fault, can produce an economic savings as the "cheapest cost avoider." See Calabresi, "Does the Fault System Optimally Control Primary Accident Costs?", 33 *Law & Contemporary Problems* 429, 447–49 (1968).

48. See Kessler, "Contracts of Adhesion—Some Thoughts About Freedom of Contract," 43 *Columbia Law Review* 629 (1943).

49. See Unico v. Owen, 50 N.J. 101, 232 A.2d 405 (1967).

50. Unconscionable Contract or Clause:

"(1) If the court as a matter of law finds the contract or any clause of the contract to have been unconscionable at the time it was made the court may refuse to enforce the contract, or it may enforce the remainder of the contract without the unconscionable clause, or it may so limit the application of any unconscionable clause as to avoid any unconscionable result.

"(2) When it is claimed or appears to the court that the contract or any clause thereof may be unconscionable the parties shall be afforded a reasonable opportunity to present evidence as to its commercial settings, purpose and effect to aid the court in making the determination."

UCC, § 2–302. See generally P. Keeton and M. Shapo, *Products and The Consumer: Deceptive Practices* (1972), pp. 110–41.

51. See notes 71 and 135 *infra*, and accompanying texts.

52. U.S. Constitution Amendment XIV.

53. Lynch v. Household Finance Corp., 405 U.S. 538 (1972); Sniadich v. Family Finance Corp., 395 U.S. 337 (1969). See also Fuentes v. Shevin, 407 U.S. 67 (1972).

54. See, for example, McKean "Products Liability: Trends and Implications, in P. Keeton and M. Shapo, *Products and the Consumer: Defective and Dangerous Products* 1233 (1970), criticizing the paucity of careful analytical discussion and consideration of the consequences of assigning liability according to the theory of enterprise liability; also Morris, "Enterprise Liability and the Actuarial Process—the Insignificance of Foresight," 70 *Yale Law Journal* 554 (1961), stressing the uncertainty of whether labor, capital or consumers in fact bear the incidence of enterprise liability.

55. For an empirical study corroborating such conclusion, see Comment, "Case Study of the Impact of Consumer Legislation: The Elimination of Negotiability and the Cooling-Off Period," 78 *Yale Law Journal* 618 (1969).

56. This is indeed the test employed by the Consumer Product Safety Act.

57. See, for example, the test enunciated by the National Commission on Product Safety, *Final Report* (1970), pp. 10–11: "In assessing individual hazards, we studied data relating frequency, severity, duration, and sequelae of injury to the frequency and degree of exposure to the product. Other variables we looked at were the degree of inherent risk, the essentiality of the product, and the feasibility and approximate cost of safety improvements.

We also considered whether there were acceptable alternatives for a hazardous product; effects on the product of aging and wear; the contribution to hazards of defective maintenance and repair; exposure to instructions or warnings; influence of product advertising or behavior; the extent and forms of abnormal uses of the product; effects of storage, distribution and disposal; and characteristics of the persons injured, including age, sex, skills, training, and experience.

Beyond the foregoing guidelines for defining "unreasonable hazards," we believe that no completely satisfactory definition is possible. Prof. Corwin D. Edwards of the University of Oregon has presented an excellent statement which supplements our guidelines:

'Risks of bodily harm to users are not unreasonable when consumers understand that risks exist, can appraise their probability and severity, know how to cope with them, and voluntarily accept them to get benefits that could not be obtained in less risky ways. When there is a risk of this character, consumers have reasonable opportunity to protect themselves; and public authorities should hesitate to substitute their value judgments about the desirability of the risk for those of the consumers who choose to incur it.

But preventable risk is not reasonable (a) when consumers do not know that it exists; or (b) when, though aware of it, consumers are unable to estimate its frequency and severity; or (c) when consumers do not know how to cope with it, and hence are likely to incur harm unnecessarily; or (d) when risk is unnecessary in . . . that it could be reduced or eliminated at a cost in money or in the performance of the product that consumers would willingly incur if they knew the facts and were given the choice.' "

58. For example, *compare* Posner §3.6, with Barber, "Government and the Consumer," *supra* note 4.

59. See Posner, chapter 15.

60. See Jordan and Warren "The Uniform Consumer Credit Code," 68 *Columbia Law Review* 387, 388–94 (1968).

61. The typical shopping patterns of the poor are described in Caplowitz, *The Poor Pay More* (1967); Note, "Consumer Legislation and the Poor, 76 *Yale Law Journal* 745 (1967).

62. Thus, do our current norms of regulation take into account the differing internalization processes of consumers in decision making or the varying noneconomic reasons that differ person to person, such as desires for status, self-esteem, or a product that fits one's own self-image? *Compare* Birdwell, "A Study of the Influence of Image Congruence on Consumer Choice," 41 *Journal of Business of the University of Chicago.* 76 (1968).

63. See generally Caplowitz, "Consumer Credit in the Affluent Society," 33 *Law and Contemporary Problems* 642 (1968).

64. Holloway v. Bristol-Meyers Corp., 485 F.2d 986 (D.C. Cir. 1973).

65. Ibid.; *cf.* Kugler v. Romain, 58 N.J. 522, 279 A. 2d 640 (1971).

66. See generally Posner, chapter 23.

67. Compare Kessler "Contracts of Adhesion—Some Thoughts About Freedom of Contract," pp. 629–32, with Posner, §3.1.

68. See generally W. Prosser, *Law of Torts* §105 at 685–86 (4th ed. 1971).

69. Posner, §3.4.

70. Compare Justice Oliver Wendell Holmes' observation in Deming v. Darling, 148 Mass. 504, 20 N.E. 107 (1889), that: "The rule of law is hardly to be regretted, when it is considered how easily and insensibly words of hope or expectation are converted by an interested memory into statements of value or

quality when the expectation is disappointed. . . ." However, puffing could become an integral part of the bargain, in which case" 'Puffing' should cease to be privileged at least when the speaker should know that it will be taken as representing the truth." Seavey, "Caveat Emptor as of 1960," *supra* note 2, p. 442.

See also Keeton, "Fraud: Misrepresentation of Opinion," 21 *Minnesota Law Review*, pp. 643, 669–70 (1937): "Some have argued that a rule of nonliability is sound social policy in that it induces people to rely on their own opinions rather than on opinions of others, especially in that type of case where reasonable men might differ. . . . It does not seem to have been emphasized sufficiently by commentators and courts that the fundamental reason why non-liability for intentional misstatements of opinion has prevailed in large measure, even today, is because society has not advanced to the stage where all such conduct is regarded as unfair. The point emphasized is that this is a question of fair conduct, just as non-disclosure is a question of fair conduct. The assumption is often made that whenever one person intends to benefit himself at the expense of another, such conduct is unfair; generally speaking, it is, but community sentiment does not condemn all conduct which the moral philosopher would condemn, and present day jurists point out that the law cannot hope to apply a standard too far in advance of the spirit of the time and place. . . . In truth, community sentiment does not condemn a vendor for using what has been called 'trade talk' or 'puffing' to deceive a vendee who is a stranger, but it does condemn the same action if the vendee was a close friend of the vendor. The test, in all cases, is what the ordinary ethical man would have done under the same circumstances, this fictitious person being endowed with the crystallized sentiment of the community."

71. The test of whether a contract or clause is unconscionable, and hence potentially unenforceable, generally turns on factors indicating peculiar vulnerability of the consumer. See Williams v. Walker-Thomas Furniture Co., 121 U.S. App. D. C. 315, 350 F.2d 445 (1965). See generally Ellinghaus, "In Defense of Unconscionability," 78 *Yale Law Journal* 757 (1969), Leff, "Unconscionability and the Code—The Emperor's New Clause," 115 *University of Pennsylvania Law Review* 485 (1967); Murray, "Unconscionability: Unconscionability," 31 *University of Pittsburgh Law Review* 1 (1969); Speidel, "Unconscionability, Assent and Consumer Protection," 31 *University of Pittsburgh Law Review* 359 (1970).

72. See Ultramares Corp. v. Touche, Niven & Co., 225 N.Y. 170, 174 N.E. 441 (1931), distinguishing the scope of a defendant's liability for negligent vis à vis intentional misrepresentations.

73. A number of states have adopted the Uniform Deceptive Trade Practices Act, a detailed listing of unfair and deceptive practices that was analyzed and discussed by its principal draftsman in Dole, "Uniform Deceptive Trade Practices Act; A Prefatory Note," 54 *Trademark Reports* 435 (1964). See also Dole, "Merchant and Consumer Protection: The Unfair Deceptive Trade Practices Act," 76 *Yale Law Journal* 485 (1967); Hester, "Deceptive Sales Practices and Form Contracts—Does the Consumer Have A Private Remedy?", 1968 *Duke Law Journal* 831. Several other states have adopted variations of The Uniform Consumer Sales Practices Act, which contains eleven specified deceptive acts or practices in consumer transactions that are actionable as a basis for private con-

sumer relief. See Dole, Henson and Richter, "The Uniform Consumer Sales Practices Act," 27 *Business Law* 139 (1971); Rice, "A Uniform Consumer Sales Practices Act—Damage Remedies: The NCCUSL Giveth and Taketh Away," 67 N.W.U.L. REV. 369 (1972), criticizing the restrictive remedy provisions that effectively negate the high standards set by the Act's substantive provisions. *Cf.* California Consumer Legal Remedies Act, California Civil Code § 1750 *ff.* (West, 1973), discussed by the legislative assistant to the Act's author, in Reed, "Legislating for the Consumer: An Insider's Analysis of the Consumers Legal Remedies Act," 2 *Pacific Law Journal* 1 (1971).

74. See Federal Trade Commission, *Report on District of Columbia Consumer Protection Program*, Attachment A (1968); FTC, Report to the Bureau of the Budget on Suggested State Legislation (1969). The Council of State Governments, in conjunction with the FTC, drafted a Model Act based on such a proposal. See Council of State Governments, Consumer Protection in the States (1970); Council of State Governments, Suggested State Legislation for 1970, Appendix (1969).

75. See National Consumer Law Center, National Consumer Act: A Model for Consumer Protection (1970). See also Magnuson and Carper, p. 64: "In writing the FTC law (it was first passed in 1914 and amended in 1938), Congress was remarkably far-sighted in making it all-inclusive—not only to meet the unfair and deceptive practices of the day but to cope with future problems, those unforeseen schemes that, as Senator Thomas J. Walsh of Montana said when debating the bill, would inevitably arise out of 'the ingenuity of the adroit rogue.' Rather than enumerate the schemes to be outlawed, Congress wisely made the FTC law flexible enough to outlaw any deceptive practice—past, present, or future."

76. See Magnuson and Carper, chapters 1 and 2, for a highly readable account of the tragedies befalling consumers lured into the quicksand of deceptive practices.

77. See, for example, California Civil Code § 1803.10 (West, 1973); Uniform Consumer Credit Code § 2.411.

78. See State by Lefkowitz v. ITM, Inc., 52 Misc. 2d 39, 275 N.Y.S.2d 303 (1966), holding that, since "somewhere along the line, the plan had to fail as a matter of economic feasibility and mathematical certainty . . . the promoters must be charged with knowledge of the fraud inherent in it." See also Sherwood and Roberts, Yakima, Inc. v. Leach, 67 Wash. 2d 630, 409 P.2d 160 (1965).

79. *Id.* See generally Comment, "Let the "Seller" Beware—Another Approach to the Referral Sales Scheme," 22 *University of Miami Law Review* 861 (1968).

80. See Magnuson and Carper, pp. 14–17.

81. Ibid., pp. 22–26; 39–41.

82. Uniform Consumer Credit Code § 2.405.

83. Ibid. § 2.415; cf. Littlefield, "Preserving Consumer Defenses: Plugging the Loophole in the New UCCC," 44 *New York University Law Review* 277, 292 (1969), arguing for outright prohibition of waiver of defense clauses in contracts on the grounds that the mere presence of such a clause, although unenforceable, may be used by the disreputable to cajole an uncounselled consumer into payment.

84. *Cf.* Fuentes v. Shevin, 407 U.S. 67,91 at n.22 (1972): "A prior hearing always imposes some costs in time, effort and expense, and it is often more efficient to dispense with the opportunity for such a hearing. But these rather ordinary costs cannot outweigh the constitutional right. . . . Procedural due process is not intended to promote efficiency or accommodate all possible interests: it is intended to protect the particular interests of the person whose possessions are about to be taken."

" 'The establishment of prompt efficacious procedures to achieve legitimate state ends is a proper state interest worthy of cognizance in constitutional adjudication. But the Constitution recognizes higher values than speed and efficiency. Indeed, one might fairly say of the Bill of Rights in general, and the Due Process clause in particular, that they were designed to protect the fragile values of a vulnerable citizenry from the overbearing concern for efficiency and efficacy. . . .' "

85. See, for example, Unico v. Owen, 50 N.J. 101, 232 A.2d 405 (1967). See generally Rosenthal, "Negotiability—Who Needs It?" 71 *Columbia Law Review* 375 (1971).

86. A holder in due course is defined in Uniform Commercial Code § 3–302.

87. Univo v. Owen, *supra* note 85 (dictum).

88. See, for example, Uniform Consumer Credit Code § 2–404. See generally Jordan and Warren, *The Uniform Consumer Credit Code* [hereinafter cited as Jordan and Warren], 68 *Columbia Law Review* 387, 433–38 (1968).

89. "The consumer sues the merchant only once or episodically. The financer, even though it does not control the merchant or participate in the breach of warranty, ordinarily has a continuing relationship with him and some experience of his performance of warranties. The financer is certainly better equipped with staff to check the merchant's reputation for reliability and fair dealing. It is submitted that the risk of cases of legitimate customer dissatisfaction should be thrown on the financer. The financer is best able to force redress by maintaining an action over against the merchant. . . . Moreover, such a rule would cut off the sources of credit of a merchant with repeated bad warranty relations with his creditors.

The clinching argument is the contrast between the legal relationships in consumer financing and the legal relationships in the financing of commercial accounts receivable. In that field the financing institutions, many of which are also engaged in the consumer field, have never sought to extend to the commercial field their assertion that they are entitled to freedom from customer defenses. There is one simple reason for this: the commercial buyers would not stand for it, for the purchase contracts in the commercial field are not contracts of adhesion. What then happens to the question of freedom from defenses in the commercial field? The financer as part of its credit determination studies the experience of the seller in respect to cusomer complaints and returned goods, and if the percentage is too high, refuses to do business with that merchant. The same type of credit thinking would provide the answer in the consumer field." Kripke, "Consumer Credit Regulation," 68 *Columbia Law Review* 445, 472 (1968) (footnotes omitted.)

90. The effect of such reallocation of costs is documented by empirical study in Comment, "Case Study of the Impact of Consumer Legislation: The Elimination of Negotiability and the Cooling-Off Period," 78 *Yale Law Journal* 618 (1968). This in turn raises the spectre of financing institutions shifting to a new and perhaps more costly "pattern of direct lending, perhaps utilizing innovative procedures yet to be devised." Murray, "Another 'Assault Upon the Citadel': Limiting the Use of Negotiable Notes and Waiver-of-Defense Clauses in Consumer Sales," 29 *Ohio State Law Journal* 667, 686 (1968); Note, "Consumer Defenses and Financers as Holders in Due Course," 4 *Connecticut Law Review* 83 (1971). But see Note, "Direct Loan Financing of Consumer Purchases," 85 *Harvard Law Review* 1409 (1972), proposing that even the unrelated lender be subject to defenses because of the lender's superior ability to police the seller's conduct and spread the costs of misconduct.

91. For example, see Unico v. Owen, *supra* note 85; Henningsen v. Bloomfield Motors, 32 N.J. 358, 161 A.2d 69 (1960).

92. Compare Posner § 3.7, with Kessler, "Contracts of Adhesion—Some Thoughts About Freedom of Contract," 43 *Columbia Law Review* 629 (1943).

93. See authorities cited in notes 71 *supra*, and 135 *infra*.

94. See, for example, Holton, "Government-Consumer Interest Conflicts and Prospects," in *Changing Market Systems* (Chicago: American Marketing Association 1967).

95. See generally text at notes 68–81 *supra*.

96. *E.g.*, California Civil Code § 1792.4 (West, 1973).

97. See David, "Potential Contributions of Social Science Research to Consumer Welfare," 1 *Journal of Consumer Affairs* 105, 108–09 (1967):

"The shopper standing in a department store ought to have immediate access to data pertinent to the performance of a durable that he contemplates buying. Repair frequency, the quality of local servicing, and a comparative summary of features and cost in competing models all ought to be broadcast to the consumer via closed circuit TV on the salesroom floor. Moreover, such a summary ought to include frequency distributions of prices paid for comparable durables in recent sales and information on the range of cost in currently available credit. The consumer might also be advised of the comparative cost of owned durables, leasing plans, and outright purchase."

98. See note 29 *supra*.

99. For example, see Kripke, "Gesture and Reality in Consumer Credit Reform," 44 *New York University Law Review* 1 (1969); Note, "Truth in Lending: The Impossible Dream," 22 *Case Western Reserve Law Review* 89, 107–12 (1970).

100. See FTC, *Economic Report on Installment Credit and Retail Sales Practices in the District of Columbia* (1968).

101. White and Munger, "Consumer Sensitivity to Interest Rates: An Empirical Study of New Car Buyers and Auto Loans, 69 *Michigan Law Review* 1207 (1971).

216 The Role of the Courts

102. See, for example, Birdwell, "A Study of the Influence of Image Congruence on Consumer Choice," 41 *Journal of Business of the University of Chicago* 76 (1968). See generally C. Bell, *Consumer Choice in the American Economy* (1970).

103. See generally Sher, "The 'Cooling Off' Period in Door-to-Door Sales," 15 *UCLA Law Review* 717 (1968).

104. See Warren, "Direct Selling Industry: An Empirical Study," 16 *UCLA Law Review* 883 (1969).

105. See State v. Direct Sellers Ass'n, 108 Ariz. 165, 494 P.2d 361 (1972).

106. See Holland Furnace Co. v. F.T.C., 295 F.2d 302 (7th Cir. 1961).

107. Comment, "Case Study of the Impact of Consumer Legislation: The Elimination of Negotiability and the Cooling-Off Period," 78 *Yale Law Journal* 618 (1968).

108. "It would have been an astonishing coincidence if the nineteenth-century system of collection laws—garnishment, wage assignments, deficiency, judgments, default judgments, repossessions, and so forth—which was conceived long before the consumer entered the credit arena, had been found appropriate in the hard-sell, easy-credit mass consumer market of the latter third of the twentieth century. These creditors' remedies are the product of an age when easy credit terms were not available, and community attitudes toward use of credit were strict; credit was reluctantly extended and warily accepted. Credit transactions were entered into with somewhat more equality of bargaining power and economic sophistication than is the case today, for the lower economic groups were not yet important participants in the credit market. The traditional remedies allowed a creditor to drive a defaulting debtor to the well. Society's only important protections for the debtor were the state exemption laws and the Federal Bankruptcy Act.

Current methods of high-pressure selling and lending make it easy for the consumer to become overcommitted. Full use of the arsenal of remedies available to the creditor—repossession, deficiency judgment, and garnishment—can leave the defaulting consumer with no goods, no job, and a substantial judgment against him. The impact of the traditional structure of creditors' remedies upon the consumer can be so catastrophic that pressure for reform on the part of consumer groups is mounting. Garnishment, wage assignments, deficiency judgments, and the holder-in-due-course concept have all come under increasing legislative attack at both state and federal levels. While the emphasis in consumer credit legislation over the past decade has been on disclosure of finance charges, indications are strong that the next ten years will focus attention on remedies." Jordan and Warren, *supra* note 88, at 433 (footnotes omitted).

See also Comment, "Consumer Protection Under the UCCC and the NCA—A Comparison and Recommendations," 12 *Arizona Law Review* 572, 573–586 (1970).

109. For example, the amount of the original debt may have been augmented by interest, loading charges, and legal fees or other costs of default.

Numerous illustrations of this phenomenon, and the desperation it provokes, are presented in Magnuson and Carper, chapter 2.

110. See California Civil Code § § 1812.2–.4 (West, 1973).

111. See Kripke, "Consumer Credit Regulation: A Creditor-Oriented Viewpoint" 68 *Columbia Law Review* 445, 469–73 (1968). But see W. Hogan and W. Warren, *Commercial and Consumer Transactions* 715–16 (1972), suggesting that restricting deficiency judgments may produce the beneficial result of limiting extension of credit to the noncreditworthy.

112. See Uniform Consumer Credit Code §5.103, prohibiting deficiency judgments in consumer sales if the amount financed is $1,000 or less.

113. A case in point is the decision that held Cutter Laboratories strictly liable to victims who contracted polio as a result of Salk vaccine inoculations. Gottsdanker v. Cutter Laboratories, 182 Cal. App. 2d 602, 6 Cal. Rptr. 320 (1960). The inevitable impact of holding Cutter Labs liable despite the jury's finding of lack of negligence was to magnify drug manufacturers' costs and need for product liability insurance and deter them from expeditious development and marketing of other promising new drugs which, as was true of the polio vaccine, could produce tremendous public benefits in drastically reducing the numbers who would otherwise have been stricken by disease. See Willis, "Product Liability Without Fault—Some Problems and Proposals," 15 *Food Drug Cosmetic Law Journal* 648 (1960). For a criticism of the court's decision, see Note, "Strict Liability For Drug Manufacturers: Public Policy Misconceived," 13 *Stanford Law Review* 645 (1961).

114. But see the proposals advanced by authorities, *id.*, for revised forms of insurance or governmental subsidization as alternative means of stimulating production without forfeiting a consumer's right to redress.

115. While it is clear that consumers must bear some responsibility for preserving their own rights, the law is unsettled as to the appropriate norm of conduct to exact. For example, should relief be denied if the consumer intentionally disregards a clear warning on use of a product, but granted if the injury occurs because he did not know how to read the warning label; or only if the danger is latent and could not have been detected by a "reasonable man?"

116. See Randy Knitwear, Inc. v. American Cyanamid Co., 11 N.Y.2d 5, 181 N.E.2d 399 (1962); Inglis v. American Motors Corp., 3 Ohio St.2d 132, 209 N.E.2d 583 (1965).

117. As to the liability of a remote manufacturer not in privity with a consumer for economic or pecuniary loss, rather than personal injury or property damage, due to negligent misrepresentations in product advertising, compare Wyatt v. Cadillac Motor Car Division, 145 Cal.App.2d 423, 302 P.2d 665 (1956), and TWA, Inc. v. Curtiss-Wright Corp., 1 Misc. 2d 477, 184 N.Y.S. 2d 284 (1955) (denying liability), *with* Lang v. General Motors Corp., 136 N.W.2d 805 (N.Dak. 1965), and State v. Campbell, 250 Ore. 262, 442 P.2d 218 (1968) (granting recovery).

118. Compare Santor v. A&M Kargheusian, 44 N.J. 52, 207 A.2d 305 (1965), with Seeley v. White Motor Co., 63 Cal.2d 9, 403 P.2d 145 (1965). See generally Note, "Economic Loss in Products Liability Jurisprudence," 66 *Columbia Law Review* 17 (1966).

119. See Littlefield, "Preserving Consumer Defenses: Plugging the Loophole in the New UCCC," 44 *New York University Law Review* 272, 280–86 (1969).

120. See, e.g., Ultramares Corp. v. Touche, Niven & Co., 225 N.Y. 170, 174 N.E. 441 (1931).

121. See, e.g., Uniform Consumer Credit Code §5.202(4) and (7).

122. See generally Rice, "Exemplary Damages in Private Consumer Actions," 55 *Iowa Law Review* 307 (1968).

123. The National Product Safety Commission, in its Final Report, recommend punitive damages as a deterrent to the merchandizing of products that fail to conform to national standards for product safety. *But cf.* Roginsky v. Richardson-Merrill, Inc., 378 F.2d 832 (2d Cir 1967).

124. See Posner, *supra* note 4, pp. 300–301.

125. See Magnuson and Carper, pp. 13–14:

Although these [deceptive] schemes are staggering in scope and diverse in their nature (the Better Business Bureau has identified 800 different varieties), they invariably have several things in common: they are lucrative, they are subtle, and their purveyors rarely come in conflict with the law. According to a nationwide survey for the President's Commission on Law Enforcement and Administration of Justice in 1966, nine out of every ten victims of consumer fraud do not even bother to report it to the police. Fifty percent of the victimized felt they had no right or duty to complain; 40 percent believed the authorities could not be effective or would not want to be bothered; 10 percent were confused about where to report.

126. See Posner, pp. 350–351.

127. See Uniform Consumer Credit Code §5.202(8).

128. See National Consumer Law Center's Model Consumer Credit Act of 1973 §8.113.

129. Henningsen v. Bloomfield Motors Inc., 32 N.J. 358, 161 A.2d 69 (1960) (dictum).

130. See *Report of Presidential Task Force Investigating Appliance Repair and Warranties* (1969). See generally Mueller, *Contracts of Frustration*, 79 *Yale Law Journal* 576 (1969).

131. Uniform Commercial Code §2–313: Express Warranties by Affirmation, Promise, Description, Sample.

(1) Express warranties by the seller are created as follows:

(a) Any affirmation of fact or promise made by the seller to the buyer which relates to the goods and becomes part of the basis of the bargain creates an express warranty that the goods shall conform to the affirmation or promise.

(b) Any description of the goods which is made part of the basis of the bargain creates an express warranty that the goods shall conform to the description.

(c) Any sample or model which is made part of the basis of the bargain creates an express warranty that the whole of the goods shall conform to the sample or model.

(2) It is not necessary to the creation of an express warranty that the seller use formal words such as "warrant" or "guarantee" or that he have a specific intention to make a warranty, but an affirmation merely of the value of the goods or a statement purporting to be merely the seller's opinion or commendation of the goods does not create a warranty.

Uniform Commercial Code §2–315: Implied Warranty: Fitness for Particular Purpose . . .

Where the seller at the time of contracting has reason to know any particular purpose for which the goods are required and that the buyer is relying on the seller's skill or judgment to select or furnish suitable goods, there is unless excluded or modified under the next section an implied warranty that the goods shall be fit for such purpose.

132. Uniform Commercial Code §2–314: Implied Warranty: Merchantability; Usage of Trade . . .

(1) Unless excluded or modified (Section 2–316), a warranty that the goods shall be merchantable is implied in a contract for their sale if the seller is a merchant with respect to goods of that kind. Under this section the serving for value of food or drink to be consumed either on the premises or elsewhere is a sale.

(2) Goods to be merchantable must be at least such as
(a) pass without objection in the trade under the contract description; and
(b) in the case of fungible goods, are of fair average quality within the description; and
(c) are fit for the ordinary purposes for which such goods are used; and
(d) run, within the variations permitted by the agreement, of even kind, quality and quantity within each unit and among all units involved; and
(e) are adequately contained, packaged, and labeled as the agreement may require; and
(f) conform to the promises or affirmations of fact made on the container or label if any.

(3) Unless excluded or modified (Section 2–316) other implied warranties may arise from course of dealing or usage of trade.

133. Uniform Commercial Code §2–316: "Exclusion or Modification of Warranties

(1) . . .

(2) Subject to subsection (3), to exclude or modify the implied warranty of merchantability or any part of it the language must mention merchantability and in case of a writing must be conspicuous, and to exclude or modify any implied warranty of fitness the exclusion must be by a writing and conspicuous. Language to exclude all implied warranties of fitness is sufficient if it states, for example, that "There are no warranties which extend beyond the description on the face hereof."

(3) Notwithstanding subsection (2)

(a) unless the circumstances indicate otherwise, all implied warranties are excluded by expressions like "as is," "with all faults" or other language which in common understanding calls the buyer's attention to the exclusion of warranties and makes plain that there is no implied warranty; and

(b) when the buyer before entering into the contract has examined the goods or the sample or model as fully as he desired or has refused to examine the goods there is no implied warranty with regard to defects which an examination ought in the circumstances to have revealed to him; and

(c) an implied warranty can also be excluded or modified by course of dealing or course of performance or usage of trade.

134. See Greenman v. Yuba Power Products, 59 Cal.2d 57, 27 Cal.Rptr. 697, 377 P.2d 897 (1963). But compare Seeley v. White Motor Co., 63 Cal.2d 9, 403 P.2d 145 (1965), allowing disclaimer of warranty to preclude manufacturer's responsibility for economic loss.

135. See J. Greenman v. Yuba Power Products, *supra* note 134 (disclaimer irrelevant to product injury); Jefferson Credit Corp. v. Marcano, 60 Misc. 2d 138, 302 N.Y.2d 390 (N.Y. Civ. Ct., 1969) (disclaimer unconscionable). The overturning of the express provision of the Uniform Commercial Code § 2–316, which authorizes disclaimer of warranties, by application of the general terms of § 2–302, dealing with unconscionability; is criticized in Leff, "Unconscionability and the Code—The Emperor's New Clause, 115 *University of Pennsylvania Law Review* 485, 516–524 (1967). *But see* Spanogle, *Analyzing Unconscionability Problems*, 117 U. PA. L. REV. 931 (1969).

136. See generally Report of Presidential Task Force Investigating Appliance Repair and Warranties (1969); *accord*, FTC, Report on Auto Warranties (1970).

137. Ibid. The complaints and sorrowful plight of consumers are often magnified by deceptive practices particularly common in automobile servicing. See Note, "Regulation of Automotive Repair Services," 56 *Cornell Law Quarterly* 1010 (1971).

138. *Cf.* California Civil Code § 1794.3 (West, 1973): "The provisions of this chapter shall not apply to any defect or nonconformity in consumer goods caused by the unauthorized or unreasonable use of the goods following sale." *But cf.* the argument for enterprise liability regardless of fault in Whitford, "A Case Study of the Automobile Warranty," 1968 *Wisconsin Law Review* 1006.

139. *Whitford, A Case Study of the Automobile Warranty, supra* note 138.

140. California Civil Code § 1790 ff. (West, 1973). See generally Thornton, "The Song-Beverly Consumer Warranty Act: New Commandments for Manufacturers," 46 L.A.B.J. 331 (1971).

141. California Civil Code § 1793 (West Supp. 1973).

142. Ibid. § § 1792.3–.4.

143. Ibid. § § 1793.2, 1795.

144. Ibid. § 1794.4.

145. Ibid. § § 1793.2–.4.

146. Ibid. § § 1794, 1794.2.

147. See Senate Committee on Commerce, 93d Congress, 2d Session, Class

Action Study 1–2 (Comm. Print June 1974). See generally Starrs, "The Consumer Class Action–Part I: Considerations of Equity," 49 *Boston University Law Review* 211; "Part II: Considerations of Procedure," Ibid. 407 (1969). For a criticism of the social costs of class actions in the form of higher consumer prices, destructive impact on businesses operating in low income areas and deterrent of advertising and hence useful information, see Comment, "Consumers Class Actions and Costs: An Economic Perspective on Deceptive Advertising," 18 *UCLA Law Review* 592 (1971).

148. The most extensively debated proposal was the Tydings-Eckhardt Bill, S. 3092, 91st Cong., 1at Sess. (1969) which would have amended the FTC Act to authorize consumer class actions for damages for violations of the FTC Act and the recovery of a reasonable attorney's fee. See Hearings on Consumer Protection before the Consumer Subcommittee of the Senate Commerce Committee, 91st Cong., 2d Sess. (1970). A later version of the consumer class action bill was introduced in the 92nd Congress, S. 984 (92nd Cong., 1st Sess. (1971). Serious objections have been raised that the enactment might inundate the federal courts. The Administration suggested a compromise proposal to permit consumer class actions to be "triggered" by prior FTC or Department of Justice actions. (i.e., class actions could only be brought after successful government actions.) S. 3201, 91st Cong., 1st Sess. (1969). See Statement of Assistant Attorney General McLaren in Hearings on S. 3092 before Consumer Subcommittee of Senate Commerce Committee, Dec. 16, 1969, 91st Cong., 1st Sess. 15–29. Oppenheim and Weston, *supra* note 3 at 523 (footnotes omitted).

149. See Consumers Legal Remedies Act, California Civil Code §1750 ff. (West 1973), commented on in Reed, "Legislating for the Consumer: An Insider's Analysis of the Consumers Legal Remedies Act," 2 *Pacific Law Journal* 1, 12–21 (1971). *Cf.* Massachusetts Consumer Protection Statute, M.G.L.A. chap. 93A, §§9 & 11, commented on in Rice, "New Private Remedies for Consumers: The Amendment of Chapter 93A," 54 *Massachusetts Law Quarterly* 307 (1969).

150. See California Civil Code §1783 (West 1973), disallowing an award of damages if the person committing the unlawful act or practice "(a) proves that such violation was not intentional and resulted from a bona fide error notwithstanding the use of reasonable procedures adopted to avoid any such error and (b) makes an appropriate correction, repair or replacement or other remedy of the goods and services according to the provisions of subdivisions (b) and (c) of Section 1782." Compare California Civil Code §1794.2(a) (West 1973), denying the right to treble damages in a class action suit, with M.G.L.A. chapter 93A, §§9 and 11, making the right turn whether the violation was willful.

151. Uniform Consumer Sales Practices Act §§9 & 11.

152. See Vasquez v. Superior Court, 4 Cal.3d 800, 94 Cal. Rptr. 796, 484 P.2d 964. But see City of San Jose v. Superior Ct., ___ Cal. 3d ___ , 115 Cal. Rptr. 797, 525 P.2d 701 (1974).

153. 394 U.S. 1025 (1969).

154. Eisen v. Carlisle and Jacquelin, 94 S.Ct. 2140 (1974).

155. G. Foster, Jr., *The Status of Class Action Litigation* (A.B.F. Monograph No. 4, 1974); Senate Comm. on Commerce, 93d Cong., 2d Sess., *Class Action Study* (Comm. Print June 1974).

156. Schrag, "Bleak House 1968: A Report on Consumer Test Litigation," 44 *New York University Law Review* 115 (1969).

157. See Kugler v. Romain, 58 N.J. 522, 279 A.2d 640 (1971). See generally Wade and Kamenshine, "Restitution for Defrauded Consumers: Making the Remedy Effective Through Suit By Governmental Agency," 37 *George Washington Law Review* 1013 (1969).

158. See Holloway v. Bristol-Myers Corp., 485 F.2d 986 (D.C. Cir. 1973).

159. See Hall v. Coburn Corp. of America, 26 N.Y.2d 396, 311 N.Y.S.2d 281, 259 N.E.2d 720 (1970). But compare P. Schrag, *Counsel for the Deceived: Case Studies in Consumer Fraud* (1972), chronicling the problems and disappointments of public enforcement.

160. See Posner, chapter 23.

161. See generally Comment, "The California Small Claims Courts," 52 *California Law Review* 876 (1964); Comment, "Small Claims Courts and the Poor," 42 *Southern California Law Review* 493 (1969); Note, "Small Claims Court: Reform Revisited," 5 *Columbia Journal of Law and Social Problems* 47 (1969); Jordan and Warren, *supra* note 88, at 427:

> In the past enforcement of consumer credit legislation by private remedies has been criticized as ineffective. The paradox of private enforcement is that the state erects a structure of laws which are supposed to protect consumers who are not in an economic position to pay for goods and services and are not sophisticated enough to protect themselves against oppressive credit practices, but, to a considerable extent, these laws provide rights that only people with economic resources and a good deal of business sophistication can enforce. The worth of these remedies to a consumer is no greater than his ability to assert them in a court of law.

162. See Note, "The Persecution and Intimidation of the Low-Income Litigant as Performed in the Small Claims Court in California," 21 *Stanford Law Review* 1657 (1969).

163. See D. Caplowitz, *The Poor Pay More* (1965); *Report of The National Advisory Commission on Civil Disorders* (1968); Note, "Consumer Legislation and the Poor," 76 *Yale Law Journal* 745 (1967).

164. See Jones, "Wanted: A New System for Solving Consumer Grievances," 25 *ARB J.* 234 (1970); Rice, "Remedies, Enforcement Procedures and the Duality of Consumer Transaction Problems," 48 *Boston University Law Review* 559, 589-592 (1968).

165. But see the suggestion for lay advocates, discussed in Eovaldi and Gestrin, "Justice For Consumers: Mechanisms for Redress," 66 *Northwestern University Law Review* 281, 322-324 (1971).

Chapter 15

Social Impact Strategies: The Experience of Legal Services Backup Centers

Kenneth F. Phillips

How can consumer rights, or the rights of low income people, be enforced once they have been granted? The issue might be whether the public has the capability, even assuming sufficient notice, to put together a response comparable in depth and documentation to that put forward by the promoters of a particular product, who have substantial resources and all of the incentives the profit motive inspires. My description of legal services backup centers should be heard in the light of that question, and I'll return to it later in this article.

The Office of Economic Opportunity (OEO)'s legal services program has been and is an unprecedented experiment in effecting social change. It involves more than 2,500 full time lawyers throughout the United States, federal funding of over $70 million a year, 800 separate law offices, the filing every year of thousands of law suits, lobbying efforts in Washington and in state capitals, assistance to low income groups in organizing themselves as pressure groups for their own interests as they perceive them, and a high level of awareness throughout of the power realities that underlie the social order and social change.

The legal services program was begun in 1965. Although not expressly contemplated by the OEO antipoverty legislation, legal services programs began to be funded within six months of the passage of the Economic Opportunities Act. The great sense of urgency in the United States at that time about race and poverty problems aided the programs in attracting many young lawyers of talent and tremendous dedication, committed to doing something about the underlying structural-legal causes of poverty in the United States.

Whereas traditional legal aid programs had concentrated on services to individual clients, many of these lawyers saw as the objectives of their converted storefront office programs the identification of and attack upon the factors that underlay the conditions they saw around them. Lawsuits were to be the principal instrument of change. But when you bring a lawsuit against a landlord, you may lose. The laws tend to protect landlords. Landlords usually can hire competent counsel, in many cases much more experienced. More frustrating yet, what if you won? So what? What's changed? These experiences produced a backwash of frustration and disappointment. It crystallized in Washington in 1967, about the same time that OEO formally promulgated a statement that law reform would be given the highest priority within the legal services program. Law reform, in fact, never commanded as much as 10 percent of the programs resources.

Two important actions were taken, however. First, law reform or appellate offices began to be established in large legal services programs around the country. A limited number of lawyers were thus freed of the tremendous caseload burdens that had accumulated and encouraged to bring law reform suits. Second, a small number of national backup centers were organized, each of them concerned with legal services strategy and operations in a specific area of law. The housing law center, which I direct, was the second backup center established. Its concern is low income housing problems and community-based economic development.

Other centers have been established in welfare law at Columbia University, consumer law at Boston College, juvenile law at St. Louis University, education law at Harvard, health and environmental law at UCLA, and employment law in New York. Also, legal problems of the elderly in New York, migrant problems in the District of Columbia, native American rights in Boulder, and a paralegal center in the District of Columbia.

The role of these centers has been to examine directions and goals, develop strategies, act as counsel or co-counsel in important litigation matters, and generally, as not only strategy but operations centers, to be participants in policy determination. The program also established a National Clearing House Review, which provides monthly information to legal services lawyers on new developments and serves as a forum for ideas, a training center, specialized recruitment centers, and a technical assistance center. In effect, the legal services program developed into a total delivery system, a systems approach to law reform and the delivery of legal services to the poor in the United States.

THE HOUSING LAW CENTER

Perhaps some description of the housing law center and its methodology will serve as a prototype to illustrate the objectives and modus operandi of the backup centers. Its approach was subsequently adopted by many other centers. The center began in 1968. Its housing law section now has eight full time staff attorneys and one planner, the section's budget is approximately $400,000 a year. The starting point for its efforts was an analysis of the low income housing problem, an analysis strikingly different from that made by the Nixon administration.

The administration's analysis, which underlay the so-called "suburban strategy," resulted from a coalescing of diverse factors and forces. Two presidential task forces, the Douglas Commission and the Kaiser Committee, had called for production of 2.6 million new housing units a year. In 1968 Congress enacted that goal into law. The builders looked to the suburbs, arguing that only there could land be aggregated, mass building techniques used, and incidentally, social problems kept at a distance. Major civil rights organizations supported the strategy as consistent with their highest priority to suburban integration objectives.

The leadership at HUD was committed to rapid production. The administration had political ties to the suburbs and had received little support from central cities. The dominating intellectual voices at that time, mostly out of Harvard and MIT, had written off the cities as beyond salvation. The result was a strategy calling for maximized suburban construction and benign neglect, coupled with grandiose urban renewal projects, for the cities.

Tenant organizations and legal services lawyers around the country took a different view. Their members and clients lived in the central cities that were being written off; Census figures demonstrated that they would continue to live there. Only solutions that would involve strengthening and rebuilding the cities, preservation and upgrading of its existing housing stock, and contracts and participation could address their problems. These realizations implied a strategy of documenting and dramatizing the reality of inner city housing and community conditions and the ineffectiveness and even counterproductive effects of the federal programs, as well as research to identify more promising approaches.

That was to be the objective. The method included the development of materials, training, organization, litigation, research, and legislative proposals. The center first prepared a comprehensive *Handbook* [1] of housing law information, strategies, and tactics for legal services lawyers and community organizations. Using the *Handbook*, it next held four major regional conferences to present proposals and refine them through discussion with field lawyers and community leaders. Then began what we have called "circuit riding." Staff attorneys from the center visited every major legal services program in the country. They asked: What is your housing problem? What are you doing about it? What resources have you allocated to housing? Do you know that in City X they are working with tenant groups in public housing, enforcing relocation rights, challenging the city's workable program, or whatever? Do you want to try it?

When the local program answered, "You do it for us," the center could say, "We don't have the resources to do it for you, but we will help if you will assign full time staff to work in collaboration with us." Through this process, more than one hundred liaison attorneys were assigned to work with the center. It thus became the hub of a network of housing specialists in cities around the country. Through its close association with the National Tenants Organization and by setting up a small Washington office, the center was able to take full advantage of the strengths these relationships created.

STRATEGIES FOR ACTION

The strategies the center has pursued fall into several categories. First were those intended to use legal techniques to demonstrate the reality of what was happening to low income housing and the inefficiency and destructive effect of the present approaches. Urban renewal has destroyed many thousands of units of poor people's housing across the country, often building expensive downtown commercial projects in their place. Laws imposing relocation requirements have been effectively ignored.

It became possible in the late sixties to overcome court-imposed standing and justiciability defenses, and a series of suits was brought to document the redevelopment agencies' pattern and practice of juggling statistics to avoid building the relocation housing that the law required. The message to redevelopment agencies was that an injunction in the course of construction can be expensive and relocation requirements would have to be taken seriously. The message for Congress and the public was the costliness and ineffectiveness of the downtown renewal approach.

A second category of strategies has had to do with assistance to organizations of poor people. Unorganized people are powerless; organization means power—it means the capability to analyze problems and develop and advocate positions. The center and other legal services programs thus have put a heavy emphasis on close support to tenant unions, on project area committees in urban renewal projects, on model cities groups and neighborhood and other similar organizations, and have used legal means to assist them. For example, the HUD Modernization Program requires that local public housing tenants participate with housing authorities in planning the use of modernization or improvement subsidies. Tenants could ask to be recognized as a tenants union in order to participate. If they were turned down, they could file administrative complaints or commence litigation.

Ultimately these local organizing efforts proved a major factor in the development of the National Tenants Organization, which in turn, with legal assistance from the center, was able to negotiate important innovations in the public housing field, at both the admininstrative and congressional levels. The combination of legal and popular action proved useful for effective public interest representation, just as ability to use more than one tool has served private interest groups in achieving their objectives.

The third critical element is research. The problems confronting public interest and consumer groups have been widely reported. It's all very well to discredit existing approaches, but what is to be put forward in their stead? A major part of the center's effort has been directed at looking for answers. Some of it may have borne fruit in provisions included in recent (1974) federal housing legislation, which, if sympathetically implemented, could provide funds for broad scale moderate rehabilitation and general improvement in central city neighborhoods which have been red-lined (denied mortgage funds) by banks.

Interestingly, no empirical systematic study has been made of the effectiveness of the legal services program in accomplishing its goal of improving the real income levels and general well-being of the poor. My comments and others you may receive are necessarily impressionistic. They are also premature, as the work is in process and incomplete. It took the housing law center years to develop a legislative approach—and to get it through Congress. Unless and until meaningfully implemented at some future time, it won't provide better housing.

Subject to these caveats, there appear to be considerable strengths in the kind of approach and organizational structure the backup centers represent. First, each of the centers has been subject matter specific. Unlike public interest law firms, which address all problems, each can hope to develop over time (and each has developed) knowledge of the causes, effects, and politics of its special field. Second, as my comments suggest, the centers have not limited themselves to litigation as a means of redress. Litigation can be an effective method, but it may be most effective employed in combination with other tactics. The public housing modernization experience offers such an example.

The implications of legal services experiences—and particularly the backup centers' experience—for consumer and environmental interests are considerable. The New Deal assumptions that regulatory agencies could regulate have been undermined by subsequent experience, as regulatory agencies have been subjected to pressures—carrots and sticks—from the bodies they were created to regulate, without correspondingly effective pressures from the plurality of consumer and public interest groups. The need is to redress that balance. To do so will require a very high level of capability, particularly where major environmental or societal issues are involved.

Public interest representatives must be able to bring to bear a capacity: lawyers, experts, research, and preparation comparable to that of proponents who stand to profit. This will require much greater concentration of resources than has yet been achieved. It implies, in turn, a high degree of selectivity of the areas to be addressed, careful selection of targets and venue. Thus, reconsiderations of the environmental and consumer laws should question where such resources can be found and how they best can be organized to ensure full presentation of public concerns.

The fast breeder nuclear reactor offers an example. The Atomic Energy Commission has joined with the major industrial actors in support of the fast breeder. Where can the level of capability come from to document and put forward a case on the merits against the giants of industry and government? Where will the funding come from? These are the questions we should address. The backup centers' experience must be analyzed in light of these questions. In my belief it suggests that, given a strategic orientation, relatively small organizations can have considerable impact. When they do so, admittedly, they invite counterattack.

The attack on the legal service program has increasingly centered on law reform, and, within that context, on the centers. As a result, in the spring of 1974 a group of conservative senators called on then President Nixon and suggested that they would take a dim view (relative to possible future impeachment proceedings) of his signing the then pending Legal Services Corporation Bill unless it was amended to discontinue the backup centers. President Nixon, accordingly, threatened to veto the entire legal services legislation if the backup centers were not eliminated. Consequently, the bill as passed prohibits their future funding. A momentum has been achieved, however, that will not easily be stopped, and hopefully, ways will be found for the centers' work to go forward.

Consumer and environmental groups could usefully study the experience of the centers to better understand the critical importance to effective public representation of (1) high level specialized capability; (2) institutionalizing that capacity and ensuring its existence over time; (3) a strategy orientation addressed both to subject area requirements and to political exigencies combined with tactical diversity; (4) subject area specificity, concentration of resources, and selectivity of issues; (5) combining the functions of research, advocacy, and technical assistance; (6) finding the considerable funding necessary for such operations, and (7) protecting them from the inevitable counterattacks that accompany their effectiveness.

NOTES TO CHAPTER 15

1. National Housing and Economic Development Law Project, *Handbook on Housing Law* (2 vols.), Englewood Cliffs, N.J.: Prentice-Hall, 1971.

Part 5

Some Special Industry Cases

Commentary

ORREN

The insurance industry is vulnerable to various types of challenges by contemporary consumers, such as class action suits, pressures for government operated insurance systems, and proposals that insurance firms be controlled by policyholders. Another group that seeks to change the present insurance system is comprised of people who cannot get insurance, for whatever reason. The insurance industry's reaction to these challenges has been a quiet one, with emphasis on continued service to policyholders to meet their changing needs. And the best response may be for the industry to point to—and count on—its many satisfied consumers.

CADY

For overall consumer benefit, the pharmaceutical industry is regulated at two distinct levels: production and distribution. At the production level this regulation serves the public interest relatively well, by requiring safe manufacturing procedures and thorough testing of products before they reach the market. There is room for improvement, however, in manufacturers' compliance with recalls of pharmaceuticals already on the market but of questionable safety. Consumers are not so well served by the regulation of pharmaceutical distribution. To date, this regulation tends to favor the retail drug industry (whose representatives make and enforce the rules) by pro-hibiting advertising of prescription drug prices. The consumer would benefit if more open and competitive policies were adopted.

Chapter 16

The Insurance Industry and the "Other" Consumer

Karen Orren

The insurance industry's public response to the current surge of consumer activism—and by public response I include the speeches executives and agents make to each other at professional meetings and editorials in trade papers, as well as presentations to government agencies—has generally sounded a positive note. Now and then an alarmist will see a threat to private property and free enterprise, while another group takes the view that there is nothing especially new in consumerism, that it will soon fade away.

But the industry spokesmen, the heads of the larger companies and the officers of the major trade associations, have counseled meeting the challenge unantagonistically, head-on, with initiative and even enthusiasm. Ralph Nader, and his incarnations within the industry, Professor Robert Belth of the University of Indiana, and Herbert Denenberg, recently insurance commissioner of Pennsylvania, are invited to speak at assemblies and their proposals debated openly. Different segments of the industry have established the predictable committees to monitor consumer affairs, and many individual companies have followed suit within their own offices. Panels on consumerism have become a regular feature at insurance conventions.

Only one rule qualifies this open-minded approach. Industry people repeatedly acknowledge the need to enter into dialogue with consumers who are "responsible," "competent," who "concentrate their fire on the first business of business—its products and services." These are distinguished from consumers characterized by "noise," who throw "curve balls," are "self-appointed," and "focus their criticism of a business on its failure to involve itself on the periphery of the business." (Note that a consumer falls into one or the other category not so much by his status—though the policyholder is definitely preferred and the one to whose service the companies claim they have been devoted all along—but by his goals and tactics) [1].

In this article, however, I will deviate from the industry rule to discuss precisely the "other" consumer, the one accused of throwing curve balls, because I think that only in relation to him can the consumer movement be understood in any but the shortest run terms. I'm not claiming that he will have his way; certainly not that he is the typical consumer, let alone policyholder; or even that his inclinations are socially beneficial. Only that if conditions are right—as they may well be in the next few years—he will be the real challenge to the industry. My hunch is also that many insurance people understand this, and the actions the industry has taken so far must be evaluated against this prospect.

CONSUMERISM: THE CONTEMPORARY VARIANT

The degree of receptivity accorded the consumer movement is understandable in light of the industry's very recent and mainly frustrating encounters in the black ghetto, both with the Life Insurance Urban Investment Program and the problems of fire and casualty coverage for inner city property. Compared to the demands of neighborhood spokesmen, the insults of gang leaders, and the threats of politicians, the appearance of an insurance shopping guide in *Consumer Reports* or a state bill to enforce truth-in-advertising is tame stuff indeed.

Many of the reforms called for are at least manageable within the parameters of selling and servicing insurance. True, they may require considerable management ingenuity if companies are to maintain their profit levels, but they call in effect for more and better of the same rather than a diversion of energy into community relations and social planning. Moreover, as the industry repeatedly points out, the phenomenon of consumerism is familiar: similar waves of activism in the 1880s and 1910s inspired the contours of state regulation as it exists today.

The industry's feeling of relief, however, may be misleading. Today's consumer activists are direct descendants of the recent civil rights and antiwar movements, and this fact has marked their nature. First there is the simple tendency and skill for organizing, resulting in a veritable effervescence of activities and pressures on every level of society and within every institutional orbit from the universities to churches, the army, even the medical profession. And the ethic and practice of *direct* participation in affairs is unprecedented certainly in this century and probably in the nation's history.

Also, the deep impressions of racial discrimination and poverty in their specific forms—structural unemployment, permanent welfare mothers, and so on—may be expected to be a constant reminder to consumers that theirs is a limited and even peripheral campaign in a much broader pursuit. Third is the disenchantment with many of the ideas central to the business system—if not with capitalism itself, then with the ideas of growth and the bounties of technology. That this is more evident in the environmental movement than in consumer groups might provide a comfort were it not for the fact that organizationally they are often one and the same, with the same or allied leadership, working out of the same offices and employing the same lawyers.

Each of these characteristics distinguishes today's consumer movement from its earlier counterpart, with which the insurance industry expresses a familiarity. The consumers of the Progressive Era were of course activists, but, especially in the area of business regulation, were willing to step aside in deference to expertise. If they more closely resembled the industry's image of the responsible consumer in that their vistas were confined to eliminating illegal, dishonest, unhealthy, or unsafe business practices, it was largely because they considered their own to be the typical (or at least presumptive) status of American citizens generally, and therefore consumer reform was seen to be at the heart of social justice. These goals were further related to their ambivalence toward the business system. Although the Progressives denounced the shame of the cities and the abuses of the trusts, there was great admiration for the material achievements of the large corporation, and particularly for the level of technology it had allowed.

There is one important similarity between the consumers today and those of 1910: both are part of larger reform movements that are distrustful—if not actually hostile—to political parties. In the case of the Progressives this hostility redounded to the benefit of business in the "independent," nonpartisan, and eventually business dominated regulatory agency [2]. In the 1970s the distrust of parties, combined with a disenchantment with business and a well deserved cynicism about public regulation, may have quite different consequences.

INDUSTRY FUNCTIONS,
INDUSTRY CONSUMERS

For the insurance industry, as for corporate business as a whole, the intensive organization of the public around issues pertaining to business behavior is in contrast to the normally general and diffuse relationship it enjoys with the public. This relationship is general in that business ordinarily dispenses its goods and services with a legitimacy grounded in a broad mandate of economic performance. It is diffuse in that the cumulative social effects—the different impact business decisions have on distinct categories of the population—are usually an artifact of socially neutral procedures for making profit, a goal itself legitimated in performance terms as contributing to overall productivity and social well-being.

To the extent that consumer activists seek to impose higher ethical standards and to perfect the systems of information and choice by which consumers may intelligently perform their designated role in the market system, they do not fundamentally alter this arrangement. Very different, however, are demands that would either alter the nature of consumer participation or structure business decisions to favor special social groups. For those who would find a nomenclature useful for comparison with other cases, the former might be thought of as product consumerism and the latter approaches as social consumerism. However, note that a too aggressive pursuit of product consumerism may alter traditional business-customer relations and thus spill over into the second category.

The functions of the insurance industry make it especially vulnerable to social consumerist demands. In the first place, its products—cushions against the hazards of crime, fire, ill health, and untimely death—are regarded by the public as basic necessities, not luxuries. *Consumer Reports* and industry advertising both aside, the mounting insecurities of modern living are likely to make this more the case rather than less so. As public opinion polls financed by the industry show, among policyholders this creates the mixture of regard and resentment characteristic of such dependency [3]. And because insurance is seen as a necessity, those persons unable to purchase what they think they need, or at a price less than prohibitive, constitute a likely pool from which those "other" consumers may be drawn, or in whose name pressures are brought.

Second, the insurance company does not simply sell the consumer a product; it enters a contract, often for a duration of many years. For the company this poses delicate decisions about renewal or termination. For the consumer it means that no matter how well informed he may be at the time of purchase, he may not be able to estimate the real value of what he has insured until he has suffered a loss. And for both parties it entails a relationship over time, whatever the nature of the services or participation on either side.

Third, however much it might wish it were so, the insurance industry's direct consumers are not limited to its policyholders. Because of the investment of over a trillion dollars of life insurance in force—and a smaller amount from other parts of the industry—it confronts the public in a different aspect, and faces a new array of potential "others": those who live or do business on property owned by insurance companies, farmers with mortgages, and many other groups of debtors. Then there are the disappointed mortgage seekers, small businessmen—in other words, a virtually endless variety of social projects, both public and private, in need of money. In normal circumstances all compete for loans according to the strictures of rules and risk; but as the insurance industry well knows from the last few years and much longer, these circumstances cannot be taken for granted.

THE "OTHER" CONSUMERISM

Lest the impression be given that the "other" consumer is presently in repose while his product oriented relative dominates consumer strategy, I shall discuss several consumer actions that fit the first connotation. All are from the last couple of years, after the national preoccupation with problems of the ghetto and during the time when consumers have been in the forefront of group politics. The list is far from comprehensive, but it does indicate the range of consumerism directed to the insurance industry beyond the "regular," good-tempered purchaser of a policy the industry favors as its own.

Class Action Suits
The first type, which has received wide public attention in the equity funding scandal, is the class action suit. This is a suit brought by a small group of policyholders on behalf of all policyholders, seeking damages for some breach of contract or law. A common complaint is consumer fraud. To select just one case with which I happen to be familiar, ten residents of Erie and Huron counties in Ohio recently sued Columbia National Life of Columbus for $10 million, charging the company with have misrepresented its policies in at least eighteen different ways. Suits of this kind have contributed significantly to the industry's initiative in the area of advertising standards, particularly in the politically sensitive health insurance field.

Another interesting example in 1973 was a "double class action," in which plaintiffs claiming to represent "all owners of participating insurance policies issued by mutual life insurance companies," sued Equitable Life, New York Life, Metropolitan Life, John Hancock, and the Prudential, as representatives of the class of "all mutual life insurance companies doing business within the United States." The charge was that, among other things, the directors of these companies fixed and inflated life insurance prices, employed arbitrary accounting and outdated mortality tables, misallocated investment monies, and arranged to perpetuate themselves in office [4].

Although the courts have lately put certain obstacles in the way of such actions by requiring notification of class members, it is probable that other consumers will find a way in this field, perhaps through aid from legislatures or insurance departments in the task and cost of notification, or by narrowing the relevant class to some subgroup that may be conveniently notified. The class action suit violates consumer "responsibility" by its tactics, in going to court rather than handling matters directly with the companies or through the state departments of insurance, and also by departing from the one-to-one relations that the industry prefers with its policyholders.

Government Operated Insurance

The second type of action that falls into the "other" category is the promotion of government operated insurance. This institution exists to any significance only in New York state, where life insurance scandals at the turn of the century provoked consumer activists such as Louis D. Brandeis and others to successfully seek a public alternative, sold through state-chartered savings banks [5]. While these policies have never been serious competition to the private industry in the past, their appeal has increased amid renewed and heightened consumer consciousness. The sale of this insurance has been restricted by law to a few states bordering on New York. Earlier this year, however, Consumers Union entered a suit to remove the limitation, and it is possible that the idea of such an alternative product may catch hold elsewhere.

Policyholder Control

Third, there is the advocacy of policyholders' control of mutual companies. Many of the largest companies in each segment of the industry are mutuals, but as the voting records submitted with annual reports show, only a handful of policyholders (e.g., in a company like Metropolitan Life only a few hundred out of millions) actually participate in choosing management. Sometimes lip service has been paid to the idea of consumer representation on the board of directors with a so-called public member, usually some prominent citizen such as an ex-governor or a judge. In fact, often the only time a policy-holder is aware that his own status in a mutual is significantly differ-ent from that in a stock company is when the company fails and he discovers that he is legally responsible for his share of the company's liabilities. This year at its annual convention, however, the Consumer Federation of America, which claims 200 affiliates with 30 million members, endorsed a resolution that policyholders in "mutual type companies be restored their due rights to control and direct the affairs of their own companies." There is something of an irony in this devel-opment, since many of the largest mutuals—Metropolitan Life, the Prudential, Western and Southern, and others—were stock companies subsequently mutualized by management as a way of freeing them-selves from stockholder interference.

It is difficult to estimate how deep the attraction toward coopera-tives runs in the consumer movement. There have long been strong organizational ties between the two, but until a few years ago both groups were relatively small. Another uncertainty is whether the disillusionment with political parties may fuel the cooperative move-ment as it has elsewhere, in western Europe, for example, or in under-developed countries like Peru. In England, the insurance industry has escaped nationalization largely through squabbles over details between the Co-operative Movement and the Labor Party [6]. In the meantime, the idea of policyholder control was given a symbolic victory in another target institution closely tied to the insurance industry when earlier this year the National Blue Cross Association decided that all of its member boards must have consumer represen-tation reflecting the makeup of their constituency populations.

Excluded Groups

The three foregoing types of consumer action have dealt with the problems and preferences of policyholders. A fourth concerns groups who seek insurance but are excluded from adequate coverage. During the late 1960s the issue surfaced as a demand for fire insurance in ghetto properties, and was handled with state and federal assistance through the FAIR plan, a system of pooled, assigned risks similar to the one for high risk automobile insurance. Today there is still evidence that residents of minority neighborhoods have difficulty getting insurance, and in a few states insurance commissioners have themselves become spokesmen for these consumers to urge change in underwriting practices in order to benefit certain social groups.

Another group that sees itself to be presently discriminated against by the industry are the farmers. They have pressured the Federal Insurance Administration and state legislatures to mandate "full insurance availability," through underwriting methods staunchly opposed by private farm insurers. Still another variation utilizes the class action suit to complain of discriminatory treatment. Thus, early this year the American Civil Liberties Union filed suit in federal court against the New York Superintendent of Insurance for approving company policies that allegedly deny adequate disability protection to women, and that particularly discriminate unfairly against low income women.

Protested Investment

A fifth "other" type of consumer action arises not from a present or policyholder relationship with an insurance company but is a consumer protest against investment related activities. This may occur in as diverse a set of circumstances as industry investments themselves. For example, recently some white residents of a Metropolitan Life-owned housing project sued the company for racial discrimination. Because of new flexibility in the requirements for federal standing, the residents won their case in the Supreme Court [7]. An indirect variety of this action may be seen in Ralph Nader's complaint filed with the Civil Aeronautics Board alleging that five insurance companies are able to control the national airline industry through their own substantial investments in the industry (without approval as required by the Federal Aviation Act) and through interlocks with major banks. Yet another is Nader's attempt as a consumer spokesman to halt the ITT–Hartford Insurance merger.

Compulsory Investment

Sixth are the proposals for compulsory investment measures to benefit specified sectors of society. These have dogged the industry throughout its history. During the nineteenth century, states, particularly western states, tried by these laws to keep locally collected premiums for use in local enterprises; and farmers attempted to secure advantages for themselves against the credit needs of heavy industry. At the time of the New Deal, the insurance industry suspected it was to be nationalized or otherwise tapped to finance various social schemes. And of course during the 1960s there were pressures from the black inner city, initially relayed by the federal government and experienced firsthand once the Urban Investments Program was under way.

The only recent compulsory investment law on the books, the Texas Robertson Act, was repealed in 1967, but between 1965 and

1972 nineteen such laws were proposed in thirteen states, most of them to funnel money into housing—and none with sufficient support to overcome fierce industry opposition. The strongest weapon against actions of this type has been the threat to withdraw from the offending state, and as such it is one of the industry's best arguments against federal regulation.

Federal Regulation

Finally, there is consumer advocacy of federal regulation of insurance. The Consumer Federation this year endorsed a resolution urging "Congress to initiate an investigation of its responsibilities to insurance consumers. Reconsideration of its position favoring state regulation, as spelled out under the 1945 McCarran-Ferguson Act, is long overdue in the face of growing revelations of failures in state regulation of insurance." The question of the adequacy of McCarran-Ferguson has also been raised by other groups in the courts, such as when the Ohio AFL–CIO, in a suit against the state Insurance Rating Board, unsuccessfully charged that state regulation of auto insurance rates was a "pretense" [8]. McCarran-Ferguson provides that federal antitrust laws apply only to the insurance industry if the business of insurance is not regulated by the states. In general the courts have been reluctant to examine the quality of existing state law.

Certain insurance executives have sometimes entertained the idea of federal regulation, but since the improved relations with state authorities dating from the last big wave of consumer reform in the 1910s, the industry as a whole has supported the decentralized state arrangement. It has, however, been inexorably drawn into the federal net through its variable annuities which are under the jurisdiction of the SEC; Medicare; mail order insurance; federal regulation of insured pension plans; and other policies. Should the Hart-Magnuson no-fault bill (which provides national standards for automobile insurance), or the Fair Credit Reporting Act pass in the coming session, they will further draw in the business. Given the realities of politics in the states compared to Washington, this progression in itself could be a serious setback for the industry's resistance to pressures brought by the "other" consumer.

INDUSTRY REACTIONS

It is perhaps premature to assess the tangible reactions of the industry to consumerism, but I might offer a few brief comments about the apparent direction of likely reforms. Needless to say, all the discussion in the numerous consumer protection committees, forums, and so on centers on the selling and servicing of insurance. But since the premise of these remarks has been that the other, social consumerism is the real challenge facing the industry, it is useful to keep that in mind.

One thing already clear is that the industry is anxious not to be pushed, not to allow consumer relations to take on the character of politics, which in itself would be a concession to those who would disturb the business-public status quo. There are no suggestions of "getting to the grass roots" through group meetings and so forth, as there were in the Urban Investments Program. Instead, the position taken is that insurance companies have always tried to serve their policyholders and will continue to do so now in light of changing consumer needs and preferences.[a]

The one major item of reform already accomplished—truth-in-advertising standards for health insurance—was designed by the industry and offered as a National Association of Insurance Commissioners "model bill" simultaneously in many states, in the standard pattern of insurance legislation. For several years, industry committees have been considering methods of disclosing the true cost of insurance policies, particularly in the life field, and it is possible that a similar model bill will eventually be passed in the states. When one insurance commissioner (Durkin of New Hampshire) attempted to hasten this progress by requiring that health and life insurance rates be disclosed at once, insurance companies and agents established a "truth squad," spread the news that companies would withdraw from New Hampshire, and Durkin was promptly retired to private life.

What is also apparent, however, is that even to respond to the product related consumer needs that the insurance industry admits are entirely legitimate poses very sticky problems. Consider the question of rate disclosure (and put aside the relatively uncomplex questions of hucksterism, misrepresentation, and so on). There is, first, the basic discomfiture of making clear to a newly attentive public that premium cost is figured on a far lower assumed rate of interest

[a]In reply to a letter asking for materials related to consumerism the vice-president of one of the major life insurance trade associations writes:

> You state in your letter that your primary concern is the changes in the industry's attitude and policy toward consumer protection and organized consumer action since 1960. This implies an assumption on your part that there has been a change, apparently as a result of consumer pressure, and I am not sure that the record warrants such an assumption. It is our belief that our business has a long record of responsiveness to and concern for consumer needs and expectations and that the past decade does not reveal a sudden movement toward that posture (August 1, 1974).

than companies actually earn. The interest-adjusted method of cost comparisons now under consideration uses an unprecedented high rate of 4 percent earnings, while the public knows interest rates are two and three times that, and not likely to come down significantly soon.

Second, a reform such as cost disclosure strains the traditionally united front of companies, agents, and insurance commissioners, which has been important to the political success of the industry. While agents are the natural middlemen between the consumers, and while companies and obviously have an interest in, say, improved handling of complaints and faster payment of benefits, a more cost-conscious environment threatens the existing system of agents' commissions. And insurance commissioners—a group accustomed to being by and large ignored by the public in the past—have responded to new public interest in their domain; several commissioners, including especially Denenberg of Pennsylvania, Mauck of Illinois, and O'Malley of Florida, have taken public positions ahead of the industry on price disclosure and other matters [9].

Third, a call for simple, comparable costs and a description of the insurance contract in plain, readable English strikes directly at what has been an extremely valuable political arsenal—industry's expertise in a subject virtually no others have felt they understand. This intimidating technicality has been the main justification for putting industry people on the vital legislative committees and having them staff or advise regulatory bodies, and for lobbying legislators with unrefuted information. The domination of insurance matters by persons who can speak authoritatively has in particular preserved industry affairs as an isolated domain into which closely related "other consumer" questions, such as the availability of finance for housing or local industry, may enter only with the greatest political difficulty [10].

Apart from the industry's strictly managerial preferences, a concentration on basic products and services is a politically sound approach, since ultimately the industry's greatest protection may have to be its satisfied customers, wary of any tampering with their insurance savings and security against hazards. But as the price disclosure issue shows, this is a difficult balancing act. There are always contrary business pressures: for example, this year life insurance companies have experienced a cash drain from policyholders' borrowing on their policies at fixed rates far lower than the market rates, but NAIC model legislation that would have modified this practice has met with predictable consumer opposition [11].

Nor is strategy made easier by the diversity of insurance fields and the absence of effective all-industry coordination. Consider, for instance, no-fault automobile insurance. In many states automobile underwriters have reached a compromise on a form of no-fault that eliminates litigation between companies and may halt the rise in liability costs, but also requires that drivers provide additional coverage for themselves. Should public dissatisfaction with still mounting costs bring federal regulation, this will be a blow not only to the auto insurers, but to those industry segments such as life insurers which are even more susceptible to the pressures of social consumerism.

ACKNOWLEDGMENT
I would like to thank my graduate assistant, Vernon Coleman, for help on the following notes.

NOTES TO CHAPTER 16

1. The best single source for materials on the insurance industry and the consumer is the weekly *National Underwriter (NU)*, both the Life & Health and Property & Casualty editions, 1971–74. However, most news items have the tendency to accent the positive, as it were, overlooking the "other" consumer and reporting on such things as the "widows' study" done by the American Life Convention, "hot lines" to unhappy consumers, efforts to find methods for disclosing true prices, and so on. A representative selection of useful articles on insurance thinking might include the following: "Kemper [president, Kemper Group] Warns that Naderism Can Wreck Consumer Movement," December 16, 1972; [Edward B. Rust, president, State Farm Companies and president, U.S. Chamber of Commerce] "Defends Nader in NALU Talk," September 29, 1973; Gerald S. Parker [vice president for health, Guardian Life Insurance Co.], "Consumerism: 'Beyond Noise to Competence,' " October 13, 1973; and "Jeffers [general chairman, Nationwide Life] Warns Industry about 'Us-vs.-Them' Approach to Consumerism," April 13, 1974 (all L. & H. edition).

2. On the relationship between hostility to parties and business regulation, see Grant McConnell, *Private Power and American Democracy* New York, 1967, chapters 6 and 8.

3. See the Yankelovich poll conducted for the Institute of Life Insurance, in *NU* (L. & H. ed.), January 2, 1971; and Harris poll, conducted with the Wharton School for Sentry Insurance, *NU* (P. & C. ed.), January 25, 1974. For example, Harris finds 74 percent (vs. 16 percent) think "if you don't look at the fine print when you buy an automobile or homeowners insurance policy, you are likely to find you are not covered in an emergency;" 46 percent (vs. 40 percent) that "in settling a claim with an insurance company, you might as well get all you can from them, since they'll pay you only what they have to;" and 41 percent (vs. 18 percent) that insurance profits are "higher than most other businesses." On the other hand, 82 percent (vs. 10 percent) believe that "considering how you need it when trouble strikes, automobile and homeowners insurance is a good buy for the money."

4. Steingart et al. v. The Equitable Life Assurance Society of the United States, 366 F. Supp. 790 (1973) at 791.

5. Still of interest is Louis D. Brandeis, "Life Insurance: The Abuses and the Remedies," in *Business—A Profession*, Boston, 1914, pp. 154–181.

6. For an account see Thomas F. Carbery, *Consumers in Politics: A History and General Review of the Co-Operative Party*, Manchester, England, 1969, pp. 162–169.

7. Trafficante et al. v. Metropolitan Life Insurance Co., 93 S. Ct. 364 (1972).

8. Ohio AFL–CIO v. Insurance Rating Board, 451 F.2d 1178 (1972).

9. See, for example, Herbert S. Denenberg, "An Insurance Policyholder's Bill of Rights," January 18, 1974; Fred A. Mauck, "Insurance Inequities Force Regulation Into Aggressive Stance . . ." May 3, 1974; and "Florida Commissioner Names Layman Group to Consider Major Consumer Problems," June 16, 1974—all in *NU* (L. & H. ed.).

10. On the role of technicality (though not with respect to consumer affairs) see Karen Orren, *Corporate Power and Social Change: The Politics of the Life Insurance Industry* Baltimore, 1974, chapter 3.

11. *Wall Street Journal* (7 August 1974).

Chapter 17

Public Policy and Consumer Interest in the Pharmaceutical Industry

John F. Cady

In an attempt to facilitate the ability of consumers to benefit from drug therapy, society has chosen to regulate the pharmaceutical industry at both the production and distribution levels.[a] The reasons for this choice stem from several unique characteristics of the market, of which the following are principal.

1. Individuals requiring drugs because of sickness or infirmity may be described as taking part in the "involuntary consumption" of one aspect of our health care system. "While personal life styles . . . are responsible for some conditions, an individual's entrance into the health care system for treatment is primarily a function of events beyond his control" [1]. If, for any reason, individuals in need of drug products to stabilize or cure an illness are unable to acquire needed medication, their ability to function in society is impaired. Both the individual and society suffer a resultant loss.

2. Because of the sophisticated technical nature of information needed to evaluate drug products, consumers are unlikely to possess the knowledge to make informed choices among these products for any given illness.

[a]Drugs fall into one of three cagegories: (1) ethical drugs, more commonly referred to as prescription drugs, are sold only on the written prescription of a physician (prescription drugs are advertised only to prescribing physicians); (2) proprietary drugs, which are available to consumers without prescription but are advertised primarily to prescribers; and (3) over-the-counter drugs, which are sold without prescription and advertised to consumers. The primary emphasis of this article is on the production and distribution of ethical drugs.

3. The inability of consumers to evaluate alternative products (or even to know the range of alternatives available to them) potentially enables suppliers in the pharmaceutical industry to engage in practices detrimental to consumer welfare—for instance, to produce and market ineffective or even harmful products.

A major thrust of public policy regarding the pharmaceutical industry is enhancing the ability of individuals to secure effective relief from illness, while at the same time developing and implementing standards serving to protect consumers from practices detrimental to their well-being. These considerations may be stated most generally as a concern for the public health and safety. This global concern may be divided into component issues. Inasmuch as these issues directly affect the ability of consumers to benefit from drug therapy, it is from them that topics of consumer interest in this market are derived. The principal issues are therapeutic quality and product availability.

Therapeutic quality (a topic related almost exclusively to the products and processes at the production level) has three aspects: manufacturing practices, with particular concern for product adulteration; product improvement, the development of superior drug products; and product efficacy, the ability of drugs to meet claimed standards of performance. Product availability, as treated here, relates to the conduct of members of the distributive sector in maintaining conditions that allow and enhance consumer access to drug products.

The remainder of this article concerns two major topics. The first section discusses the respective roles for maintaining therapeutic quality taken on by pharmaceutical manufacturers and the Food and Drug Administration. The second section examines distributors of pharmaceutical products and distributive regulations, relative to their impact on pharmaceutical product availability.

THERAPEUTIC QUALITY: PUBLIC POLICY
AND PHARMACEUTICAL PRODUCTION

Drug production is regulated at the federal level. Statements of concern for the public health and safety with respect to drug production may be traced to Congressional debate preceding the enactment of the 1906 Pure Food and Drug Act. The 1938 Food Drug and Cosmetic Act reiterated a concern for the production and sale of drug products and delegated the responsibility for regulating standards of safety, quality, and purity to the Food and Drug Administration.

The 1962 amendments to the 1938 Act took implemented policy in this market a step beyond the regulation of safety. Of primary importance were provisions of the amendments requiring that all new drugs be approved for efficacy prior to marketing and that standards in labeling of products be developed and maintained. As of 1962 the Food and Drug Administration was designated by statute as the agency responsible for maintaining and enforcing not only standards of drug purity and safety in production but standards of efficacy and labeling as well. How well does this system of surveillance and regulation protect the consumer interest? The answer will derive from the following assessment of the two parties involved in the process of drug production and marketing—the pharmaceutical manufacturers, and the FDA.

Manufacturing Practices

A basic requirement of therapeutic quality for the products of the pharmaceutical industry is that drugs be pure and unadulterated.

> Adulterated drugs are defined as those which are not produced in conformity with good manufacturing practices (GMP). Good manufacturing practices include a host of detailed regulation covering every aspect of the drug manufacturing process, from the nature of the buildings and equipment to the packaging, labeling and maintenance of distribution records of finished products [2].

The FDA, by provision of the 1962 Kefauver-Harris Amendments, has been given the power to regulate drug quality and enforce good manufacturing practices through the mandate to inspect every drug manufacturing plant biannually, to present a report to the manufacturer regarding the results of the inspection, and to take action against the manufacturer of any adulterated or misbranded drugs. Once discovered, there are three sequential steps by which the FDA is able to remove adulterated drugs from the market: recalls, seizures, and notices of judgment.

Recalls. Recalls of drugs from the market may be initiated by a manufacturer if he recognizes some product-quality problem, or by the FDA. Recall is the first line of action against adulterated drugs and thus is the most frequently used method of removing potentially harmful drugs from the market. There are three types of recalls, each related to the hazard the drug poses to consumers.

1. Recalls of drugs posing *immediate harm to consumers*—these drugs are recalled from every purchaser and user.
2. Recalls of drugs posing a *potential threat to consumers*—these drugs are recalled from every retail distributor.
3. Recalls of drugs posing a *minor health hazard to consumers*—these drugs are recalled from the wholesale level. [b]

Seizures. If a company does not comply with an FDA initiated recall, seizure procedures may be initiated.

> The FDA must go to court to institute the seizure as a civil procedure. If the court concurs with the FDA then the seizure is carried out by the U.S. Attorney's office, which, as in a recall, sends out a letter to all consignees, requiring that the product be returned or destroyed [3].

Seizures are limited to the specific quantity and location of a product identified in the complaint filed by the U.S. Attorney. The FDA must identify the quantity of a product at each location and recommend a separate seizure for each location. Removal of a drug from the market after it has been distributed nationally is, therefore, very difficult.

Notices of Judgment. If a company contests seizure, the FDA may bring the case to court as a notice of judgment. Notices of judgment represent criminal actions against the company contesting or failing to comply with a seizure order.

The Council on Economic Priorities obtained data in 1973 on recalls, seizures, and notices of judgment for sixteen major drug manufacturers for the period 1966–1973. [c] Authors of the study assumed that the number of notices of judgment and seizures should be good indicators of the seriousness of adulteration in drug production; "... they [seizures and notices of judgment] also indicate unwillingness on the company's part to accept FDA rulings, since seizures represent refusals to deal with recall requests, and notices of

[b]After June 1971, drugs in this category were no longer treated as recalls. The reasons cited for this decision were the amount of resources devoted to these recalls that might better be spent elsewhere; the contention being that these drugs posed little danger to consumers.

[c]The sixteen were the pharmaceutical divisions of the following companies: Hoffman La Roche, American Home Products, Merck, Eli Lilly & Co., Warner Lambert, CIBA-Geigy, Smith Kline & French, Squibb, Charles Pfizer & Co., Bristol-Myers, Searle, Upjohn, Abbott, Burroughs Wellcome, Schering, and Sterling. These manufacturers held approximately 68 percent of the domestic ethical drug market in 1972.

judgment often represent appeals of seizure judgments, or failure to comply with seizure procedure" [4].

Recalls. Under all three classifications of recalls listed above, 186 recalls occurrred during the study period. Twenty-two were initiated by the FDA, the remainder by the firm concerned. Of all recalls, twenty-three constituted immediate health hazards and were recalled from all purchasers and users. Twenty-six constituted minor health hazards and were withdrawn from the wholesale level. The bulk, therefore, constituted potential health hazards and were recalled from the retail level. Compliance with an FDA initiated recall is voluntary. This occasionally leads to abuse of the procedure by manufacturers; such abuse inevitably exposes consumers to unnecessary health hazards.

> A firm produced a prescription drug that did not meet federal standards for dissolution. . . . FDA considered this defect to be a moderate-to-serious health hazard. FDA notified the firm of the problem on March 19, 1971. The firm initiated the recall 55 days later. According to the firm's estimated consumption rates, this delay permitted about 75,000 of the tablets to be sold to the public [5].

Seizures. During the study period twelve seizures were carried out for drugs produced by the sixteen companies. The principal reasons for the seizures were product contamination, preparation under unsanitary conditions, incorrect strength, and inadequate labeling.

Notices of Judgment. During the seven-year period spanned by the study, the sixteen companies received a total of six notices of judgment. Two of these were for a lack of balance in advertising between claims of effectiveness and potential adverse reactions. The remaining four were for inadequate labeling, false or misleading claims, or inadequate directions for use.

The seriousness of problems of adulteration resulting from deviations from good manufacturing practices and the problems the FDA has in dealing with particular firms is clearly conveyed in the conclusion of an FDA recommendation to prosecute a manufacturer for a record of violations over a three-year period.

> [The manufacturer] is one of the major drug manufacturers in this country. . . . It is unfair and detrimental to the public at large that this firm should have allowed itself to operate under such extremely poor manufacturing practices that resulted in numerous mixups, recalls, adulterated and

misbranded drug products. When a firm the stature of [manufacturer] . . . operates under conditions whereby their entire output is open to question it is cause for serious concern. . . . We cannot condone any excuse for a firm of this size that prepares drug products, which are anything but safe, reliable, and potent. [Although the firm spent huge sums to correct manufacturing conditions] this was only done after the seriousness of the situation, which they allowed to develop, was forcibly brought to their attention by the Food and Drug Administration [6].

The willingness and ability of the FDA to monitor and enforce compliance with good manufacturing practices are apparently necessary to insure the production and sale of unadulterated, adequately labeled drug products. Consequently, the agency's record of surveillance and enforcement of the mandates of the act is of singular importance.

A report by the General Accounting Office (GAO), *Problems in Obtaining and Enforcing Compliance with Good Manufacturing Practices for Drugs*, was highly critical of FDA inspection procedures. The study found that the agency had not carried out a biannual inspection of all plants, that over 200 of the 1,300 plants in three districts were not inspected during one two-year period. The GAO attributed this apparent laxity to problems in scheduling, the placement of priorities of producers with a history of violations, the diversion of employees to other tasks, and a general lack of manpower [7]. The GAO report noted also that the FDA ". . . often neglects to use the legal methods at its disposal to enforce compliance with good manufacturing practices. This contributes to the continued recurrence of violations, and the continued production of adulterated or contaminated drugs" [8].

With respect to this latter criticism it should be noted, however, that for recalls, ". . . there is no law requiring removal. Because FDA cannot enforce recalls they are a matter of negotiation between industry and FDA and can be delayed or ineffectively carried out by the companies involved" [9]. The success of a recall in terms of the proportion of a recalled product removed from the market is extremely sensitive to the speed with which the recall is initiated. Delay by the manufacturer can significantly affect the recall procedure. A delay of over 30 days results, on average, in less than one-half as much product being removed from the market compared to a recall initiated within ten days of request. Despite this because of the costs incurred and the revenues foregone, firms often successfully delay carrying out recalls.

FDA notified a drug company . . . that the production of one of its drugs . . . was super-potent and considered a potential health hazard. Although

FDA had tested the drug, the firm requested time to retest and perform its own analysis. After 111 days and an appeal to the firm by the Deputy Associate Commissioner for FDA the firm agreed . . . to recall the superpotent drug. However, this delay made the recall less effective, because about 84,000 pills or about 42 percent of the amount distributed were not recovered. FDA officials advised . . . that seizure of the drug was not practical because of national distribution [10].

From the preceding discussion it is apparent that deviations from "good manufacturing practices" do occur, resulting in the production of adulterated drugs. There are two bases for these deviations. The first is the FDA which, according to agency spokesmen and the GAO, does not have the resources to comply with its legislative mandate for inspection. Coupled with this lack of resources is the absence of an enforceable mechanism for the swift removal of adulterated products from the market. Recalls are voluntary; seizures are impractical for nationally distributed products. The second reason for the observation of deviations from good manufacturing practices lies with the producers themselves. It is too apparent that some pharmaceutical companies are either unable or unwilling to initiate and implement standards of quality control and labeling consistent with "good manufacturing practices." The exhibition of good records of manufacturing practice by several firms demonstrates that it is technically possible to comply with current regulatory standards.[d]

Product Improvement
The second aspect of therapeutic quality—product improvement—is also controlled by the producing sector of the pharmaceutical industry. Product improvement is measured by research and development (R&D) efforts. Research and development efforts, in turn, may be measured by inputs (expenditures on research) or by outputs (some measure of research productivity).

---

[d]The performance in maintaining good manufacturing practices varied considerably among the individual companies examined. One domestic producer had a total of four seizures and notices of judgment, while five companies had none. One manufacturer alone accounted for 38 recalls. The root causes of the variability in the number and seriousness of adulterated products withdrawn from the market among manufacturers are not clearly defined. Conceivably sales volume differences among firms may be related to the number of product withdrawals, with larger firms having more withdrawals. However, diversity among firms in the number of withdrawals is still in evidence when differences in sales size are controlled for. Using a base of the number of recalls per $100 million in prescription sales, the firms studied varied from 2 to 19.7. The Council on Economic Priorities attributes the variability to substantial differences in the manufacturing and quality control procedures of the studied firms.

Inputs. A recent study analyzed the R&D patterns for six major pharmaceutical manufacturers. These six had combined pharmaceutical sales of over $3.5 billion in 1972 [11]. At first glance the gross expenditures of these firms are impressive. Private R&D expenditures (excluding government financed expenditures), both foreign and domestic, for the six averaged $181 million or 9 percent of sales for the period 1961–1973. This figure is compared to R&D expenditures of 1.3 percent of sales for all manufacturing to highlight the relative emphasis placed on research by pharmaceutical manufacturers.

These figures seem to indicate two things: (1) if these six firms can be taken as representative of the pharmaceutical industry as a whole (the six accounted for 26 percent of 1972 domestic prescription drug sales) and the figures are roughly correct, the pharmaceutical industry is, indeed, research intensive relative to all U.S. manufacturing; (2) at an average of 40.2 percent, research and development expenditures represent a significant proportion of pharmaceutical manufacturers net income.

Despite these impressive statistics, the measurement of dollar research inputs is probably not a very effective index for measuring product improvement efforts. There is, for example, evidence suggesting that much of what is classified as expenditure on research is actually expenditure on promotion [12]. In addition, input measurement allows no assessment of the efficiency or productivity of research efforts. So while it is obvious that the measurement of research outcomes is what one desires in the attempt to measure product improvement, the development of a meaningful index of output is not without problems. For example, it is frequently stressed that the number of "new" products forthcoming from pharmaceutical research is not meaningful as a measure of product improvement since many of these merely represent patentable compounds without any significant therapeutic benefit over a product currently on the market [13, 14].

Outputs. Several possible candidates exist as measures of significant research output. One is the total number of new drug applications processed. Another is the number of new chemical entities, defined as new and different chemical compounds never before marketed in the U.S. Both of these measures, however, have the major drawback of including drugs that are variations of currently existing products. One measure of research productivity does not have this drawback. *The Medical Letter*, an independent source of information on the clinical use of drugs, compiles a list of new products considered to be "significant therapeutic advances."

The Council on Economic Priorities in its attempt to measure productivity in research among pharmaceutical manufacturers examined *The Medical Letter's* list of significant new drugs developed from 1966–1973. A high proportion (67 percent) of the 56 drugs considered by *The Medical Letter* to be significant therapeutic advances were developed by the sixteen study firms. That is, these companies accounted for two-thirds of the significant new drugs developed over an eight-year period. Of particular interest is the relationships among the number of significant new drugs, new chemical entities, and all new drug applications (Table 17–1).

On an outcome basis, using the list compiled by *The Medical Letter* as the criterion of productivity, less than 20 percent of the new drugs developed through the R&D expenditures of these sixteen firms are considered significant. There was a great deal of variability among the firms studied in terms of the ratio of significant new drugs to new applications. However, further analysis by the Council uncovered no correlation between either the number of new drug applications or the number of new chemical entities and the number of significant new drugs developed by a firm. The conclusion derived is that the majority of products that are developed as a result of the relatively large R&D expenditures of pharmaceutical manufacturers are duplicative drugs and their development is stirred by a desire to market a patented version of a currently profitable drug on the market.

Product Efficacy

With slightly less than one-fifth of new drugs marketed between 1966 and 1973 rated as significant, and some substantial portion of the remainder representing duplication of current products, the issue of product efficacy arises. Product efficacy refers to the extent to which the claims made for drugs match their performance.

The Kefauver-Harris Amendments required that all new drugs be evaluated for efficacy before being marketed [15]. Although the

Table 17–1. New Drug Applications, New Chemical Entities, and Significant New Drugs, 1966–1973

(1) *New Drug* *Applications*	*(2)* *New Chemical* *Entities*	*(3)* *Significant* *New Drugs*	*(4)* *(3) ÷ (1)*
185	152	34	.183

Derived from "Safety, Efficacy and Research Productivity in the Pharmaceutical Industry," *Economic Priorities Report*, Vol. 4, No. 4–5, August/November, 1973, p. 7.

amendments did not provide for the reevaluation for efficacy of drugs on the market prior to 1962, in 1966 "new drugs" (previously defined as those introduced after 1962) were redefined to include all drugs which had not undergone review as required by the amendments. Some 4,300 drugs (both prescription and over-the-counter) marketed between 1938 and 1962 were evaluated for efficacy. The task of evaluation was assigned to scientific specialists of the National Academy of Sciences of the National Research Council. Each of the approximately 16,000 claims for the over 4,000 drugs was classified into the following categories:

1. *Effective*: Substantial evidence of effectiveness.
2. *Probably Effective*: Additional evidence required to rate the drug "effective."
3. *Possibly Effective*: As it stands there is little evidence of effectiveness, and in the absence of substantial evidence, the claim is considered inappropriate.
4. *Ineffective*: There is lack of substantial evidence of efficacy [16].
   Among the results of the classification procedure were the following: a "considerable number" of the drugs reviewed have been rated as effective for all claims made for their use; a few (about 7 percent) have been rated as ineffective for all claims cited (this represents slightly over 300 drug products); 41 percent of the products were rated effective for one or more claims. However, of the 16,000 claims that were made for the drugs, effectiveness was found for only 19 percent.

As part of their report, the Council on Economic Priorities also examined the efficacy review study data for the sixteen drug firms mentioned above and derived the following evaluations (Table 17−2).

Table 17−2. Classification of Drug Products by Efficacy: All Pharmaceutical Firms and C.E.P. Study Firms

Classification	Percent of Drugs for All Companies	Percent of Drugs for 16 Companies Studied
Ineffective	15	18
Possibly effective	19	12
Effective for all indications	12	16
Effective for at least one indication	60	62

Source: "Safety, Efficacy and Research Productivity in the Pharmaceutical Industry," *Economic Priorities Report*, Vol. 4, No. 4−5 (August/November 1973), p. 20.

There was substantial variation among the firms studied in the number of ineffective drugs marketed. The percentage of totally effective drugs marketed ranged from a high of 31.5 to a low of 1.6. The percentage of totally ineffective drugs marketed by the firms varied from 23.3 to 7.4 [17]. From the single perspective of the proportion of drugs marketed that were ineffective for treating some or all of the problems for which they were claimed effective, it appears that the requirements for proof of efficacy included in the 1962 amendments were necessary and in the interest of consumers of drug products. As Peltzman points out:

> The 1962 amendments seek to reduce the cost of new-drug information to the consumer by substituting FDA-produced information for drug-company promotion and information obtained from actual usage. That is, the FDA today restricts what the drug company may claim, but provides the user with independent assurance about the accuracy of what is claimed. This independent assurance is produced by preventing actual usage until the FDA has what it considers sufficient clinical test evidence to make the assurance valuable [18].

Peltzman finds, however, that the amendments have had an unanticipated effect on consumers. That effect relates to the decline in new drug innovation since 1962. One of Peltzman's main findings is ". . . that benefits forgone on effective new drugs exceed greatly the waste avoided on ineffective drugs. The estimated net impact is equivalent to a 5–10 percent tax on drug purchased" [19]. This argument has not gone unchallenged. The Council on Economic Priorities, in finding no relationship between significant new drugs and the number of new chemical entities marketed, concluded that there is "no reason to assume that the decline in the number of new chemical entities signals a decline in new drug innovation" [20].

Regardless of whether one considers the proof of efficacy requirements of the 1962 amendments to be unduly restrictive to the marketing of new drugs [21], it is clear that these requirements reduced (probably to zero) the number of ineffective drugs marketed. In view of the relatively large proportion of drugs marketed between 1938 and 1962 that were totally or partially ineffective, this reduction is not a minor consideration.

PRODUCT AVAILABILITY: PUBLIC POLICY AND PHARMACEUTICAL DISTRIBUTION

A major segment of the pharmaceutical industry has been largely ignored with regard to its impact on consumer welfare—the distributive sector. Consumer expenditures on prescription drugs in 1973 are estimated at close to $8 billion. The bulk of these expenditures (85 percent) are consumer out-of-pocket costs; the majority of these costs are incurred for purchases of drugs in retail pharmacies.

Like the producing sector of the pharmaceutical industry, the distributive sector, particularly at the retail level, is regulated. The method of regulation and the scope of regulation at retail are quite different from the producing sector, and these differences are felt to promote conditions that are more likely to be in the interest of suppliers than consumers.

In order to address the issue of whether the practices of the suppliers in this sector are, or appear to be, in the best interest of consumers, an examination of the methods by which regulations are implemented as well as the regulations and their impact is necessary.

Regulation of Pharmacy Retailing—Method

The enactment of policy consistent with federal provisions regarding the distribution and sale of pharmaceutical products is undertaken by the various states. State regulation is implemented through two mechanisms: pharmacy board regulation, and legal statute.

Pharmacy Regulation and Pharmacy Boards. State boards of pharmacy, in structure and function, are similar to other trade regulation agencies. Their primary function is occupational licensing; they are created to assess the competence and insure continued competence of those engaged in a trade or profession. Aside from licensing, however, pharmacy boards are granted broad discretionary powers in the regulation of the profession of pharmacy and the conduct of retail trade.

> Most of the states do not contain provisions that are concerned with the minutiae of retail drugstore operations, but rather . . . empower the pharmacy boards to adopt the detailed rules necessary for [the administration of] other enactments. The boards are also generally responsible for securing compliance with state drug adulteration laws and for promulgation and enforcement of rules to govern the practice of retail pharmacy.
>
> The pharmacy laws and rules of the various states give the boards a powerful weapon to force compliance with the provisions—license suspension and/or revocation. A pharmacist must be registered to practice his profession. Threat of revocation of his license is a menace to his livelihood, so he is apt to abide by the board's wishes [22].

Because of the power and legislatively granted means of control vested in state pharmacy boards, the regulations enacted by them have a potentially great effect on the manner in which trade is carried on in the sector. Pharmacy boards are predominantly controlled by retail pharmacists. Within the retail pharmacist population, the independent owner exerts the greatest control over boards. Enacted regulations, not surprisingly, are characterized as being supportive of independent owner-pharmacists.

Pharmacy Regulation and Legal Statute. In the consideration of legislation regulating a specialized sector such as retail drug distribution, legislators rely on three sources of guidance: public opinion, expert knowledge, and lobbying organizations. Historically, in the absence of major abuses, public opinion has had a small role in shaping the structure of retail drug legislation. Pharmacy boards have provided expert knowledge. The primary source of lobbying influence over state legislatures is found in a major organization representing members of the retail sector of the pharmaceutical industry.

The National Association of Retail Druggists (NARD) in 1965 represented over 90 percent of the pharmacies in the U.S. in that year. NARD has been characterized as ". . . the politically most powerful of all retail trade associations . . . [23] and has a long history of actively lobbying and campaigning for the economic interests of the independent pharmacist. It is primarily through the efforts of NARD spanning forty years that state resale price maintenance laws, the Miller-Tydings Act, and the McGuire Act were passed. Through the experience gained in lobbying for resale price maintenance, NARD has developed what can only be described as a highly efficient, powerful organization which has consistently pressed for the enactment of legislation in the interest of the independent owner-pharmacist.

Regulation of Pharmacy Retailing—Scope

The scope of activities regulated through the pharmacy board and legislative mechanisms is wide. Table 17–3, listing regulations currently in effect in the U.S., clearly shows that virtually every aspect of pharmacy retailing subject to discretionary managerial action is regulated by one or several states. One area of regulation more than any other has been singled out as having potentially adverse effects on consumers. That area is the regulation of prescription drug price advertising and other price-based promotional practices. As of 1973, thirty-four states by regulation or statute, prohibited the advertisement of prescription drug prices. The issue of whether prescription drug price advertising should or should not be restricted is a subject of current debate. The topics of debate are the relationships among price advertising and public health and safety and prescription drug prices.

Table 17-3. Regulations Enacted by State Legislatures and Boards of Pharmacy Concerning the Retail Distribution of Pharmaceuticals

---

I. Ownership Regulations

   1. No physician ownership of pharmacies
   2. Pharmacist ownership of pharmacies required

II. General Prohibitions and Limitations

   1. No pharmacy permit for a general merchandise store
   2. No pharmacy permit for a Fair Trade violator
   3. Limitation on the number of pharmacies in a state

III. Physical Requirements

   1. Physical separation of prescription department in a general merchandise store
   2. Separate entrance mandatory for prescription department in a general merchandise store
   3. Entrance between pharmacy and adjoining store prohibited
   4. Minimum floor space requirement for pharmacy department (expressed as a percentage of total store size)
   5. Self service prohibited for proprietary products
   6. Minimum inventory requirement for pharmacy (as a percent of total inventory)

IV. Advertising Regulations

   1. Outdoor signs controlled
   2. Prohibition from *implying* discount prescription prices in advertising
   3. Advertising of prescription drug prices prohibited
   4. Promotional schemes prohibited

V. Employee Regulations

   1. Pharmacist manager requirement
   2. Pharmacist must be on duty whenever store is open
   3. Number of pharmacists to be employed
   4. Prescription dispensing rules

The Debate—Price Advertising and Public Health and Safety

Proponents of drug price advertising regulations have commonly cited the following arguments for prohibiting advertising with the objective of providing for public welfare:

Drug price advertising encourages patients to importune physicians to prescribe medication that may not be therapeutically necessary or that would be dangerous to their health.

It tends to encourage the prescribing and use of larger than needed quantities of drugs.

It would be contrary to the interests of the consumer and a possible threat to public health. There is most likely a relationship between illegal drug use and over-the-counter drug commercials. If advertising of prescription drugs is allowed, that can be added to the list of probable offenders.

Proponents of drug price advertising are quick to discount these allegations. They assert that:

The prescribing physician has the ultimate control of both drugs and doses of medication. No competent physician would submit to pressure to prescribe unneeded or dangerous medication.

Drugs would not be consumed in quantities larger than needed for proper treatment because: (a) physicians would have no reason to prescribe such quantities; (b) individuals would receive no physical benefit from taking drugs in quantities larger than those needed to control or cure an ailment or condition. To do so would be to incur the cost of drugs with no concomitant benefit.

The asserted relationship between advertised drug prices and illegal drug use is fallacious. There is no evidence from which to conclude that advertising drug prices is causally linked to illicit drug use.

The resolution of the debate on the relationship between advertised drug prices and consumer health and safety is far from concluded. Suffice it to say that in states permitting price advertising no evidence has been forthcoming demonstrating adverse consequences attributable to price advertising.

The Debate Continued—Price Advertising
and Drug Prices

The economic issues of debate concerning price advertising primarily concern prescription drug prices. This topic has three components: (1) price levels in areas restricting advertising compared to areas permitting advertising; (2) price variations among sellers; and (3) price discrimination.

Proponents of advertising restrictions assert:

Advertising will not lower prices of drugs because the cost of advertising will be passed on to the consumer.

Price variations among pharmacies reflect the "true value" of the pharmacy dispensing function. Variations in price exist because some pharmacies provide services, while "discounters" provide none.

Opponents of current advertising restrictions contend that the foregoing arguments are basically in error:

There is evidence to suggest that prescription prices are lower where advertising is permitted. In any event, even if prices are not lowered, the public has a basic right to know the price of a product prior to actual sale.

Price variations for identical prescription drugs are found among pharmacies in limited geographic areas. In the absence of price information consumers are not able to make informed decisions as to where they might prefer to purchase a prescription.

There is evidence of price discrimination on the part of some pharmacists. This discrimination can be linked to a lack of price information on the part of consumers.

Opponents of current advertising restrictions also point out that the conditions of high relative price levels, large price variations, and price discrimination related to a lack of consumer information are most costly to those who can least afford it—the elderly and the poor. These groups have a disproportionate incidence of illness and resultingly large drug expenditures. The immobility associated with illness and age and poverty makes these individuals unable to physically shop around for low prescription prices.

Price Levels

Surveys sponsored by consumer interest groups and other researchers quite conclusively demonstrate that prescription drug prices are lower in areas permitting price advertising. "Retail price advertising—where it exists—reveals the immense disparity between prices for the identical drug and shows conclusively that where there is open price competition, the consumer pays less for the same product" [24]. For example, one survey found that a consumer in Philadelphia pays" . . . an average of 34 percent less for his prescription than does the New York patient. . . . The reason can only be attributed to the competition created by advertising" [25].

Price Variations

Large prescription price variations among pharmacies in limited geographic areas is another condition that critics of advertising contend would be eliminated by price information. Studies in Virginia, California, New York, and Michigan have found variations of 300 to 400 percent for identical prescriptions purchased from pharmacies located in a limited area. The magnitude of these variations has led critics to contend that the ignorance of consumers regarding a "normal" level of price coupled with an unwillingness of pharmacists to compete on a price basis are the sources of these variations. Proponents of advertising restrictions contend that prescription charges reflect the provision of services such as credit, delivery, and the maintenance of customer health records. A second source of price variation stems, they contend, from purchasing economies of "discounters."

A recent study sought to separate out the effects of service provision, economies in purchasing and other characteristics affecting prescription prices from regulatory impact on prices [26]. While not limited to examining advertising restrictions, the study concluded that the costs to consumers in 1970 of advertising regulations were nearly $200 million.

Variance in Prices—Price Discrimination

An issue of concern apart from variations in price per se is price variation in the form of price discrimination. Critics have contended that the absence of seller-supplied price information and the consequent ignorance of consumers regarding price are conditions under which the observation of price discrimination is highly probable.

Three studies have examined the issue of retail price discrimination in the sale of prescription drugs [27—29]. None of these was able to identify characteristics of the purchaser (age, race, attire) as a basis for price discrimination. All three, however, observed intrastore price variation among purchasers of the same prescription. Price differences of over one dollar per prescription within the same pharmacy were found. A general conclusion of these surveys is that in pharmacy retailing there is a general lack of consistency in the pricing of prescription drugs. A result of this inconsistency is that the price any given purchaser is charged for any given prescription has a large random component.

Current Direction of Public Policy Regarding Pharmaceutical Distribution

Large costs have been shown by several studies to accrue to prescription drug purchasers attributable to regulations initiated by retail drug distributors. The initial impetus for regulation of this sector of the industry was much the same as that which prompted federal legislation—practices such as the sale of adulterated drugs, which were clearly detrimental to public welfare. Over time the offensive practices disappeared. This is due at least in part to the success of regulation in meeting its objectives. But regulation not only remained, over time the realm of control encompassed by regulation expanded to include virtually every area of management decision making. Accompanying the increase in the span of regulation was a change in the character of regulation.

Today retail pharmacy regulations are generally characterized as economically supportive to small scale independent pharmacies, restrictive toward chains and other potential discounters, and of questionable benefit to consumers. While it may be demonstrated that there are benefits to be derived by consumers from regulation equaling or even surpassing the costs of regulation, no one has yet pointed them out. Acting on the premise that the regulation of advertising represents a "cost without benefit" for consumers, recent court decisions have overturned pharmacy regulations, particularly advertising restrictions. The U.S. District Court in Eastern Virginia recently declared:

> The right-to-know is the foundation of the First Amendment; it is the theme of this suit. Consumers are denied this right by the Virginia statute. ...Why the customer is refused this knowledge is not convincingly explained by the State Board of Pharmacy and its members. Enforcement of the ban gives no succor to public health; on the contrary access by the infirm or poor to the price of prescription drugs would be for their good [30].

SUMMARY AND CONCLUSIONS

In the attempt to provide for consumer welfare, the production and distribution sectors of the pharmaceutical industry are regulated. Consumers, however, do not always benefit from these attempts. Regulation of the producing sector is an effective mechanism for serving the public interest. Whatever faults may be imbedded in the system of drug regulation at the production level, the combined activities of drug producers and the FDA result in preserving a flexible system for the marketing of drugs while reducing the number of unsafe and ineffective drugs sold to the public.

A critical notion is that these results derive from the interrelated activities of these agents. It is unlikely that the consumer interest would be served in the absence of regulation at the production level. This conclusion follows from our examination of the relationship between pharmaceutical manufacturers and the FDA with respect to requests for product withdrawals and for provision of data substantiating claims for efficacy.

While one is always loath to suggest some increase in regulatory activity, the hesitancy of producers to comply with FDA-initiated recalls makes it difficult not to agree with the General Accounting

Office call for new measures combining speed, flexibility, and some degree of mandatory compliance for removal of products considered harmful.

Regulation of the retail sector of the pharmaceutical industry is not always in the best interest of consumers. Regulations are promulgated and enforced by representatives of the retail pharmacists. Consequently, such regulations tend to favor current market members rather than consumers. This is particularly evident with respect to prohibitions on prescription drug price advertising. No evidence has shown that price advertising results in negative consequences for consumers; the prohibition of price advertising is associated with high drug prices, large interstore price variation, and price discrimination. Accordingly, the consumer interest is best served by deregulating those areas of pharmaceutical distribution currently covered by regulation but contributing little to consumer welfare.

NOTES TO CHAPTER 17

1. T. Donals Rucker, "Public Policy Considerations in the Pricing of Prescription Drugs in the United States," *International Journal of Health Services* (1974), p. 171.

2. "Safety, Efficacy and Research Productivity in the Pharmaceutical Industry," *Economic Priorities Report* (August/November 1973), p. 10.

3. *Ibid.*, p. 12.

4. *Ibid.*, p. 13.

5. "Competitive Problems In the Drug Industry," Hearings Before The Subcommittee on Monopoly, Ninetieth Congress, Part 22, p. 9099.

6. Ibid., Part 3, p. 1119.

7. "Safety, Efficacy and Research Productivity," p. 11.

8. Ibid.

9. "Lack of Authority Limits Consumer Protection: Problems in Identifying and Removing from the Market Products Which Violate the Law," Report to the Congress by the Comptroller General of the United States, September 1972, p. 3.

10. *Ibid.*, p. 28.

11. "Economic Aspects of R&D Intensity in the Pharmaceutical Industry: A Composite Profile of Six Major Companies," Jesse J. Friedman and Associates, Washington, D.C. September 1973. The six companies were: Abbott Laboratories, Eli LIlly & Co., Merck & Co., G.D. Searle & Co., SmithKline Corp., and Upjohn Co.

12. "Competitive Problems In the Drug Industry," Hearings Before the Subcommittee on Monopoly, Ninetieth Congress, Part 5.

13. William Comanor, "Research and Technical Change in the Pharmaceutical Industry," Hearings Before the Subcommittee on Monopoly, Ninetieth Congress, Part 5, p. 2078, (from) *The Review of Economics and Statistics* (May 1965).

14. The patent system provides a strong stimulus to incur research expenditures to achieve product differentiation. "Since a large proportion of pharmaceuticals have some degree of patent protection, entry into a specific therapeutic market requires, in most cases, some form of scientific or chemical product differentiation. In a world of competing monopolists, rivalry requires the ability to acquire a monopoly position." William Comanor, "Research and Competitive Product Differentiation in the Pharmaceutical Industry in the United States" (in) Hearings Before the Subcommittee on Monopoly, Ninetieth Congress, Part 5, p. 2074, (from) *Economica* (November 1964).

15. The Amendment requires that proof of efficacy be in the form of "substantial evidence." This is defined as "adequate and well controlled investigations including clinical investigations, by experts qualified by scientific training and experience. [The results of such investigations must be such that it may] reasonably be concluded by such experts that the drug will have the effect it purports to have or is represented to have." "The Drug Efficacy Study," *FDA Drug Bulletin* (23 June 1971), p. 1.

16. Ibid.

17. "Safety, Efficacy and Research Productivity," pp. 20–21.

18. Sam Peltzman, "An Evaluation of Consumer Protection Legislation: The 1962 Drug Amendments," *Journal of Political Economy* pp. 1049–1091.

19. *Ibid.*, p. 1049.

20. "Safety, Efficacy and Research Productivity," p. 25.

21. The view that the 1962 Amendments were restrictive to new drug development may be found in Richard L. Landau (ed.), *Regulating New Drugs*, Chicago: University of Chicago Center for Policy Study.

22. F. Marion Fletcher, *Market Restraints in the Retail Drug Industry*, Philadelphia: University of Pennsylvania Press, 1967, p. 39.

23. J.C. Palamountain, *The Politics of Distribution*, Cambridge, Mass.: Harvard University Press, 1955, p. 94.

24. Benjamin Rosenthal, *Retail Prescription Drug Prices*, U.S. Congress, House Document, March 19, 1973, p. 1880.

25. *Ibid.*, p. 1890.

26. John F. Cady, *Drugs on the Market: The Impact of Public Policy in the Retail Market for Prescription Drugs* (Lexington, Mass.: Lexington Books), in press.

27. G.E. Hastings and R. Kunnes, "Predicting Prescription Prices," *The New England Journal of Medicine* (September 1967):625–628.

28. J.A. Kotzan and C.L. Braucher, "A Multivariate Analysis of Retail Prescription Prices," *Journal of Marketing Research* (November 1970):517–520.

29. John F. Cady and Alan R. Andreasen, "Price Levels, Price Practices and Price Discrimination in the Retail Market for Prescription Drugs," *Journal of Consumer Affairs* (Summer 1975).

30. "Opinion of the Court," U.S. District Court Eastern District of Virginia, No. 73–336–R, p. 10.

Index

About the Contributors

Babette B. Barton is a professor of law at the University of California, Berkeley where she took her bachelors' degree and attended law school. She has also taught on the Davis campus.

William W. Bradley is currently the Executive Assistant for Scientific Affairs at The Proprietary Association, a trade association for the non-prescription drug industry in Washington, D.C. He is the founder and charter member of the Society of Consumer Affairs Professionals and is a senior member of the Society for Quality Control. He established the Consumer Affairs Department at Miles Laboratories where he served as manager for three years. Mr. Bradley holds an A.B. in chemistry from Olivet Nasarene College in Kankakee, Illinois and has worked in the non-prescription medicine industry for sixteen years.

John F. Cady, a graduate of the State University of New York, Buffalo, is Assistant Professor of Marketing in the College of Business and Public Administration at the University of Arizona, Tucson. He is consultant to the Federal Trade Commission's Bureau of Consumer Protection, Division of Marketing Practices. His recent publications include *Drugs on the Market: The Impact of Public Policy on the Retail Market for Prescription Drugs*, published by D.C. Heath, *Restricted Advertising in Competition*, published by the American Enterprise Institute for Public Policy Research, and several articles on public policy issues.

Myron Kandel is editor and publisher of two newsletters: *Review of the Financial Press* and *Yanks Abroad*. He previously served as a reporter for the *New York Times*, as business editor of the *New York Herald Tribune*, and editor of the *New York Law Journal*. He also was founding editor and publisher of the *Wall Street Letter*. A graduate of Brooklyn College and Columbia University School of Journalism, he has taught at the City College of New York and at Columbia.

Benny L. Kass graduated from Northwestern University, received law degrees from Michigan University and from George Washington University, and practices law in association with the firm of Boasberg, Hewes, Klores and Kass in Washington, D.C. He is a member of the District of Columbia Bar and the Federal and American Bar Associations. He served on the Subcommittee on Administrative Practices and Procedure, of the Senate Judiciary Committee from 1965 through 1968, and was a member of Mayor Washington's Committee on Economic Development from 1966 through 1970. He has served on the Commission on Uniform State Laws as a representative of the District of Columbia since 1969.

Robert N. Katz is a member of the faculty of the University of California, teaching in the area of the legal, political and social environment of business. He also serves as editor of the *California Management Review*. Prior to joining the faculty at Berkeley he served as The Solicitor of the Federal Maritime Commission. Prior thereto he was engaged in the private practice of law serving as counsel to government contractors and to a national trade association. He has practiced law before the courts of California, the United States Supreme Court, and various other state and federal courts. He is a graduate of the University of Texas Law School and the Harvard School of Business Administration.

Thomas G. Krattenmaker is a Professor of Law at Georgetown University's Law Center specializing in trade regulation and constitutional law. He attended Swarthmore College, earned his J.D. from Columbia University and has served as the Assistant Director for Evaluation for the Bureau of Consumer Protection of the Federal Trade Commission.

Robert N. Mayer attended Columbia University and is presently a doctorial candidate in sociology specializing in consumer and environmental affairs at the University of California, Berkeley. He has coauthored two monographs entitled *Technology, the Consumer and*

Information Flows, a study for the National Research and Development Assessment Program of the National Science Foundation; and *Changing a Car's Engine Oil at Home: A Consumer Survey*, done for the United States Environmental Protection Agency. He is also the co-author of "Toward a Sociology of Consumption" which appears in the volume *Synthesis of Knowledge of Consumer Behavior*, edited by Robert Ferber and published by the National Science Foundation in 1976. Mr. Mayer has addressed the American Sociological Association and has been published in the *Journal of Consumer Research*.

Mark Nadel, who is a staff aide in the United States Senate, graduated from the University of California, Berkeley, took his Ph.d. at Johns Hopkins University, and was a Brookings Institution Research Fellow. He is the author of *Politics of Consumer Protection* (Bobbs-Merrill, 1971) and a variety of articles on regulation and public administration that have appeared in *The Handbook of Political Science*, *Public Administration Review* and *The Journal of Politics*. His latest book, *Corporations and Political Accountability*, will be published by D.C. Heath in 1976.

Francesco M. Nicosia is Professor of Business Administration, Graduate School of Business Administration and Director of the Consumer Research Program (sponsored jointly with the Survey Research Center), University of California, Berkeley. He is author of the book *Consumer Decision Processes, Marketing and Advertising Implications*, published by Prentice-Hall in 1966 and translated into four languages. He serves the Wadsworth Publishing Company as the Consulting Editor for Marketing. He was elected to the Board of Directors, San Francisco Chapter of the American Marketing Association for 1963 through 1964, and for 1974–1975. He has also been elected Chairman, Publications Committee, and member of the Executive Council of the American Association of Public Opinion Research (publisher of the *Public Opinion Quarterly*) for 1973–1975, and reelected for 1975–1977. The San Francisco Chapter of the American Marketing Association has elected Mr. Nicosia President-Elect 1975–1976 and President for 1976–1977.

Karen Orren earned her doctorate at the University of Chicago in 1972. She is an associate professor of political science at the University of California, Los Angeles, where she specializes in interest groups in American politics. Her book, *Corporate Power and Social Change: The Politics of the Life Insurance Industry* (Johns Hopkins University Press, 1974), and various other articles and publications reflect her interest in group politics.

Kenneth F. Phillips is a member of the California Bar and Adjunct Professor of Law at the University of California, Berkeley. He is also acting director of the University's Earl Warren Legal Institute. From 1968 through 1974, he was director of the Institute's National Housing and Economic Development Law Project. Prior to that time he practiced law in San Francisco as a member of the firm of Feldman, Waldman and Kline, and from 1962 through 1965 he served as Assistant General Council of the United States Agency for International Development. He is a graduate of the Harvard Law School.

R. David Pittle, Commissioner of the Consumer Product Safety Commission in Washington, D.C., received his doctorate from the University of Wisconsin in 1969. He has taught at Carnegie-Mellon University and the University of Wisconsin, and is frequent lecturer on consumer protection. He was the principal investigator of a three-year National Science Foundation grant entitled "Research on Improving Consumer Safety Through Innovative Consumer Education," and from 1971 through 1973 served as president of Alliance for Consumer Protection, a voluntary consumer organization in Pittsburg. In 1972 he received, on behalf of the Alliance, the Federal Executive Board's Award for outstanding public service in consumer protection.

Francis Pollock is the editor of the publication *Media and Consumer* published in Norwalk, Connecticut.

Lee E. Preston graduated from Vanderbilt and received his doctorate from Harvard in 1958. He is the Director of the Center of Policy Studies at the State University of New York, Buffalo. His areas of specialization are economics, marketing and public policy and he has numerous publications in these fields.

Ernest S. Rosenberg attended the New York University School of Law and graduated in 1971. He is a former staff member of the Federal Trade Commission's Bureau of Consumer Protection and is presently the chief of the Regulatory Management Staff of the Office of Mobile Source Air Pollution Control, of the U.S. Environmental Protection Agency.

S. Prakash Sethi is an associate professor at the School of Business Administration, University of California, Berkeley, where he teaches in the fields of international business and the social and political environment of business. He holds an M.B.A. and a Ph.d. from Columbia University, and is also a graduate of the Delphi School of

Economics, Delphi University, India. He has published numerous journal articles and four books including *Up Against the Corporate Wall: Modern Corporations and Social Issues of the Seventies* (1971, 1974); *The Corporate Dilemma: Traditional Values, Contemporary Problems* (1973); *Multinational Business Operations* (1973); and *Management of the Multinationals: Policies, Operations, and Research* (1974). He is consultant to American and European multinational corporations and is a contributing editor of *Business and Society Review/Innovation*.

Frederick D. Sturdivant, who holds the M. Riklis Professorship of Business and Its Environment at The Ohio State University, Columbus, received his doctorate from Northwestern University in 1963. He has taught at the University of Southern California, the University of Texas, Austin, and Harvard Business School. His recent publications include *The Ghetto Marketplace* (1966), *Managerial Analysis in Marketing* (1970), and *The Credit Merchants: The History of Spigel* (1973).

David Vogel took his doctorate in political science at Princeton University and has served on the faculty of the School of Business Administration at the University of California, Berkeley since 1973. He has published articles in *Business and Society Review, Social Policy, California Management Review* and *Polity.* With Leonard Silk he has written *Ethics and Profits: The Crisis of Confidence in American Business* published by Simon and Schuster in 1976. Mr. Vogel is currently consultant to the Council of Foreign Relations of Multinational Corporations.